HOW TO ATTRACT
GARDEN BIRDS

HOW TO ATTRACT GARDEN BIRDS

BUILDING BIRD FEEDERS, NEST BOXES, BIRD TABLES AND BIRDBATHS

What to plant where, to welcome birds into your garden
• Backyard birdwatching • Illustrated bird spotter guides

DAVID ALDERTON
CONSULTANT: DR JEN GREEN

LORENZ BOOKS

This edition is published by Lorenz Books
an imprint of Anness Publishing Ltd
info@anness.com
www.annesspublishing.com

Publisher: Joanna Lorenz
Editor and layout: Lucy Doncaster
Design: Nigel Partridge
Wildlife gardening expertise: Christine and Michael Lavelle
Birdhouse project contributors: Mary Maguire, Deena Beverley,
    Andrew Newton-Cox and Stephanie Donaldson
Editorial contributor: Dr Felicity Forster
Photographers: Peter Anderson, Michelle Garrett, David Parmiter,
    Robert Pickett and Peter Williams
Illustrators: Peter Barrett, Studio Galante, Stuart Jackson-Carter,
    Martin Knowelden, Liz Pepperell and Tim Thackeray
Maps: Anthony Duke
Index: Marie Lorimer
Production controller: Ben Worley

© Anness Publishing Ltd 2022

All rights reserved. No part of this publication may be reproduced,
stored in a retrieval system, or transmitted in any way or by any
means, electronic, mechanical, photocopying, recording, or
otherwise, without the prior written permission of the copyright
holder. A CIP catalogue record for this book is available from the
British Library.

PUBLISHER'S NOTE
Although the advice and information in this book are believed to be
accurate and true at the time of going to press, neither the authors
nor the publisher can accept any legal responsibility or liability for
any errors or omissions that may have been made nor for any
inaccuracies nor for any loss, harm or injury that comes about from
following instructions or advice in this book.

Front cover: starling (main); tree sparrows (left); European robin (top
left); black-capped chickadee (top right).
Page 1: House sparrows.
Page 2: Finches using a seed tube feeder with feeding ports.
Page 3: Northern flicker; red-breasted nuthatch.
Page 4: European robin.
Page 5: European greenfinch; American redstart.

CONTENTS

INTRODUCTION

Birds are an endless source of fascination and inspiration. Attracting birds to your garden or backyard and observing the variety of species that visit can develop into an absorbing pastime – and one that offers an unparalleled insight into the natural world.

Birds have influenced human cultures across the world, featuring in customs, religious festivals and also in many common sayings. The European robin (*Erithacus rubecula*), for example, has become inextricably linked with the celebration of Christmas, while the return of the cuckoo (*Cuculus canorus*) or bluebirds (*Sialia* species) from their wintering grounds is awaited as a sure sign of spring.

Whether your garden or backyard is in the countryside, a town or a city, it can play an important part in the conservation of wildlife, and especially birds. As farming becomes more intensive, and more and

Below: *Collared doves (*Streptopelia decaocto*) increased their range in the last century, and are now common visitors to rural and urban gardens.*

more of the countryside is swallowed up by new housing and industrial developments, the natural habitats of many birds are being reduced or lost altogether. Gardens are now more essential for the survival of birds than ever. A little planning will ensure that your garden is a welcoming haven for birds.

HELPING BIRDS

The average garden or backyard is regularly visited by 15–20 species of birds, with occasional visits from 10 less common species. By erecting a bird table and nest box, you will not only be offering nature a helping hand, but you will also provide yourself with hours of interest and entertainment. Your garden friends will also return the favour by controlling pests, such as aphids, slugs and snails, that threaten your flowerbeds and vegetable patch.

ABOUT THIS BOOK

This book is a celebration of garden and backyard birds, and sets out to reveal just some of the diversity in their form and lifestyles. The opening section describes the main physical and behavioural features of birds and explores how they live. The second section offers advice on how your garden can be planted or adapted to attract birds, providing food, drink and shelter, and how you can greatly increase the number and variety of birds that visit. There are tips on what to feed birds and when, where to site feeders and birdhouses, as well as how to keep birds safe from predators. There are planting suggestions for flowers, shrubs and trees that offer the most suitable natural environment for birds.

Birdhouses are a charming addition to any garden. They help to ornament and personalize it, and give an even greater satisfaction if you have made them yourself. The third section of this book offers a selection of projects for those keen on craft and DIY. These projects range from simple decorated nest boxes to elaborately constructed houses. There are creative ideas for feeders and birdbaths, with something to suit every garden, and every level of practical expertise.

The directory sections that follow provide illustrated guides to some of the typical bird species that are likely to be seen in British and North American gardens. It is impossible to profile every bird that you might encounter, but noting the bird's overall profile and the habitat where you spot it will provide a pointer to the group to which it belongs, and an informative starting point for identification.

Creating a haven for birds is a hugely satisfying activity. It is pure joy when you see a bird visiting your feeding station, or even starting to build its new home in a nest box that you have made.

Right: *Once you have set up bird feeders in your garden, you will be rewarded with sights such as this.*

HOW BIRDS LIVE

Birds display many diverse characteristics, but have several key features in common. The most obvious of these is the presence of feathers. The need for birds' bodies to be lightweight so that they can fly with minimum effort has led to evolutionary changes in their anatomy, and yet the basic skeletal structure of all birds is remarkably similar, irrespective of size. The other feature unique to birds is that all species reproduce by means of calcareous eggs. Actual breeding habits are very diverse, however. There is even greater diversity in the feeding habits of birds, as reflected by differences in bill structure and also in their digestive tracts.

Left: *The male Virginian cardinal (*Cardinalis cardinalis) *is a scarlet colour. It defends its territory aggressively against other males in the area.*

Above: *A stout, conical bill, such as that of this male rose-breasted grosbeak* (Pheucticus ludovicianus), *helps crack seeds.*

Above: *Thrushes such as this song thrush* (Turdus philomelos) *are welcome visitors to gardens because of their tuneful singing.*

Above: *Woodpeckers (such as this great spotted,* Dendropocus major) *are among the largest birds that might visit a garden.*

PARTS OF A BIRD

The bird's skeleton has evolved to be light yet robust, both characteristics that help with flight. To this end, certain bones, particularly in the skull, have become fused, while others are absent, along with the teeth. The result is that birds' bodies are very light compared to those of other vertebrates.

In order to be able to fly, a bird needs a lightweight body so that it can become airborne with minimal difficulty. It is not just teeth that are missing from the bird's skull, but the associated heavy jaw muscles as well. These have been replaced by a light, horn-covered bill that is adapted in shape to the bird's feeding habits. Some of the limb bones, such as the humerus in the shoulder, are hollow, which also cuts down on weight. At the rear of the body, the bones in the vertebral column have become fused, which gives greater stability as well as support for the tail feathers.

AVIAN SKELETON

In birds, the greatest degree of specialization is evident in the limbs. The location of the legs is critical to enable a bird to maintain its balance. The legs are found close to the midline, set slightly back near the bird's centre of gravity. The limbs are powerful, helping to provide lift at take-off and absorb the impact of landing. Strong legs also allow most birds to hop over the ground with relative ease.

There are some differences in the skeleton between various groups of birds. For example, the neckbones of hornbills are slightly different to those of other birds.

FEET AND TOES

Birds' feet vary in length. The feet of wading birds are noticeably extended, which helps them to distribute their weight more evenly when moving over soft mud or floating vegetation. The four toes may be arranged either in a typical 3:1 perching grip, with three toes gripping the front of the perch and one behind, or in a 2:2 configuration, known as zygodactyl, which gives a surer grip. The zygodactyl grip is seen in a few groups of birds, notably woodpeckers (Piciformes) and also parrots (Psittaciformes). Having two toes pointing in either direction gives the woodpecker a firm hold as it scales vertical tree trunks. The same arrangement helps some parrots to use their feet like hands for holding food.

Birds generally have claws at the ends of their toes, which have developed into sharp talons in the case of birds of prey, helping them to catch their quarry even in flight. Many birds also use their claws for preening, and they can provide balance for birds that run or climb.

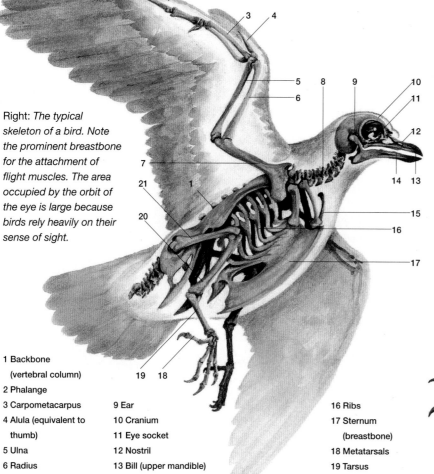

Right: *The typical skeleton of a bird. Note the prominent breastbone for the attachment of flight muscles. The area occupied by the orbit of the eye is large because birds rely heavily on their sense of sight.*

Parrot

Bird of prey

Above: *Parrots use their feet for holding food, rather like human hands.*

Above: *In birds of prey, the claws have become talons for grasping prey.*

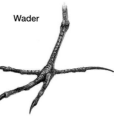

Wader

Duck

Above: *Long toes make it easier for waders to walk over muddy ground or water plants.*

Above: *The webbed feet of ducks provide propulsion in water.*

1 Backbone
   (vertebral column)
2 Phalange
3 Carpometacarpus
4 Alula (equivalent to
   thumb)
5 Ulna
6 Radius
7 Humerus
8 Cervical vertebrae

9 Ear
10 Cranium
11 Eye socket
12 Nostril
13 Bill (upper mandible)
14 Bill (lower mandible)
15 Clavicle (wishbone)

16 Ribs
17 Sternum
   (breastbone)
18 Metatarsals
19 Tarsus
20 Tibia and Fibula
21 Femur

BILLS

The bills of birds vary quite widely in shape and size, and reflect their feeding habits. The design of the bill also has an impact on the amount of force that it can generate. The bills of finches such as chaffinches and American goldfinches are strong enough to crack seeds. A bird's bill has many purposes, being used not only for feeding but also for preening, nest-building and, where necessary, defence.

Above: *The narrow bill of waders such as this curlew* (Numenius arquata) *enables the bird to probe for food in sand or mud.*

Above: *Woodpeckers, such as this pileated woodpecker* (Dryocopus pileatus), *have straight bills ideal for chiselling under bark.*

Above: *The chaffinch* (Fringilla coelebs) *has a short, stout, cone-shaped beak suited to cracking seeds.*

WINGS

A bird's wing is built around just three digits, which correspond to human fingers. The three digits of birds provide a robust structure. The power of the wings is further enhanced by the fusion of the wrist bones and the carpals to create the single bone known as the carpometacarpus, which runs along the rear of the wing.

At the front of the chest, the clavicles are joined together to form what in chickens

Above: *Birds of prey such as the sparrowhawk* (Accipiter nisus) *rely on a sharp bill with a hooked tip to tear their prey apart.*

Above: *The broad bill of the mallard* (Anas platyrhynchos) *allows it to filter plant food from the water.*

Above: *Hummingbirds* (Trochilidae) *have long, slender bills that they use to probe tubular-shaped flowers to gain nectar.*

is called the wishbone. The large, keel-shaped breastbone, or sternum, runs along the underside of the body. It is bound by the ribs to the backbone to provide stability, especially during flight. In addition, the major flight muscles are located in the lower body when the bird is airborne.

DARWIN'S FINCHES

In the 1830s, a voyage to the remote Galapagos Islands off South America helped the British naturalist Charles Darwin formulate his theory of evolution. The finches on the Galapagos Islands are all believed to be descended from a single ancestor, but have evolved in different ways. The changes are most obvious in their bill shapes. For example, some species have stout, crushing beaks for cracking seeds, while others have long, slender beaks to probe for insects. These adaptations have arisen to take full advantage of the range of edible items available on the islands, where food is generally scarce.

Below: *The finches of the Galapagos Islands helped to inspire Charles Darwin's theory of evolution. Some species have stout bills for crushing seeds, while those with pointed bills eat insects. Others have bills specialized for eating cactus, buds and fruit. The woodpecker finch* (Camarhynchus pallidus) *(bottom) uses a cactus spine to winkle out grubs hiding in tree bark.*

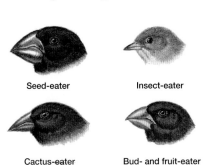

Seed-eater   **Insect-eater**

Cactus-eater   **Bud- and fruit-eater**

Grub-eater

FEATHERS

The presence of feathers is one of the main distinguishing characteristics that set birds apart from all other animals on the planet. The number of feathers on a bird's body varies considerably – a swan may have as many as 25,000 feathers, for instance, while a tiny hummingbird has just 1,000 in all.

Aside from the bill, legs and feet, the entire body of the bird is covered in feathers. The plumage does not grow randomly over the bird's body, but develops along lines of so-called feather tracts, or pterylae. These are separated by bald areas known as apteria. The apteria are not conspicuous under normal circumstances, because the contour feathers overlap to cover the entire surface of the body. Plumage may also sometimes extend down over the legs and feet as well, in the case of birds from cold climates, providing the extra insulation that is needed there.

Feathers are made of a tough protein called keratin, which is also found in our hair and nails. There are three main types of feathers on a bird's body: the body, or contour, feathers; the strong, elongated flight feathers on the wings; and the warm, wispy down feathers next to the bird's skin.

A diet deficient in sulphur-containing amino acids, which are the basic building blocks of protein, will result in poor feathering, creating 'nutritional barring' across the flight and tail feathers. Abnormal plumage coloration can also have nutritional causes in some cases. These changes are usually reversible if more favourable environmental conditions precede the next moult.

FUNCTION OF FEATHERS

Plumage has a number of functions, not just relating to flight. It provides a barrier that retains warm air close to the bird's body and helps to maintain body temperature, which is higher in birds than mammals – typically between 41 and 43.5°C (106 and 110°F). The down feathering that lies close to the skin and the overlying contour plumage are vital for maintaining body warmth. Most species of birds have a small volume relative to their surface area, which can leave them vulnerable to hypothermia.

A special oil produced by the preen gland, located at the base of the tail, waterproofs the plumage. This oil, which is spread over the feathers as the bird preens itself, prevents water penetrating the feathers, which would cause the bird to become so waterlogged that it could no longer fly.

Below: *The American robin (*Turdus migratorius*), a member of the thrush family, has a characteristic red breast. The sexes look similar, although the female is paler.*

Left: *A bird's flight feathers are longer and more rigid than the contour feathers that cover the body, or the fluffy down feathers that lie next to the skin. The longest, or primary, flight feathers, which generate most thrust, are located along the outer rear wing edges. The tail feathers are often similar in shape to the flight feathers, with the longest in the centre.*

1 Primaries
2 Secondaries
3 Axillaries
4 Rump
5 Lateral tail feathers
6 Central tail feathers
7 Breast
8 Cere
9 Auricular region (ear)
10 Nape
11 Back
12 Greater under-wing coverts
13 Lesser under-wing coverts

Above: *Like other birds, tree sparrows* (Passer montanus) *spend time each day preening. This helps to keep feathers clean and tidy and also reduces parasites.*

The contour feathers that cover the body are also important for camouflage in many birds. Barring in particular breaks up the outline of the bird's body, helping to conceal it in its natural habitat.

The plumage has become modified in some cases, reflecting the individual lifestyle of the species concerned. Woodpeckers, for example, have tail feathers that are short and rather sharp at their tips, providing additional support for gripping on to the sides of trees. The woodpecker's stiff tail and feet with toes pointing forwards and backwards create a sturdy, tripod-like stance.

SIGNIFICANCE OF PLUMAGE

Plumage can be important in social interactions between birds. Many species have differences in their feathering that separate males from females, and often juveniles can be distinguished from their parents by their plumage. Although the rule does not apply in every case, cock birds are generally more brightly coloured than hens, which helps them to attract mates, while the female's dull colours help conceal her while she incubates eggs on the nest.

The difference between the sexes in terms of their plumage can be quite marked, for example in mallards. Cock birds of a number of species have feathers forming crests as well as magnificent tail plumes, which are seen to greatest effect in peacocks (*Pavo cristatus*), whose display is one of the most remarkable sights in the avian world.

Waterfowl may display eclipse plumage, at the time of year when they are not breeding, being much plainer in appearance at this stage.

Recent studies have confirmed that birds that appear relatively dull in colour to our eyes, such as the starling, with its blackish plumage, are seen literally in a different light by other birds. They can visualize the ultraviolet component of light, which is normally invisible to us, making these seemingly dull birds appear greener. Ultraviolet coloration may also be significant in helping birds to choose their mates.

MOULTING

Birds' feathering is maintained by regular preening, but even so, it becomes frayed and worn over time. It is therefore replaced by new plumage during the process of moulting, when the old feathers are shed. Many birds moult their feathers according to a given pattern that varies according to species. In many cases the flight feathers are shed symmetrically, the same number being lost from each wing at a time. This helps the bird to remain balanced.

Moulting is most often an annual event. However, many young birds shed their nest feathers before they are a year old. Moulting may also be triggered by the onset of the breeding season. Some birds become more strikingly coloured at this time. Hormonal alterations in the body are important in triggering this process, with external factors such as changing day length also playing a part.

IRIDESCENCE

Some birds are not brightly coloured, but their plumage literally sparkles in the light, thanks to its structure, which creates an iridescent effect. One of the particular features of iridescence is that the colour of the plumage alters, depending on the angle at which it is viewed, often appearing quite dark or almost black from a side view. This phenomenon is particularly common in some groups of birds, notably members of the starling family (Sturnidae), which are described as having metallic feathers as a result.

In some cases, the iridescent feathering is localized, while in others it is widespread over most of the body. Green and blue iridescence is common, with reddish sheens being seen less often. Iridescence is especially seen in cock birds, helping them to attract their mates.

Below: *A common starling* (Sturnus vulgaris) *displays its iridescent plumage.*

Right: *The feather shaft holds the feather in place in the skin. The barbs run off the shaft at regular intervals, like the branches of a tree, and divide into smaller branches called barbules. These have tiny hooks attached to them that reinforce the structure of the flight feather.*

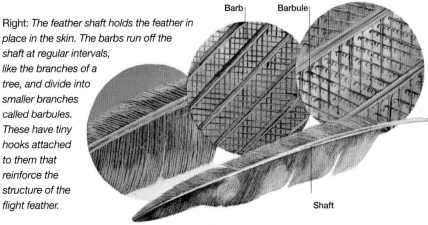

Barb   Barbule

Shaft

FLIGHT

Some birds seen in gardens spend much of their lives in the air, whereas others will only fly as a last resort if threatened. The mechanics of flight are similar in all birds, but flight patterns vary significantly, which can help you to identify the various groups in the air.

The structure of the bird's body has evolved to facilitate flight. It is important for a bird's body weight to be relatively light, because this lessens the muscular effort required to keep it airborne. The powerful flight muscles, which provide the necessary lift, can account for up to a third of the bird's total body weight. They are attached to the breastbone, or sternum, in the midline of the body, and run along the sides of the body from the clavicle along the breastbone to the top of the legs.

WEIGHT AND FLIGHT
There is an upper weight limit of just over 18kg (40lb), above which birds would not be able to take off successfully. Some larger birds, notably swans, need a run-up in order to gain sufficient momentum to lift off, particularly from water. Smaller birds can dart straight off a perch. Some of the heavier flying birds, such as pheasants, prefer to run rather than fly because of the effort involved in becoming airborne.

WING SHAPE AND BEAT
The shape of the wing is important for a bird's flying ability. Birds that remain airborne for much of their lives, such as swifts, have relatively long wings that allow them to glide with relatively little effort.

Above: *The feathers of the barn owl (Tyto alba) have fringed edges. This allows it to fly without the slightest sound, and swoop down on its prey without being detected.*

The swift's narrow wings make it fast and also manoeuvrable. Some larger predatory birds such as kites and falcons use rising columns of air called thermals, caused by warm air rising from the ground, to provide uplift, and then circle around in them.

The number of wing beats varies dramatically between different species. Hummingbirds are renowned for beating their wings more frequently than any other bird as they hover in front of flowers to harvest their nectar. Their wings move so fast – at over 200 beats per minute – that they produce a buzzing sound and appear

Above: *Predatory birds such as red kites (Milvus milvus) use rising air currents to stay aloft. Such species may struggle to fly early in the day when little warm air is rising.*

as a blur to the eyes. At the other extreme, heavy birds such as swans fly with slow, deliberate wing beats.

LIGHTENING THE LOAD
The lightness of a bird's skeleton helps it to fly. There have been evolutionary changes in body organs, too, most noticeably in the urinary system. Unlike mammals, birds do not have a bladder that fills with urine. Instead, their urine is greatly concentrated, in the form of uric acid, and passes out of the body with their faeces, appearing as a creamy-white, semi-solid component.

Below: *These illustrations show a typical take-off sequence, in this case by a large bird of prey.*

1 When resting, a bird typically has a relatively upright stance.

2 As it leans forwards for take-off, it raises its wings and starts to lift its legs.

3 Leaving its perch, the bird pushes off into the air, and opens its wings.

Above: *Waterfowl such as this mallard (*Anas platyrhyunchos*) have few difficulties becoming airborne from water, as their plumage is designed to prevent waterlogging.*

FLIGHT PATTERNS

Different species of birds have various ways of flying, which can aid the bird-watcher in helping to identify them. For example, small birds such as tits and finches alternately flap their wings and fold them at their sides, adopting a streamlined shape, which helps to save energy. This produces a characteristic dipping flight that aids recognition. Large birds such as ducks and geese maintain a straighter course at an even height.

In some cases, it is not just the individual flying skills of a bird that help it to stay airborne, but those of its fellows nearby. Birds flying in formation create a slipstream, which makes flying less effort for all the birds behind the leader. This is why birds often fly in formation, especially when covering long distances on migration.

THE AEROFOIL PRINCIPLE

Once in flight, the shape of the wing is crucial in keeping the bird airborne. Viewed in cross-section from the side, a bird's wing resembles an aeroplane's wing, called an aerofoil, and in fact aeroplanes use the same technique as birds to fly.

The wing is curved across the top, so the movement of air is faster over this part of the wing compared with the lower surface. This produces reduced air pressure on top of the wing, which provides lift and makes it easier for the bird to stay in the air.

The long flight feathers at the rear edge of the wings help to provide the thrust and lift for flight. The tail feathers, too, can help the bird remain airborne. The kestrel (*Falco tinnunculus*), for example, having spotted prey on the ground, spreads its tail feathers to help it remain aloft while it hovers to target its prey.

A bird's wings move in a regular figure-of-eight movement while it is in flight. During the downstroke, the flight feathers join together to push powerfully against the air. The primary flight feathers bend backwards, which propels the bird forwards. As the wing moves upwards, the longer primary flight feathers move apart, which reduces air resistance. The secondary feathers further along the wing provide some slight propulsion. After that the cycle repeats itself.

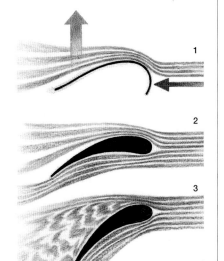

Above: *The way the air flows over a bird's wing varies according to the wing's position.*
1 When the wing is stretched out horizontally, an area of low pressure is created above the wing, causing lift.
2 As the wing is tilted downwards, the flow of the air is disrupted, causing turbulence and loss of lift.
3 When the wing is angled downwards, lift slows, which results in stalling. The bird's speed slows as a consequence. Splaying the tail feathers also increases drag and so slows the bird down, particularly prior to landing.

4 Powerful upwards and downwards sweeps of the wings propel the bird forwards.

5 When coming in to land, a bird lowers its legs and slows its wing movements.

6 Braking is achieved by a vertical landing posture, with the tail feathers spread.

SENSES

The keen senses of birds are vital to their survival, in particular helping them to find food, escape from enemies and find mates in the breeding season. Sight is the primary sense for most birds, but some species rely heavily on other senses to thrive in particular habitats.

All birds' senses are adapted to their environment, and the shape of their bodies can help to reflect which senses are most significant to them.

SIGHT

Most birds rely on their sense of sight to avoid danger, hunt for food and locate familiar surroundings. The importance of this sense is reflected by the size of their eyes, with those of starlings (*Sturnus vulgaris*), for example, making up 15 per cent of the total head weight. The enlargement of the eyeballs and associated structures, notably the eye sockets in the skull, has altered the shape of the brain. In addition, the optic lobes in the brain, which are concerned with vision, are also enlarged, whereas the olfactory counterparts, responsible for smell, are poorly developed.

The structure of the eye also reveals much about a bird's habits. Birds of prey have large eyes in proportion to their head, and have correspondingly keen eyesight. Species that regularly hunt for prey underwater, such as kingfishers, can see well in the water. Some aquatic birds have a muscle in each eye that reduces the diameter of the lens and increases its thickness on entering water, so that their eyes can adjust easily to seeing underwater. In addition, diving birds such as the common kingfisher have a lens that forms part of the nictitating membrane, or third eyelid, which is normally hidden from sight. Underwater, when this membrane covers the eye, its convex shape serves as a lens, helping the bird to see in these surroundings.

The positioning of the eyes on the head gives important clues to a bird's lifestyle. Most birds' eyes are set on the sides of their heads. Owls, however, have flattened faces and forward-facing eyes that are critical to their hunting abilities. These features allow owls to target their prey.

There is a disadvantage to this arrangement. Owls' eyes do not give a rounded view of the world, so they must turn their heads to see about them. It is not just the positioning of owls' eyes that is unusual. They are also able to hunt effectively in almost complete darkness. This is made possible in two ways. First, their pupils are large, which maximizes the amount of light passing through to the retina behind the lens, where the image is formed. Second, the

Above: *Sight is very important for birds, like this blackbird (*Turdus merula*). Birds have excellent colour vision, and can see more colours than us.*

cells here consist mainly of rods rather than cones. While cones give good colour vision, rods function to create images when background illumination is low.

The positioning of the eyes of game birds such as woodcocks (*Scolopax rusticola*) and American woodcocks (*Scolopax minor*) allows them to spot danger from almost any angle. It is even possible for them to see a predator sneaking up from behind. The only blind spot of these birds is just behind the head.

SMELL

The chemical senses (smell and taste) are relatively undeveloped in most birds, and garden birds are no exception. Very few birds have a keen sense of smell, with kiwis and vultures providing notable exceptions. Birds' nostrils are normally located above the bill, opening directly into the skull, but kiwis' nostrils are positioned right at the end of the long bill. They probably help these birds to locate earthworms in the soil. Vultures have very keen eyesight, which helps them to spot dead animals on the ground from the air, but they also have a strong sense of smell, which helps them to home in on a carcass.

FIELD OF VISION

The positioning of a bird's eyes on its head affects its field of vision. The eyes of owls are positioned to face forwards, producing an overlapping image of the area in front known as binocular vision. This allows the owl to pinpoint its prey exactly, so that it can strike. In contrast, the eyes of birds that are likely to be preyed upon, such as woodcocks, are positioned on the sides of the head. This eye position gives a greatly reduced area of binocular vision, but it does give these birds practically all-round vision, enabling them to spot danger from all sides.

Woodcock
(*Scolopax*
species)

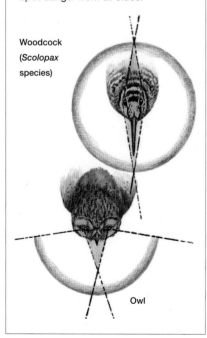

Owl

ECHOLOCATION

This technique helps Mascarene swiftlets (*Collocalia francica*) to navigate inside dark caves. These birds utter a stream of high-frequency clicks, which echo back off surrounding surfaces. The time lapse between clicks and echoes indicates the proximity of objects within range, which helps to prevent collisions.

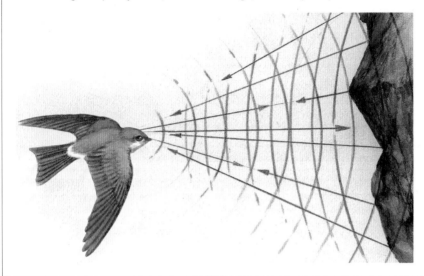

TASTE

The senses of smell and taste are linked, and most birds also have correspondingly few taste buds in their mouths. The number of taste buds varies, with differences between groups of birds. Blue tits and some titmice may have as few as 24 taste buds. Pigeons have around 50, while parrots have up to 400. This compares to around 10,000 taste buds in our own mouths.

Below: *The common kingfisher (*Alcedo atthis*) is able to use sight to track prey such as fish underwater, thanks to a protective membrane that covers the eyes while the bird is submerged.*

Birds' taste buds are located all around the mouth, rather than just on the tongue, as in mammals. The close links between smell and taste can lead vultures, which feed only on fresh carcasses, to reject decomposing meat. They may start to eat it, but then spit it out once it is in their mouths, probably because of a combination of bad odour and taste.

HEARING

Birds generally do not have a highly developed sense of hearing. They lack any external ear flaps that would help to pinpoint sources of sound. The openings to their hearing system are located on the sides of the head, back from the eyes. These openings are usually hidden by the plumage, and so cannot be seen. Some owls have ear tufts, but these are usually unrelated to hearing.

Hearing is of particular significance for nocturnal species, such as owls, which find their food in darkness. These birds are highly attuned to the high-pitched squeaks and rustling noises made by rodents. The broad shape of their skull has the additional advantage of spacing the ear openings more widely, which helps them to localize the source of the sounds with greater accuracy. Hearing is also important to birds during the breeding season. They are able to pinpoint the calls of their own species within a chorus of birdsong, which helps to find mates. Later in the season, parent birds show particular sensitivity to sounds falling within the vocal range of their chicks, which helps them to locate their offspring easily in the critical early days after fledging.

TOUCH

The sense of touch is more developed in some birds than others. Those such as snipe (*Gallinago* species), which have long bills for seeking food, have sensitive nerve endings called corpuscles in their bills that pick up tiny vibrations caused by their prey. Vibrations that could suggest approaching danger can also register via other corpuscles located particularly in the legs, so that the bird has a sensory awareness even when it is resting on a branch.

INTELLIGENCE

Birds have considerable intelligence, with species such as tits noted for their problem-solving abilities. Some species are more intelligent than others. Field studies of wild birds suggest that corvids (members of the crow family, such as jays and magpies), have quite keen intellects. Jays are able to remember where they have cached food items such as acorns. Both corvids and parrots do well in laboratory tests, including tests involving recognition, tool-using and basic counting.

Below: *Owls, such as this eastern screech owl (*Otus asio*), have forward-facing eyes specialized for hunting in dim light. Keen hearing also helps this nocturnal hunter to track prey, such as rodents.*

FINDING FOOD

The birds that visit your garden feed on a wide range of foods including seeds, berries, insects, slugs and worms. A few hunt larger prey, including other backyard or garden birds. The shape of a bird's body and especially its bill is suited to finding and dealing with its particular diet.

As small flying creatures, birds have a high-energy lifestyle. Finding an adequate supply of food is vital to daily survival, and particularly essential in the breeding season. Birds' mating habits are timed so that abundant food is available during the period when parents must supply huge amounts of it to their hungry young.

Food not needed to fuel immediate activity is stored as fat, which is 'burned' when food is scarce. The aim of every feeding bird is to gain maximum nutrition with the minimum of effort. For this reason, many birds switch between various foods as they become abundant at particular times of year.

MEAT-EATERS

Animal foods such as insects, spiders, slugs and worms are high in energy and protein, but may take considerable effort to capture and swallow. Large insects such as bees and butterflies are high in nourishment but are less numerous, compared with tiny insects such as midges. They, however, have to be caught and consumed in large quantities to meet the bird's food requirements. Backyard

Below: *Tanagers, such as this summer tanager (*Piranga rubra*), mostly eat insects, though they also eat berries in autumn.*

THE DIGESTIVE SYSTEM
Birds lack teeth, so their food must be small enough to be swallowed and digested easily. Birds have a storage organ known as the crop, located at the base of the neck. From here, food passes down into the proventriculus, where the digestive process starts, before entering the gizzard, which is equivalent to the mammalian stomach. Nutrients are then absorbed through the wall of the small intestine.

The digestive system of plant-eaters differs in various respects from that of predatory species. For example, plants are a less nourishing food than meat, so plant-eaters must possess longer digestive tracts than other birds, to process the large quantities of food they consume in order to obtain enough nourishment.

In addition, digesting plant matter poses certain difficulties. The gizzards of seed-eating species such as finches have especially thick muscular walls, which serve to grind up the seeds. These birds often swallow small stones and grit, which remain in their gizzards and help to break down the seeds.

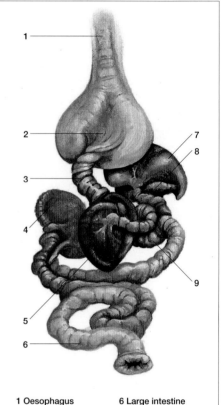

1 Oesophagus	6 Large intestine
2 Crop	7 Liver
3 Proventriculus	8 Spleen
4 Pancreas	9 Small intestine
5 Gizzard	

birds that are insect-eaters aid gardeners in helping to control invertebrate pests. Species such as woodpeckers, kinglets and treecreepers hunt for bugs beneath the bark of tree trunks. Other birds hunt among leaves or on the ground. Swifts, swallows, martins, flycatchers and nightjars hunt their food on the wing. Aerial hunters such as flycatchers prefer to feed on bluebottle-size insects. Worms satisfy most of the moisture requirements for species such as blackbirds, American robins and some other thrushes, so these birds rarely need to drink. The same birds can die if they consume slugs or snails containing conventional garden pesticides, so use environmentally friendly brands if these pests frequent your garden.

PREDATORS AND SCAVENGERS
Some birds that visit backyards are active predators, seeking and killing prey including smaller birds, such as sparrows. American kestrels (*Falco sparverius*), prairie falcons (*Falco mexicanus*) and sparrowhawks (*Accipiter nisus*) feed mainly on other birds. Another occasional garden visitor, the peregrine falcon (*Falco peregrinus*) is among the most agile of hunting birds. Many predatory birds are opportunistic feeders, hunting when food is plentiful but scavenging when it becomes scarce.

Corvids (members of the crow family) such as magpies and jays are both scavengers and hunters. They are unpopular with bird-lovers because of their habit of stealing the

Above: *Pied wagtails (*Motacilla alba*) feed on a wide range of invertebrates, including flies, snails and this earthworm.*

eggs and nestlings of songbirds. The same species also alight on road kills and other casualties to find rich pickings to eat.

PLANT-EATERS

Many different types of birds are primarily plant-eaters, whether feeding on flowers, fruit, nuts, seeds or other plant matter. Plant-eaters have to eat a large volume of food compared to meat-eating species,

Below: *The goldfinch (*Carduelis carduelis*) can pluck seeds from pits in the seedhead of a teasel with its fine-tipped beak.*

because of the low nutritional value of plants compared to that of prey such as invertebrates. In the last century or so, many species have benefited from the spread of agriculture, which now provides them with large acreages of suitable crop plants to feed on. These birds' feeding habits bring them into conflict with farmers when they breed rapidly in response to an expansion in their food supply.

FLOWER- AND FRUIT-EATERS

A number of birds rely on flowers as a source of food. Pollen is a valuable source of protein, while nectar provides sugars. Not surprisingly, flower-feeders tend to be confined to mainly tropical areas, where flowers are in bloom throughout the year.

Hummingbirds (Trochilidae) use their narrow bills to probe flowers for nectar. Some hummingbirds have developed especially curved or elongated bills, which allow them to feed on particular flowers. These birds help to pollinate the plants on which they feed by transferring pollen from flower to flower as they feed. Sunbirds (Nectariniidae) of Africa and Asia fill a similar evolutionary niche to hummingbirds, which they resemble in their small size and bright, often iridescent plumage.

Exclusively frugivorous (fruit-eating) birds such as fruit doves (*Ptilinopus* species) are found only in the tropics, where fruit is available throughout the year. Fruit- and berry-eaters help plants to reproduce. The seeds of the fruits they eat pass right through their digestive tracts unharmed, to be deposited far from the parent plant, which helps the plants to spread.

NUT- AND SEED-EATERS

Dry foods are a valuable resource to many different types of birds, ranging from parrots to finches. However, cracking nuts' tough outer shells or husks can be a problem. Finches such as grosbeaks have evolved a particularly strong bill for this purpose. Hawfinches (*Coccothraustes coccothraustes*) are able to crack cherry stones to extract the kernel.

The most bizarre example of bill adaptation for eating seeds is seen in the crossbills (*Loxia* species) of northern coniferous forests in North America. These birds have twisted upper and lower mandibles, which enable them to crack open the seeds inside larch cones, on which they feed.

OMNIVORES

These are birds that eat both animal and plant foods. Most of these species are opportunists, switching between foods as they come into season. Many feed mainly on plant foods such as seeds or nuts in autumn and winter, and switch to insects to nourish themselves and their young in the breeding season.

ADAPTING TO THE SEASONS

Birds from temperate areas exist on a varied diet that is closely related to the seasons. Bullfinches (*Pyrrhula pyrrhula*), for example, eat buds in apple orchards in spring – when they can become a pest – while later in the year, they consume seeds and fruit. Pine grosbeaks (*Pinicola enucleator*), too, consume seeds, buds, fruit, berries, and also invertebrates at different times of year. The bills of both these species, like those of most other members of the finch family, are stout and relatively conical, which helps them to crack seeds effectively.

Some birds store plant food when it is plentiful, in order to sustain them through the leaner months. Nutcrackers (*Nucifraga* species) collect hazelnuts to feed on in winter, and corvids, particularly jays, collect nuts and acorns to feed on during winter. Acorn woodpeckers (*Melanerpes formicivorus*) drill holes in trees that they fill with acorns, creating an easily accessible larder for the winter, when snow may cover the ground.

Below: *Red-bellied woodpeckers (*Melanerpes carolinus*) are omnivores, even feeding on songbird nestlings.*

SINGING, COURTSHIP AND PAIRING

Birdsong is a key element in courtship and pairing, serving to establish territory and attract mates. It is of particular interest to birdwatchers because it helps in species identification. Birds' breeding habits vary greatly. Some species pair up only fleetingly in the breeding season, while others pair for life.

In songbirds, the start of the breeding season generally coincides with the time of abundant food we know as spring. A number of factors trigger the onset of the breeding period. In temperate areas, as the days start to lengthen in spring, the increase in daylight is detected by the pineal gland in the bird's brain, which starts a complex series of hormonal changes in the body. Most birds form a bond with a single partner during the breeding season, which is often preceded by an elaborate display by the cock bird.

BIRDSONG

Many cock birds announce their presence by their song, which both attracts would-be mates and establishes a claim to a territory. Once pairing has occurred, the male may cease singing, but in some cases he starts to perform a duet with the hen, with each bird singing in turn.

Singing serves to keep members of the pair in touch with each other. In some species, the pair co-ordinate their songs so precisely that although the cock bird may

sing the first few notes, and then the hen, it sounds as if the song is being sung by just one bird. Other birds may sing in unison. In a few species, it may even be possible for experts to tell the length of time that the pair have been together by the degree of harmony in their particular songs.

Above: *Feral pigeons, also known as rock doves (*Columba livia*) are sociable birds that often gather to feed in flocks. This pair of pigeons is exhibiting a type of courtship behaviour known as kissing, which is linked to ritualized feeding.*

Studies have revealed that young male birds start warbling quite quietly, and then sing more loudly as they mature. Young songbirds know just the basics of their species' song by instinct. As they mature, they refine their singing by copying the songs of the adults around them. Finally, when their song pattern becomes fixed, it remains constant throughout the bird's life.

It is obviously possible to identify different species by differences in their song patterns. However, there are sometimes marked variations between the songs of individuals of the same species that live in different places. Local dialects have been identified in various parts of a species' distribution, as in the case of chiffchaffs (*Phylloscopus collybita*) from neighbouring valleys separated by hills or mountains or white-crowned sparrows (*Zonotrichia leucophrys*) from different regions. In addition, studies have shown that over the course of several generations, the pattern of songs produced by individuals can alter markedly.

Below: *In blue-winged warblers (*Vermivora cyanoptera*), as in other species, males sing to attract females and warn away rival males.*

Below: *Reed buntings (*Emberiza schoeniclus*) identify their mates by song and also by the different colours of the male and female.*

Above: *Ritualized feeding plays a role in the courtship behaviour of hawfinches (Coccothraustes coccothraustes). During courtship, the male offers the female food items, such as seeds, to prove he is a suitable partner. Initially the birds may only touch bills, but as the bond grows, so they share food in this way.*

SONG PRODUCTION

Birds produce their sounds – even those species capable of mimicking human speech – without the benefit of a larynx and vocal cords like humans. The song is created in a voice organ called the syrinx, which is located in the bird's throat, at the bottom of the windpipe, or trachea.

The structure of the syrinx is very variable, being at its most highly developed in the case of songbirds, which possess as many as nine pairs of separate muscles to control the vocal output. As in the human larynx, it is the movement of air through the syrinx that enables the membranes here to vibrate, creating sound as the bird exhales. The pitch of notes is controlled by rings of cartilage that tighten or loosen to vary the sounds produced.

An organ called the interclavicular air sac also plays an important role in sound production; birds cannot sing without it. The distance over which bird calls can travel is remarkable – up to 5km (3 miles) in the case of species such as the bittern (*Botaurus stellaris*) or American bittern (*B. lentiginosus*), which have a particularly deep, penetrating song. High, shrill notes can also carry long distances. Wrens produce a very loud song relative to their small size.

Song complexity also varies greatly among types of garden birds. Species such as the cuckoo and doves seem content to repeat a single phrase with little variation that human ears can detect. In contrast, species such as thrushes have several hundred different phrases in their repertoire. These are combined in many different ways to produce a song that is constantly changing.

COURTSHIP DISPLAYS

Many birds rely on their breeding finery to attract their mates. The bright or bold colours of male birds are designed to warn off rival males and attract the females. Thus it is usually the female that selects her mate. She bases her choice not only on her potential mate's appearance but also on his singing

talents, and in some cases, on his ability to demonstrate nest-building or food-providing skills. Male kingfishers and pine siskins present their mates with fish to vouchsafe their ability to provide food for their young, while male robins may proffer worms.

Some types of birds, though not generally garden birds, assemble in communal display areas known as leks, where hens witness the males' displays and select a mate. A number of different species, including some game birds and also hummingbirds, establish leks. In a few species, such as the bowerbirds of Australia, the male constructs elaborate bowers of grass that he decorates with items of a particular colour, such as blue, varying from flowers to pieces of glass.

PAIR BONDING

Many male and female birds form no lasting relationship, although the pair bond may be strong during the nesting period. It is usually only in potentially long-lived species, for example, storks and waterfowl such as swans, that a lifelong pair bond is formed.

Pair bonding in long-lived species has certain advantages. The young of such birds are usually slow to mature, and are therefore often unlikely to nest themselves for five years or even more. By remaining for a period in a family group, the adults can improve the long-term survival prospects of their young.

Below: *Studies of the song patterns of chiffchaffs (*Phylloscopus collybita*) in neighbouring valleys show slight variations.*

NESTING AND EGG-LAYING

Birds vary in their nesting habits, some constructing very simple nests and others making elaborate ones. All birds reproduce by laying eggs, which are covered with a hard, calcareous shell. The number of eggs laid at a time – known as the clutch size – varies between species, as does egg coloration.

Most birds construct their nests from vegetation, depending on which materials are locally available. In coastal areas, some seabirds use pieces of seaweed to build theirs. Artificial materials such as plastic wrappers or polystyrene may even be used by some birds.

Different types of birds build nests of various shapes and sizes, which are characteristic of their species. Groups such as finches build nests in the form of an open cup, often concealed in vegetation. Most pigeons and doves construct a loose platform of twigs. Swallows are among the birds that use mud to construct their nests. They scoop muddy water up from the surface of a pond or puddle, mould it into shape on a suitable wall, and then allow it to dry and harden like cement.

The simplest nests are composed of little more than a pad of material, resting in the fork of a tree or on a building. The effort entailed in nest construction may reflect how often the birds are likely to nest. The platforms of pigeons and doves can disintegrate quite easily, resulting in the loss

Below: *House martins (*Delichon urbita*) are so-named for their habit of forming their mud nests under the protective eaves of houses. This largely aerial bird touches down only when breeding. It raises up to three broods between April and September.*

of eggs or chicks. However, if disaster does befall the nest, the pair will often breed again within a few weeks.

Cup-shaped nests are more elaborate than platform nests, usually made by weaving grasses and twigs together. The inside is often lined with soft feathers. Raised sides of the cup nest lessen the likelihood of losing eggs and chicks, and also offer greater security to the adults during incubation. The hollow in the nest's centre is created by the birds compressing the material here before egg-laying begins.

Suspended nests enclosed by a domed roof offer even greater security. They are less accessible to predators because of their design and also their position, often hanging from slender branches.

NEST SITES

Many birds use tree holes for nesting. Woodpeckers are particularly well equipped to create nesting chambers, using their powerful bills to enlarge holes in dead trees. The diameter of the entry hole thus created is just wide enough to allow the

Above: *Birds' nests are often located in secluded spots. If detected, they should always be left undisturbed and untouched.*

birds to enter easily, which helps to prevent the nest being robbed.

Some birds rely on safety in numbers to deter would-be predators, building communal nests that are occupied by successive generations and added to regularly. Rooks (*Corvus frugilegus*) are highly social corvids. Their communal sites, known as rookeries, may contain several hundred nests. Pine siskins (*Carduelis pinus*) are among the American birds that nest communally, in northern conifer forests.

Other birds, such as the common cuckoo (*Cuculus canorus*) and the cowbirds (*Molothrus*) of North America, lay and abandon their eggs in the nests of other species. The foster parents-to-be do not seem able to detect the difference between their own eggs and that of the intruder, so they do not reject the latter. They incubate it along with their own brood, and feed the foster chick when it hatches out.

Above: *This songbird chick is the first to hatch in the nest. Different types of birds will utilise different styles of nest, which helps to indicate the occupants.*

Birds that nest on the ground in open country, such as the horned lark (*Eremophila alpestris*) and lark bunting (*Calamospiza melanocorys*) are especially vulnerable to predators and rely heavily on their fairly drab colours as camouflage. Skylarks (*Alauda arvensis*) have another means of protecting the nest – they hold one wing down and pretend to be injured to draw a predator away.

Some birds return to the same nest site each year, but many birds simply abandon their old nest and build another. This may seem a waste of effort, but it actually helps to protect the birds from parasites such as blood-sucking mites, which can otherwise multiply in the confines of the nest.

MATING
For most birds, mating is a brief process. The male usually mounts the female, twisting his rump so that the cloacas, or body openings, of the two birds touch for a second. Spermatozoa swim up the hen's reproductive tract, and fertilize the ova at an early stage in the process. Generally, only one mating is required to fertilize a clutch of eggs. Hens can also lay unfertilized eggs if no male is around, but these eggs will not hatch however long they are incubated. The period between mating and egg-laying varies according to species. In small birds, the interval may be as little as ten days, while in larger species such as owls, it may be several months.

THE REPRODUCTIVE SYSTEMS
The cock bird has two testes located within his body. Spermatozoa pass down the vas deferens, into the cloaca and then out of the body. Insemination occurs when the vent areas of the male and female bird are in direct contact during mating. Cock birds do not have a penis for penetration, although certain groups, such as waterfowl, may have a primitive organ that is used to assist in the transference of semen in a similar way.

Normally only the left ovary and oviduct of the hen bird are functional. Eggs pass down through the reproductive tract from the ovary.

1 Testes	8 Isthmus
2 Kidneys	9 Egg with shell
3 Vas deferens	contained in
4 Cloaca	the hen's
5 Ova	reproductive tract
6 Infundibulum	10 Cloaca
7 Magnum	

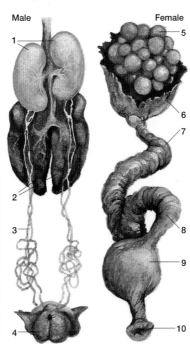

Male   Female

EGG SIZE AND COLOUR
The size of eggs produced by different species of birds varies dramatically. An ostrich's egg is thousands of times heavier than the eggs laid by wrens or hummingbirds. The coloration and markings of a bird's eggs are directly linked to the nesting site. Birds that usually breed in hollow trees produce white eggs, because these are normally hidden from predators and so do not need to be camouflaged. The pale coloration may also help the adult birds to locate the eggs as they return to the nest, thus lessening the chances of damaging them. Birds that build open, cup-shaped nests tend to lay coloured and often mottled eggs that are camouflaged and so less obvious to potential nest thieves.

CLUTCH SIZES
The number of eggs laid at a time varies according to species, as does the number of clutches produced in a year. Birds such as blue tits (*Cyanistes caeruleus*) lay one clutch of 10–12 eggs in spring, and American bushtits (*Psaltriparus minimus*) lay one or two clutches of 5–13 eggs. In contrast, female blackbirds (*Turdus merula*) can produce three clutches of up to 4 eggs in a single season and female American robins (*Turdus migratorius*) produce two or three clutches of 3–6 eggs.

Birds' breeding habits are often related to the food that will be fed to the nestlings. For example, blue tit nestlings are fed on caterpillars, which are most abundant in springtime, and bushtit nestlings are fed on tiny insects, which are most abundant in spring and summer. Robin nestlings are reared on berries and earthworms, found throughout the year.

Below: *Ostriches (*Struthio camelus*) lay the largest eggs in the world, which can weigh up to 1.5kg (3.3lb). In comparison, a chicken's egg looks tiny. The egg at the front is a hummingbird egg. These tiny birds lay the smallest eggs in the avian world, weighing only about 0.35g (0.01oz).*

HATCHING AND REARING CHICKS

Birds are vulnerable to predators when breeding, especially when they have young in the nest. The chicks must be fed frequently, necessitating regular trips to and from the nest, which makes it conspicuous. The calls of nestlings represent a further danger, so the breeding period is often short.

Most birds incubate their eggs to keep them sufficiently warm for the chicks to develop inside. Larger eggs are less prone to chilling during incubation than small eggs, because of their bigger volume. In the early stages of the incubation period, when the nest may be left uncovered while the adult birds are foraging for food, eggs can withstand a lower temperature. Temperature differences also account for the fact that, at similar altitudes, incubation periods tend to be slightly longer in temperate areas than in tropical regions.

The eggshell may appear to be a solid barrier but in fact contains many pores, which are vital to the chick's wellbeing. These tiny holes allow water vapour and carbon dioxide to escape from the egg, and oxygen to enter it to reach the embryo.

INCUBATION TIMINGS

The incubation period often does not start until more than one egg has been laid, and sometimes not until the entire clutch has been completed. The interval between the laying of one egg and the next varies – finches lay every day, whereas birds such as gannets may lay only one egg every six

days. If incubation does not start until egg-laying has finished, the chicks will all be of a similar size when they hatch, which increases their overall chances of survival. Among species such as owls, incubation generally starts after the first egg is laid. This results in one chick that is larger than its fellows. This large individual frequently bullies its nest mates.

The cock and hen may share incubation duties, as in the case of most pigeons

Above: Spring sees the onset of the nesting season, when parent birds work hard to gather food such as insects for their chicks.

and doves, or just one member of the pair may incubate. Among garden birds, this is usually the hen, but there are exceptions in the wider bird world. For example, in ostriches (*Struthio camelus*) and most other large flightless birds, it is the male who incubates the eggs and cares for the

Below: A fertile chicken's egg, showing the development of the embryo through to hatching. 1. The fertilized egg cell divides to form a ball of cells that gradually develops into an embryo. 2. The embryo develops, nourished by the yolk sac. 3. The air space at the rounded end of the egg enlarges as water evaporates. 4. The chick is almost fully developed and ready to hatch. 5. The chick cuts its way out, and its feathers quickly dry off.

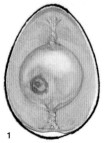
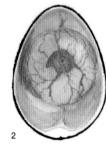
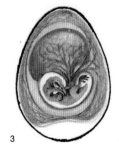

1   2   3   4   5

NEST PARASITISM
This is common in many species of cuckoo, such as the European cuckoo (*Cuculus canorus*). The males do not establish breeding territories, but mate with females at random. The females lay a single egg in the nests of host species such as reed warblers (*Acrocephalus scirpaceus*). The rapid development of the cuckoo's egg is vital so that the chick hatches first, and can then throw the other eggs or chicks out of the nest. In this way, it monopolizes the food supply brought by its foster parents. Any other chicks that do survive this initial stage die later, as they lose out in competition for food with their gigantic nest mate.

Below: *Foster parents such as this reed warbler continue to feed the young cuckoo even when the imposter dwarfs them in size.*

resulting chicks. Anis (*Crotophaga*) breed communally, and all members of the group share the task of incubation. Incubation periods vary among species, ranging from as few as 11 days in the case of American cowbirds (*Molothrus*), to over 80 days in some albatrosses (Diomedeidae).

HATCHING
When hatching, the chick uses the egg tooth on the tip of its upper bill to cut through the inner membrane into the air space at the blunt end of the shell, which forms as water evaporates from the egg. The chick starts to breathe atmospheric

air for the first time. About 48 hours later, it breaks through the shell to emerge from the egg.

Chicks hatch out at various stages of development, and are accordingly able to leave the nest sooner or later. Species that remain in the nest for some time after hatching, including finches (Fringillidae), hatch in a blind and helpless state and are entirely dependent on their parents at first. Birds in this group are known as nidicolous. If not closely brooded, they are likely to become fatally chilled. In contrast, species that leave the nest soon after hatching, known as nidifugous, emerge from the egg and are able to move around on their own at this stage. They can also see and feed themselves almost immediately. The offspring of many game birds such as pheasants as well as waterfowl and waders are nidifugous, which gives them a better chance of survival, as they can run to escape from predators. Young waterfowl cannot take safely to the water at first, however, because they lack the oil from the preen gland above the base of the tail to waterproof their feathers.

REARING AND FLEDGING
Many adult birds offer food to their offspring, even some nidifugous species. This can be a particularly demanding period, especially for small birds that have relatively large broods. Great tits (*Parus major*) and titmice (Paridae), for example, must supply their offspring with huge quantities of insects. They typically feed their chicks up to 60 times an hour, as well as keeping the nest clean by removing faeces.

Young birds usually leave the nest from about 12 to 30 days after hatching. However, some species develop much more slowly. Among birds generally, albatross chicks are particularly slow developers, spending up to 8½ months in the nest.

Above: *The broad and often colourful gape of chicks lets parent birds feed their offspring quickly and efficiently. Weak chicks that are unable to raise their heads and gape at the approach of a parent will quickly die from starvation.*

When they first leave the nest, many young birds are unable to fly, simply because their flight feathers are not fully functional. If these feathers are not completely unfurled from the protective sheaths in which they emerged, they cannot work effectively. The strength of the wing muscles also needs to be built up, so it is not uncommon for young birds to rest on the sides of the nest, flapping their wings occasionally, before finally taking to the air independently for the first time. Chicks that are unable to fly immediately on fledging remain reliant on the adults, especially the cock, for food until they become fully independent. It is a common sight to see immature songbirds following a parent around the garden, begging them for food.

Below: *Blue tits (Cyanistes caeruleus) are typical of many birds that leave the nest before they are able to fly effectively. The young are fed by their parents in the critical early days after leaving the nest.*

BIRD BEHAVIOUR

The field of bird behaviour, or avian ethology as it is known, is very broad. Some patterns of behaviour are common to all birds, whereas other actions are very specific, just to a single species or even to an individual population. Interpreting behaviour is a fine art, and of special interest to keen birdwatchers.

All bird behaviour essentially relates to various aspects of survival, such as avoiding predators, obtaining food, finding a mate and breeding successfully. Some behaviour patterns are instinctive, while others develop in certain populations of birds in response to particular conditions. Thus the way in which birds behave is partly influenced by their environment as well as being largely instinctual.

AGGRESSION

Birds can be surprisingly aggressive towards each other, even to the point of sometimes inflicting fatal injuries. Usually, however, only a few feathers are shed before the weaker individual backs away, without sustaining serious injury. Conflicts of this type can break out over feeding sites or territorial disputes.

The risk of aggressive outbreaks is greatest at the start of the breeding season, when the territorial instincts of cock birds are most aroused. Size is no indicator of the potential level of aggression, since some of the smallest birds, such as wrens and hummingbirds, can be extremely ferocious.

Below: *A dispute breaks out between a pair of great tits* (Parus major) *over food. Birds often fight with wings outstretched as they seek to batter their opponent into submission.*

Above: *A gila woodpecker (*Melanerpes uropygialis*) is feeding on a cactus flower. These desert-dwelling woodpeckers will bore into larger cacti to create a nest site.*

Age, too, plays a part in determining behaviour, since young birds often behave in a very different way to the adults. Some forms of bird behaviour are relatively easy to interpret, while others are a great deal more difficult to explain.

ADAPTING BEHAVIOUR

One of the first studies documenting birds' ability to adapt their behaviour in response to changes in their environment involved blue tits (*Cyanistes caeruleus*) in Britain. The study showed that certain individuals learned to use their bills to tap through the shiny metallic foil covers on milk bottles to reach the milk inside. Other blue tits followed their example, and in certain areas householders with milk deliveries had to protect their bottles from the birds. In addition, the tits concerned demonstrated the ability to distinguish bottles containing creamy milk from ones holding skimmed milk by the colours of their tops. The study showed that the birds directed the overwhelming majority of their raids at bottles containing the creamier milk.

The way in which birds have learned to use various types of backyard feeders

Above: *In birds such as common starlings (*Sturnus vulgaris*), preening may serve to reinforce bonds between individuals, as well as keeping the feathers clean.*

also demonstrates their ability to modify their existing behaviour in response to new conditions when it benefits them. A number of new feeders on the market designed to thwart squirrels from stealing the food exploit birds' ability to adapt in this way. The birds have to squeeze through a small gap to reach the food, just as they might to enter the nest. Once one bird has been bold enough to enter in this fashion, others observe and soon follow suit.

PREENING

Although preening serves a variety of functions, the most important aspect is keeping the feathers in good condition. It helps to dislodge parasites and removes loose feathers, particularly during moulting. It also ensures that the plumage is kept waterproof by spreading oil from the preen gland at the base of the tail.

Preening can be a social activity too. It may be carried out by pairs of males and females during the breeding season, or among a family group. This behaviour is seen in a variety of birds, including members of the finch family. In some cases preening may be a prelude to mating.

BATHING

Preening is not the only way in which birds keep their plumage in good condition. Birds often bathe to remove dirt and debris from their plumage. Small birds wet their feathers by lying on a damp leaf during a shower of rain, in an activity known as leaf-bathing. Other birds immerse themselves in a pool of water, splashing around and ruffling their feathers.

Some birds, especially those found in drier areas, prefer to dust-bathe, lying in a dusty hollow known as a scrape and using fine earth thrown up by their wings to absorb excess oil from their plumage. They then shake themselves thoroughly and preen their feathers to remove the excess oil.

SUNBATHING

This may be important in allowing birds to synthesize vitamin D3 from the ultraviolet rays in sunlight, which is vital for a healthy skeleton. This process can be achieved by rays of sunlight falling on the bird's skin and preen gland, which is located at the base of the tail. This explains why birds ruffle their plumage at this time. Some birds habitually stretch out while sunbathing, while others, such as many pigeons, prefer to rest with one wing raised, leaning over at a strange angle on the perch.

MAINTAINING HEALTH

Some people believe that when birds are ill, they eat particular plants that have medicinal properties, but this theory is very

Below: *A wren (*Troglodytes troglodytes*) sunbathing. Many birds sunbathe with wings outstretched and an open beak.*

difficult to prove. One form of behaviour that does confer health benefits has been documented, however: it involves the use of ants. Instead of eating these insects, some birds occasionally rub them in among their feathers. This causes the ants to release formic acid, which acts as a potent insecticide, killing off lurking parasites such as mites and lice. Jays (*Garrulus glandarius*), blue jays (*Cyanocitta cristata*), common starlings and Eurasian blackbirds (*Turdus merula*) are among the species that have been observed using insects in this way.

Members of the crow family (Corvidae) have also been seen perching on smoking chimney pots or above bonfires, ruffling their feathers and allowing the smoke to penetrate their plumage. The smoke is thought to kill off parasites in a process that confers the same benefits as anting.

Above: *When bathing, birds frequently dip down and use their wings and tail to splash the water. This ensures their whole body receives a wetting.*

DISPLAYS

Birds often signal their intentions to one another using displays, or ritualized gestures. Such actions are used in courtship, to co-ordinate flock behaviour, and also to reinforce territorial claims and resolve disputes. A songbird wishing to warn another off a food source will fluff itself up and spread its wings to look as big as possible. Its rival may indicate submission by crouching low to minimize its size.

Below: *A greenfinch (*Chloris chloris*) dive-bombs another. Birds show aggression with feathers fluffed.*

MIGRATION

Some birds live in a particular place all year round, but many are only temporary visitors. Typically, species fly north into temperate latitudes in spring, and return south at the end of summer. They have a wide distribution, but are seen only in specific parts of their range at certain times of the year.

Many species of birds take long seasonal journeys. The birds that regularly undertake such seasonal movements on specific routes are known as migrants, and the journeys themselves are known as migrations. Migrations are different from so-called irruptions, when flocks of certain types of birds suddenly move to an area where conditions are more favourable.

Birds migrate to seek shelter from the elements, to find safe areas to rear their young and, in particular, to seek places where food is plentiful. Birds such as waxwings (Bombycillidae) irrupt to a new location to find food when supplies become scarce in their habitat, but such journeys are less frequent and are irregular.

The instinct to migrate dates back millions of years, to a period when the seasons were often much more extreme, which meant that it was difficult to obtain food in a locality throughout the year. This forced birds to move in search of food. Even today, the majority of migratory species live within the world's temperate zones, particularly in the Northern Hemisphere, where seasonal changes remain pronounced.

ROUTES AND ALTITUDES

The routes that the birds follow on their journeys are often well defined. Land birds try to avoid flying over large stretches of water, preferring instead to follow coastal routes and crossing the sea at the shortest point. For instance, many birds migrating from Europe to Africa prefer to fly over the Straits of Gibraltar, and many of those migrating between North and South America prefer to fly over the isthmus of Central America. Frequently, birds fly at much greater altitudes when migrating. Cranes (Gruidae) have been recorded flying at 5,000m (16,400ft) when crossing mountainous areas, and geese (Anatidae) have been observed crossing the Himalayas at altitudes of more than 9,000m (29,500ft). Even if the migratory routes are known, it is often difficult to spot migrating birds because they fly so high.

Above: *The routes taken by birds migrating back and forth to Africa from parts of Europe and western Asia are shown here. Crossings are not always made by the most direct route, if this would entail a long and possibly dangerous sea journey.*

SPEED AND DISTANCE

Migrating birds also fly at greater speeds than usual, which helps to make their journey time as short as possible. The difference can be significant – migrating swallows travel at speeds between 3 and 14kmh (1.8–8.7mph) faster than usual, helped by the altitude, where the air is thinner and resistance is less.

Some birds travel huge distances on migration. Arctic terns (*Sterna paradisea*) are renowned for covering distances of over 15,000km (9,300 miles) in total, as they shuttle between the Arctic and Antarctic. They fly an average distance of 160km (100 miles) every day. Among garden birds, British barn swallows (*Hirundo rustica*) travel

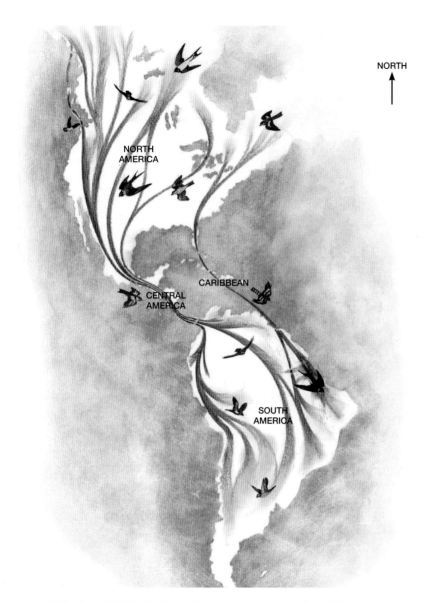

NORTH

NORTH
AMERICA

CARIBBEAN

CENTRAL
AMERICA

SOUTH
AMERICA

Above: *This diagram illustrates the main migratory routes in the Americas, where birds fly either down the Central American isthmus, or across the Caribbean via the local islands. In following traditional routes over or close to land, the birds avoid long and potentially hazardous sea crossings.*

all the way to South Africa to overwinter. Experienced birds may complete the return journey in around five weeks, covering about 300km (185 miles) a day. However studies suggest that as few as 25 per cent of young swallows complete the round trip.

Size does not preclude some birds from migrating long distances. The tiny ruby-throated hummingbird (*Archilochus colubris*) flies over the Gulf of Mexico from the eastern USA every year, a distance of more than 800km (500 miles).

PREPARING FOR MIGRATION

The migratory habits of birds have long been the subject of scientific curiosity. As late as the 1800s, it was thought that swallows hibernated in the bottom of ponds because they were seen skimming over the pond surface in groups before disappearing until the following spring. Now we know that they were probably feeding on insects to build up energy supplies for their long journey ahead.

Even today, the precise mechanisms involved in migratory behaviour are not fully understood. We do know that birds feed up before setting out on migration, and that various hormonal changes enable them to store more fat in their bodies to sustain them on their journey. Feeding opportunities are likely to be more limited than usual when birds are migrating, while their energy

requirements are, of course, higher. In addition, birds usually moult just before migrating, so that their plumage is in the best condition to withstand the inevitable buffeting that lies ahead.

NAVIGATION

Birds use both learned and visual cues to orientate themselves when migrating. Young birds of many species, such as swans, learn the route by flying in the company of their elders. However, young birds such as European cuckoos set out on their own and reach their destinations successfully without the benefit of experienced companions, navigating by instinct alone. Birds such as swifts (Apopidae) fly mainly during daytime, whereas others, including ducks (Anatidae), migrate at night. Many birds fly direct to their destination, but some may detour and break their journey to obtain food and water.

Experiments have shown that birds orientate themselves using the position of the sun and stars, as well as by following landmarks. They use the Earth's magnetic field to find their position, and thus do not get lost in cloudy or foggy weather. The way in which these factors come together has, however, yet to be fully understood.

BANDING BIRDS

Much of what we know about migration and the lifespan of birds comes from banding studies carried out by ornithologists. Bands placed on birds' legs allow experts to track their movements when the ringed birds are recovered again. The rings are made of lightweight aluminium, and have details of the banding organization and when banding was carried out. Unfortunately, only a very small proportion of ringed birds are ever recovered, so the data gathered is incomplete. However, other methods of tracking, such as radar, are also used to follow the routes taken by flocks of birds, which supplement the information from banding studies.

SURVIVAL

The numbers of a particular species of bird can vary significantly over time, affected by factors such as the availability of food, climate, disease and hunting. When the reproductive rate of a species falls below its annual mortality rate, it is in decline, but this does not mean it will inevitably become extinct.

For many birds, life is short and hazardous. Quite apart from the risk of predation, birds can face a whole range of other dangers, from starvation and disease through to either deliberate or inadvertent human persecution. The reproductive rate is higher and age of maturity is lower in species that have particularly hazardous lifestyles, such as blue tits (*Cyanistes caeruleus*) and titmice (Paridae). Such species often breed twice or more each year in rapid succession.

RISING AND FALLING NUMBERS

Some birds have a reproductive cycle that is geared to allow them to increase their numbers rapidly under favourable conditions. In parts of the world where rainfall is erratic, for example, seed-eating birds multiply quickly when the rains come. Rainfall not only ensures the rapid germination of the grasses that form the basis of their diet, but also replenishes rivers, lakes and other water sources. During periods of drought when food and

Below: *As grain-eaters, pigeons in rural areas worldwide have benefited from the spread of agriculture, while in cities, food scraps are available in refuse. These opportunists have also adapted to other changes in their environment, for example, the chance to roost on power lines.*

water become harder to find, the same bird populations may well plummet, but they can grow again rapidly when conditions become more favourable.

Regular fall-offs in populations can occur on a cyclical basis in the case of predatory birds such as owls, that feed mainly on one type of food, such as rodents. In years where conditions favour rodents, the parent birds are able to rear more chicks. When rodent numbers decline, the owls' breeding success plummets, only to recover when the rodent population rises again.

Above: *Predatory birds such as barn owls (*Tyto alba*) do well in years when conditions favour prey such as rodents, allowing them to multiply. In years when rodent populations are lower, there is less food for barn owl adults and their young.*

GROUP LIVING

Living within a group offers several major advantages to birds such as starlings (Sturnidae) and pigeons (Columbidae). Flocks of birds are able to exploit large supplies of food as they become available. Birds that live in flocks also find their mates more easily than other birds. Another advantage is the safety of numbers. An aerial predator such as a hawk will find it harder to recognize and target individuals in a flying mass of birds, although stragglers are still likely to be picked off.

Coloration can increase the safety of birds in flocks. In Florida, USA, there used to be feral budgerigar (*Melopsittacus undulatus*) flocks made up of multicoloured individuals. The different colours reflected the diversity of colour varieties that were developed through domestication. Today, however, green is by far the predominant colour in such flocks, as it is in genuine wild flocks, simply because predators found it much easier to pick off individuals of other colours. Greater numbers

CRYPTIC COLORATION

Camouflage, also known as cryptic coloration, enables a bird to hide in its natural surroundings. It offers distinct survival benefits in concealing the bird from would-be predators. Cryptic coloration has the effect of breaking up the bird's outline, allowing it to blend in with the background in its habitat. Posture and, in particular, keeping still can also aid concealment, as movement often attracts the attention of potential predators.

Below: *Camouflage allows birds such as this pheasant to forage while remaining undetected by enemies. However, cryptic coloration is also useful to predators such as owls.*

urban areas, road systems, mines, farms and other developments worldwide has greatly reduced the amount of wild habitat that is available to birds. In Britain and North America the modernization of agriculture has led to the creation of larger fields in some areas, and increased use of chemicals, both of which have had consequences for many species of native birds.

However, the expansion of agriculture has not always had a negative effect on bird populations. In countries such as Australia, it has resulted in the greater availability of water in what was formerly arid countryside, which has enabled birds such as galahs (*Eolophus roseicapillus*), a type of cockatoo, to spread.

Other birds have benefited more directly from human intervention, as is the case with the common starling (*Sturnus vulgaris*). These birds have spread across North America, following their introduction from Europe in the late 1800s. Similarly, the common pheasant (*Phasianus colchicus*) is now native across most of Europe, thanks to human interest in these game birds, which are bred in large numbers for sport shooting. Many more survive than would otherwise be the case, thanks to the attention of gamekeepers who not only provide food, but also help to curb possible predators in areas where the birds are released.

ENVIRONMENTAL CHANGE

In the last decade or so, scientists believe that global warming has started to affect habitats worldwide, producing generally warmer conditions and in some regions, making extreme weather events such as droughts more common. Research

Above: *Meadowlarks (*Sturnella *species) have generally benefited from the spread of agriculture. However, they often nest in hay fields, where their nests are sometimes destroyed by harvesting machinery.*

shows that this has started to affect birds' breeding habits and migration patterns. Some species appear to be benefiting from environmental changes. However birds that reproduce slowly are likely to be highly vulnerable to any changes in their surroundings, whether caused by climate change or other factors, such as habitat loss, hunting or disease.

Below: *Group living provides safety in numbers for birds such as starlings (*Sturnus vulgaris*). These birds spend much of the year together in a flock.*

of the green budgies survived to breed and pass on their genes to their descendants, and so green became the dominant colour in the feral flocks.

Group living also means that when the flock is feeding and at its most vulnerable, there are extra eyes to watch out for predators and other threats. Within some flocks, individual birds take it in turns to act as sentinels, and screech loudly at any hint of danger.

EFFECTS OF HUMANS

It is generally assumed that human interference in the landscape is likely to have harmful effects on avian populations. In the last century or so, the expansion of

BIRDS IN TOWNS AND CITIES

Some birds display a remarkable ability to adapt to modern life, settling in the heart of towns and cities. They use buildings for nesting and, in the case of predatory birds, as vantage points for hunting, as trees or rocky crags are used in the wild. This means that cities can be great places to watch birds.

Cities tend to be slightly warmer than the surrounding countryside, and this warm microclimate offers a number of advantages for birds. Drinking water is less likely to freeze in cold weather, and in spring, insects are more abundant at an earlier time, as plants bud and grow more quickly because of the warmth.

RESIDENTS AND VISITORS
Some birds live permanently in cities, taking advantage of parks, whereas others are less regular visitors, flying in to roost at night from outlying areas, or pausing here on migration. Deserted buildings offer a snug and relatively safe retreat for birds that roost in flocks, whereas birds of prey

Above: *Some species such as the common starling* (Sturnus vulgaris) *have travelled from Europe and do well in North American urban parks and backyards.*

Below: *City parks offer the best chance of spotting a wide range of species in urban environments, particularly if a pond or lake offers a habitat for species such as ducks.*

Above: *Out of all birds, the feral pigeon* (Columba livia), *which is a descendant of the wild rock dove, has adapted best to urban life, to the extent that it is now a common sight in cities around the world.*

seek the inaccessible ledges of high-rise buildings. The abundance of feral pigeons (*Columba livia*) in built-up areas attracts peregrine falcons (*Falco peregrinus*), proving that these predators are just as adaptable as their prey. The falcons may keep pigeon populations in check but, if not, the latter's numbers can also be curbed by feeding them with corn, which acts as a contraceptive.

Migrating birds still pass through cities on occasions, notably huge flocks of common starlings (*Sturnus vulgaris*). These congregate not just in city parks, but also roost on buildings and tree-lined streets when breaking their journey, creating a noisy chatter and plenty of mess.

BENEFITS AND DANGERS
A life above the bustle of city streets generally offers predatory species a fairly safe existence, compared with more rural areas where they risk being shot illegally. There are still dangers lurking on the city streets, however. Homes or high-rise office blocks with large expanses of glass can lure birds to a fatal collision.

Right: *Many bird species thrive in towns and cities. There are plenty of places for perching, nesting and rearing young. However, the spread of cities also causes many avian populations to decline, by altering neighbouring habitats. When new development encroaches on surrounding land, it becomes hard for many birds to find food.*

TIPS FOR OBSERVING BIRDS IN TOWNS AND CITIES
• Early morning is a good time to spot birds at close quarters in cities, before many people are out and about to disturb avian residents.
• Join the local ornithological society to gain insight into the more unusual species that have been observed in local towns and cities.
• If you venture outside your garden to spot birds, don't forget about the dangers of traffic in your enthusiasm.

Typical sightings in towns and cities, depending partly on location:
• Pigeons and doves
• Sparrows and juncos
• Magpies, jays and crows
• Finches, tits and titmice
• Gulls, ducks and moorhens

1 Sparrows
2 Starlings
3 Peregrine falcon
4 Feral pigeons
5 Crows
6 Mallards
7 Moorhen
8 Gull

BIRDS IN COUNTRY GARDENS

A wide variety of birds are likely to be seen in country gardens. As well as the species that naturally visit in search of food among the trees and shrubs, the addition of feeding stations will help to draw birds to rural garden settings. As many as 40 species have been observed regularly visiting bird tables.

Tidy, immaculately manicured gardens generally support less bird life than well-established gardens with plenty of mature shrubs that can be used for roosting and nesting. If there are stands of trees nearby, or even just lining the road outside, the range of birds visiting the garden will increase, and larger species will become more common. Artificial nesting sites, such as nest boxes of various types and sizes, can also help to increase the variety and numbers of birds that visit your garden on a regular basis.

TIPS FOR OBSERVING BIRDS IN RURAL BACKYARDS

• Positioning a bird table near a window will allow you to watch birds from inside the house, but take care to site it well away from cover where cats could lurk and ambush birds.
• Keep a pair of binoculars handy indoors so you can get a good view of the bird table and any unexpected visitors to it, plus a notepad to record any unusual birds you see.
• You can encourage invertebrate-eating birds to visit your garden by creating a wild area or by establishing a compost heap where invertebrates can multiply.
• Try to avoid using insecticides on your garden, as these reduce the food that would otherwise be available for birds.
• Ordinary slug pellets will poison slug-eaters such as thrushes feeding in your garden. Use pellets that are described as safe for birds instead.

Typical sightings in rural gardens, depending on location:
• Tits
• Titmice and chickadees
• Thrushes and cardinals
• Finches
• Sparrows and juncos
• Grackles and starlings

1 Rooks
2 Spotted flycatchers
3 Collared dove
4 European robin
5 Chaffinch
6 Thrush
7 Blue tit
8 Wren
9 Dunnock
10 Blackbirds

Birds face a major danger in gardens in the guise of the domestic cat. Huge numbers of individuals fall victim to these pets annually. The majority of the casualties are young fledglings, which lack the awareness and caution of adult birds. In areas where the cat population is especially high, there may be local declines in bird numbers. However, studies suggest that bird populations do not seem to be adversely affected by cats overall.

Above: *Rural gardens such as this typical British scene can offer an ideal habitat for birds. Food is readily available in these surroundings, as well as trees and shrubs, which provide good opportunities for roosting and nesting. Unfortunately, gardens can often be dangerous places, thanks to pet cats. What's more, predatory birds, notably magpies (Pica pica) and jays (Garrulus glandarius) will raid the nests of smaller birds, taking both eggs and chicks.*

Above: *Fieldfares (*Turdus pilaris*) arrive from their northerly breeding grounds to winter in European gardens and farmland, where they feed on fruit.*

Above: *Bird feeders attract birds, such as blue jays (*Cyanocitta cristata*), into backyards. The additional food sources are especially valuable during the cold months.*

Above: *Bluebirds (*Sialia *species), such as this eastern bluebird, bring colour to backyards in spring and summer. These are members of the thrush family (*Turdidae*).*

HELPERS AND PESTS

Birds are often regarded as gardeners' friends because they help to control the number of invertebrate pests in gardens. For example, tits and titmice (Paridae) eat aphids on rose bushes, and thrushes (Turdidae) hunt snails. At certain times of year, however, some birds can themselves become pests. Pigeons (Columbidae), in particular, often dig up newly planted seeds and eat them before they can germinate, unless the seeds are protected in some way. Later in the year, some species eat ripening berries.

RESIDENTS AND VISITORS

Some songbirds are resident in garden settings throughout the year. Others are temporary visitors, migrating to warmer climes for the winter period. For example, swallows, warblers and hummingbirds frequent gardens in spring and summer only, then head south for the winter. Meanwhile, winter migrants from farther north may appear in gardens at about the same time, as in the case of fieldfares, redpolls and pine grosbeaks. Yet other species, such as waxwings, appear infrequently when food becomes scarce in wild habitats. Studies provide clear evidence that shifts in the behaviour and distribution of birds are currently occurring because of the availability of garden habitat and the provision of food there.

Right: *In North America, threats to birds in rural backyards include woodpeckers and corvids, which raid the nests of songbirds in springtime to take both eggs and chicks.*

1 Downy woodpecker	7 Common grackles
2 Purple martins	8 Ruby-throated
3 Eastern bluebird	hummingbird
4 Cardinal	9 Eastern phoebe
5 Blue jay	10 Black-capped chickadees
6 Purple finches	11 Tufted titmouse

WOODLAND BIRDS

If your home lies near a woodland habitat, be it a forest plantation, countryside copse or even a tree-lined avenue in a city centre, your garden will be visited by woodland birds. However, many of these species are quite shy and secretive by nature, which can make them difficult to observe.

Bird life is more prolific and varied in and near deciduous, broad-leaved woodlands than in coniferous forests, largely because of greater feeding opportunities in the former setting. Nonetheless some species manage to thrive in coniferous forests.

DECIDUOUS WOODLANDS

A wide variety of food types exists for birds in deciduous forests. The species here may eat all sorts of foods, ranging from seeds to berries and invertebrates, depending on the time of year. Deciduous woodlands are more open than coniferous ones, particularly in winter when trees lose their leaves. This means that there is a significant understorey of vegetation and insects are more plentiful. Migratory birds feed in these woods in summer.

Ground birds of various types, including pheasants (*Phasianus colchicus*), may be found here, along with wood warblers, owls

1 Wood warbler
2 Hobby
3 Redstart
4 Treecreeper
5 Tawny owl
6 Blackcap
7 Eurasian jay
8 Great spotted
   woodpecker
9 Pheasant
10 Song thrush

TIPS FOR OBSERVING WOODLAND BIRDS
• Spring is a good time to spot woodland species, before the trees are covered in foliage, providing concealment for birds.
• In summer, woodland trees teem with invertebrates, which attract insectivorous birds in search of prey.
• Stand quietly in wooded areas and listen. Hidden among foliage, woodland birds use song to announce their presence to others. Such species are as frequently detected by sound as by sight.

Typical sightings in gardens with or near wooded areas, depending on location:
• Woodpeckers (below) and flickers
• Finches and grosbeaks
• Nuthatches
• Wood warblers

Left: *Deciduous woodlands offer an ideal habitat for birds during the warmer months of the year, providing a variety of food, excellent cover and a range of nesting sites to attract woodland species. Selective planting can help to recreate these conditions in your gardens. Depicted left are some typical woodland birds in the UK.*

and woodpeckers. During the breeding season woodland birds gather in clearings to display and mate. However, in winter these leafless woods provide little shelter and food for birds, so at this time these birds may visit gardens.

CONIFEROUS WOODLANDS

Birds such as crossbills (*Loxia* species) thrive in coniferous woodlands in both Europe and North America. Their curving bills allow these specialized members of the finch family to extract the seeds from pine cones effectively. Woodpeckers and corvids, such as jays, prepare for the cold winter weather by gathering and burying stores of nuts or hiding them in trees.

Owls are frequently found in coniferous forests, preying on the rodents that can be quite plentiful there. However, they may be forced to hunt elsewhere if their prey numbers plummet following a shortage of pine cones.

Evergreen coniferous woodlands provide shelter all year round for birds, but here too food supplies are far from guaranteed. There are barren years when the trees do not produce as many cones as usual, forcing the birds to abandon their regular haunts and seek food elsewhere, including in gardens and backyards. These unpredictable movements, known as irruptions, occur when birds such as waxwings (*Bombycilla* species) suddenly appear in large numbers outside their normal range, searching for alternative sources of food. They later disappear just as suddenly as they arrived, and may not return again for many years.

1 Black-capped chickadee	5 White-breasted nuthatch
2 Goshawk	6 Pine siskins
3 Pileated woodpeckers	7 Yellow warbler
4 Long-eared owl	8 Winter wren
	9 Hermit thrush

Above: *Some typical species found in US woodlands. During winter, life in deciduous woods can become harsher. Once the leaves have fallen, the birds will be more conspicuous and food is likely to be scarce.*

Far left: *The yellow warbler (*Dendroica petechia*) is one of North America's most common warblers. These birds will nest in backyards with mature trees, and like to take suet, baked goods and raisins from bird tables.*

Left: *Black-capped chickadees (*Poecile atricapillus*) nest in wooded backyards in spring. They spend the winter surviving on handouts from bird feeders, such as peanuts, and sunflower and mixed seeds.*

AQUATIC BIRDS

Some birds are drawn to gardens with or near ponds and streams because of feeding opportunities, while others seek sanctuary from would-be predators in these surroundings. Aquatic species can be attracted to your garden by the presence of even a small water feature, such as a pond or bog.

A wide variety of birds haunt streams, ponds and lakes, but not all are easy to observe because of their camouflage. The dense plant growth often found by water also provides concealment.

FINDING FOOD

Many predatory birds hunt in wetland habitats including garden ponds, swooping low over the water to seize fish by day or even at night. Some fish-eating birds, notably kingfishers (Alcedinidae), dive to seize their prey, which they may feed to their young in nest sites built into the banks of streams. Other hunters rely on different strategies to catch food. Herons (Ardeidae) lurk by the water's edge and seize fish that swim in range of their sharp, powerful bills. Rails (Rallidae) often forage by slow-flowing or still water with well-established reed beds, but these birds are shy by nature. Their mottled plumage and slim body shape make them hard to spot.

NESTING

Some birds are drawn to ponds, bogs or streams in gardens not so much by food but by the nesting opportunities there.

Below: *Moorhens (*Gallinula chloropus*) are more commonly seen by the water's edge than in open water. Long toes spread their weight as they walk across boggy ground.*

Above: *Kingfishers (*Alcedo atthis*) may venture into gardens with ponds in search of fish and other prey. Despite their bright colours, they are difficult to spot.*

Swallows (*Hirundo rustica*) collect damp mud from the water's edge to make their nests, and may also catch midges flying above the water surface. Many birds that actually nest by ponds and streams, such as ducks, geese and moorhens, seek seclusion when breeding. They hide their nest away, or make it hard to reach by choosing a spot surrounded by water.

Swans and geese have been known to nest by large ponds in gardens. Mute swans (*Cygnus olor*) construct large nests, which restricts their choice of sites. Both sexes defend the nest ferociously. These largish birds are capable of inflicting painful blows with their wings on intruders, so be careful not to venture too close.

Above: *Carolina wood ducks (*Aix sponsa*) will use duck nest boxes near ponds in backyards. These rank among the most common waterfowl in North America.*

Right: *Open ponds and lakes in parks offer a good opportunity to view many aquatic birds, although some such as coots may prefer to hide away in reeds at the water's edge where this has been planted. Birds swimming into open water will be much easier to spot.*

TIPS FOR OBSERVING AQUATIC BIRDS
• Patience is essential when watching aquatic birds, as many are shy and easily frightened away.
• Plant cover can make birdwatching difficult, but can also provide concealment for birdwatchers.
• Great care must always be taken near water. If you have a water feature in your garden, you may need to install steps to ensure children will not be in danger if they are drawn to the water's edge.

Typical sightings in gardens with or near ponds, lakes or streams, depending on location:
• Coots and moorhens
• Kingfishers and belted kingfishers
• Herons
• Ducks, including wood duck, teal, wigeon and mergansers
• Geese and swans

1 Crows
2 Starlings
3 Magpie
4 Feral pigeons
5 Gulls
6 Coots
7 Mallards
8 Tufted ducks
9 Mute swan
10 Wigeons
11 Pintails
12 Wood duck
13 Goldeneye
14 House sparrow

WATCHING BIRDS

Birds can be seen in virtually any locality, even in the middle of cities. You don't need any special equipment to watch them, but a pair of binoculars will help you to gain a better insight into avian behaviour, by allowing you to study birds at close range.

Observing the birds that visit your garden can give hours of pleasure. It will also allow you to build up a detailed picture of the species that frequent your area. You may be surprised at the variety of visitors. Some species visit on a daily basis, others only at certain times of year. As you become an experienced birdwatcher, you will become attuned to seasonal changes that occur through the year, as birds moult, court a mate, nest and raise their families, and as migrants depart for warmer climes in autumn and return again in spring.

Birds may be observed at any time of day, with the early morning being a prime time of feeding activity. You may be able to observe bird behaviour from behind the cover of tall vegetation in the garden, or from the house, particularly if you position a bird table or feeder nearby. You could even construct your own backyard hide.

GETTING A GOOD VIEW
Binoculars can be purchased from bird reserves, camera shops and similar outlets, but it is important to test them before

Above: *To get a really close-up view, you can buy a special camera for installing inside a nest box. This provides a wonderful opportunity to observe behaviour without disturbing either the chicks or their parents.*

deciding which model to buy, particularly as they vary significantly in price. When buying binoculars, you need to consider not only the power of magnification, but also how closely they can be focused, especially as you are going to use them at home, where the bird table is likely to be relatively close.

Of course, you can also take them on birdwatching ventures to local parks, woods or wetlands for example. There you will be able to observe different birds and probably a greater variety of species than can be seen at home.

CAPTURING IMAGES
It is now possible to obtain photographic digital binoculars, so that you can get good pictures of your bird table visitors through the binocular part of the unit, but it helps if you put your binoculars on a stand to keep them steady. Alternatively, a camera with a suitable lens can be used. Video can be shot in the same way.

FIELDSCOPES
As well as binoculars, dedicated bird-watchers often use birding telescopes, called fieldscopes. These are ideal for use indoors or in hides as they can be mounted

---

DRAWING BIRDS FOR REFERENCE

1 Sketching birds is relatively straight-forward if you follow this procedure. Start by drawing an egg shape for the body, with a smaller egg above, which will become the head, and another to form the rump. A centre line through the head circle will form the basis for the bill. Now add circles and lines to indicate the position of the wings and tail. Add lines for the legs and then sketch in the feet and claws.

2 Use an fine-line felt-tip pen to ink in the shape of the bird that you have drawn previously in pencil, avoiding the construction lines (which can be erased).

3 Coloured pencils will allow you to add more identifying features and details.

4 If you take a number of pre-prepared head shapes with you into the field, you can fill in the detail quickly and easily, enabling you to identify birds later.

Right: *Binoculars allow you to observe details of anatomy, plumage and also behaviour that cannot be seen easily with the naked eye.*

in various ways, using either a clamp fitting or a tripod.

Fieldscopes are equipped with lenses similar to those in binoculars, but are more suited to long-term use, when you are watching a nest or the bird table for example, as you do not have to keep holding the scope while waiting for birds to appear. Instead, set up the scope so it is trained on the nest or feeder, then simply be patient until the birds appear.

MAKING NOTES

When observing birds either in the garden or farther afield, it is always useful to have a notebook handy to write down details and make sketches. When sketching, proceed from a few quick pencil lines to a more finished portrait if and as time allows.

A handful of coloured pencils are helpful for adding details of colour and pattern, or even a small waterpaint travel set.

If you spot a bird you cannot identify, jot down the details quickly in your notebook. Note any sound the bird makes, and also

its colours and markings. Notice the length of neck and legs, and the shape of the bill. Assess the bird's size in relation to familiar species, and which family you think it might belong to. Compare your notes later with a field guide or other bird identifier.

MAKING A TEMPORARY HIDE

1 To make this hide you'll need a large cardboard box, chalk, paints, a decorating sponge, a paintbrush and a knife.

2 Draw circular, square and rectangular holes in the front of the box in chalk. Cut off the back flap, and cut out the shapes.

3 Use a piece of chalk to sketch on different leaf shapes to create a camouflage design that will blend in with your garden.

4 Use a decorating sponge to daub on green and brown paint. Paint on some streaks of black to look like leaf shadows.

5 Place the hide among greenery or against a similar-looking backdrop to the camouflage design, with the open side of the box to the back. Hang bird feeders in front of the hide for at least a week before you want to use it.

ATTRACTING BIRDS TO YOUR GARDEN

Birds are a delight in the garden at all times of year. In spring and summer their singing provides uplifting sound, while in winter their colourful plumage helps to brighten dull days. Urban and suburban backyards can be havens for wild birds, especially if you put out food and water. Birds will soon come to know it as a food source and it will become a regular stopping-off point. If nest boxes are provided, birds may well set up home too. There is immense pleasure to be had from knowing that you are helping wild bird populations to thrive and from watching the species that come to feed.

Left: *In spring, the provision of foods and also nesting materials may help many types of birds to rear their young successfully.*

Above: *Feeders containing different foods placed at varying heights in the garden will help to attract a greater variety of birds.*

Above: *House sparrows (Passer domesticus) are among the bird species that will benefit from seeds and nuts in feeders.*

Above: *Planting shrubs such as holly will attract berry-eating birds in winter when there is a scarcity of food.*

BIRDS IN DOMESTIC GARDENS

Birds have always lived around people. As human settlements developed, birds were happy to move into buildings which provided cosy roosts and also food scraps. The art of domesticating wild birds has a long history, though in the early days this was generally because birds were seen as a source of food.

Pigeons were probably the first birds to be domesticated, because they were good to eat, their food requirements were simple and they were prolific breeders. Both the Egyptians and the Romans built towers for pigeons on their rooftops, fitted with internal ledges on which the birds could roost and nest.

The Native Americans had a different reason for inviting wild birds to share their homes. They used bottle-shaped gourds to make nest boxes for purple martins, whose massed presence helped to deter vultures from raiding the meat left out to

Below: *Birds will make use of even the smallest urban spaces. This compact courtyard area contains a small tree, a mixture of flowers, herbs, vegetables and climbers, and an open-fronted nest box positioned in a sheltered place on the wall.*

dry in the sun. Nest boxes made from gourds are still used in North America today, and east of the Rocky Mountains the entire purple martin population lives in sites provided by humans.

HISTORY OF BEFRIENDING BIRDS

It was not until fairly recently that people began to encourage birds into their gardens purely for the joy of watching them. The English naturalist Gilbert White noted in his diary for June of 1782 that his brother Thomas had nailed up scallop shells under the eaves of his house, with the hollow side facing upwards against a wall, for house martins to nest in. This strategy proved successful, as the martins began to move in almost immediately.

In the early 19th century the pioneering naturalist Charles Waterton, who turned his estate in Yorkshire, England, into a nature

Above: *Barn swallows are among the species that establish their own homes on buildings, forming mud nests under eaves.*

reserve, developed stone nest boxes for barn owls and built a tower for jackdaws, similar to a garden dovecote.

Baron von Berlepsch was an early popularizer of nest boxes in Britain. During the late 19th century he spent much time experimenting, eventually creating a design that replicated a natural woodpecker's nest, consisting of a section of tree trunk that had been hollowed out at one end, an entry hole that went into this chamber from the front, and a wooden lid with an attachment for fixing at the back. This simple rustic design was effective, and similar nest boxes are still used today. Since then, designs for nest boxes and birdhouses have burgeoned, ranging from purely functional structures to ornate miniature versions of people's homes.

PLANNING A GARDEN FOR BIRDS

If you wish to make your garden a haven for wild birds, it's important to take the birds' needs into account throughout the planning and planting process. A long-established garden or backyard, with mature trees, flowering plants and a diverse selection of shrubs, surrounded by a thick hedge, is

Above: *Pyracantha, also known as firethorn, shelters birds from the elements. In autumn the scarlet berries provide food.*

Above: *Sunflowers provide blazing colour in gardens, and many types of birds feed on the oil-rich seeds.*

ideal, and if your house is old it probably has lots of nooks and crannies in its walls which are good for roosting.

Not everyone is lucky enough to have such perfect conditions, but if you are considering making some changes, it is often not difficult to improve on what you already have. An urban garden may not get as great a variety of visitors as a rural one, but it has some advantages. The city air is warmer so there is less threat of frost. Town birds are also used to co-existing with people, so will tolerate close observation.

CHOOSING PLANTS FOR BIRDS

You need varied vegetation that will attract insects, which will be needed once the birds are nesting. The best plants are ones that will produce plenty of nuts, berries and seeds. Birds require cover for protection, so hedges are perfect. Shrubs such as hawthorn and pyracantha are a good choice, as they provide shelter from wind and rain, and for nesting. In the autumn their berries make fine pickings. If possible, keep one part of your garden

Right: *This garden is ideal for attracting birds. It contains shrubs and hedges for protection, a variety of flowering plants for seeds and insects, and a lawn with a bench where you can sit and observe your feathered friends.*

wild. If you can find room for a tree, plant a native species that the birds are adapted to. Shrubs such as elder produce luscious berries which are enjoyed by dozens of species. A fruit tree such as apple or pear will benefit both you and the birds.

Many border plants attract bees, moths and butterflies, which the birds feed on in the summer, as well as providing seeds in the autumn. Good choices include

cornflowers, Michaelmas daisies (asters), cosmos, marigolds, zinnias, bee balm, penstemons, cow parsley, primroses, poppies, snapdragons and sunflowers, whose seeds are irresistible to finches and nuthatches.

Water lawns regularly in dry weather to bring the worms to the surface. Let the grass grow long around trees – the weeds will provide seed for finches.

GARDEN MENACES

In the last hundred years or so, birds generally have been threatened by changes to or loss of the wild habitats where they feed and breed. In gardens and parks, birds may be at constant risk from menaces such as cats, squirrels and predatory birds from hawks to magpies.

Most of the songbirds that visit your garden die young through either predation or natural causes, such as cold. The average life expectancy for an adult songbird is less than 2 years. This compares to a potential lifespan of 7 or 8 years for titmice, 9 years for tits, 12 years for robins and sparrows, and up to 20 years for larger species such as blackbirds and starlings.

It is not only winters that are perilous; summers claim as many lives, and breeding time is as dangerous as migration. If you encourage birds to visit your garden, it is also your duty to protect them, especially from 'unnatural' predators such as cats.

PREDATORY BIRDS

Birds of prey such as sparrowhawks, falcons and to a lesser extent, kestrels, can be a danger to garden birds. Most falcons and sparrowhawks approach fast and low, appearing as if out of nowhere to seize small birds in their talons. Kestrels hover in the air and then drop like a stone

Below: *Corvids, such as the black-billed magpie* (Pica hudsonia), *are omnivorous, with a diet that includes songbirds' eggs and nestlings in the breeding season.*

to capture their prey. However the latter species is less of a danger since kestrels usually hunt in open country, and nowadays over motorways. American kestrels mostly hunt on the ground. A number of falcons are known after their favoured prey. For example, the merlin is also known as the pigeon hawk. The peregrine falcon is called the duck hawk.

In the 1950s and 1960s, populations of sparrowhawks, falcons, hawks, eagles and other predatory birds declined due to use of the powerful pesticide DDT, but they have risen again since DDT has been banned in most countries. Scientists estimate that a breeding pair of sparrowhawks needs to kill 2,000 small birds to raise their family.

Members of the crow family, known as corvids, are a danger to nesting birds worldwide. Crows, rooks, jays, jackdaws and especially magpies raid songbirds' nests to steal eggs and nestlings. Magpies in particular conduct systematic raids, returning to raided nests after a suitable interval to take replacement clutches. These habits make magpies and their kin unpopular with songbird-lovers. However, there is no hard scientific evidence that predation by corvids has any long-term effect on populations of songbirds.

Above: *Sparrowhawks* (Accipiter nisus) *are bold enough to hunt in gardens. Their broad wings and long tail make these predators speedy and also agile.*

Providing thick cover for nesting birds, such as dense shrubs and hedges, increases their chance of survival. You could also put wire mesh over the nest entrance to exclude corvids while allowing small nesting birds to enter. This is best done once the eggs are laid and the birds start incubating, otherwise there may be a real danger that the parent birds could abandon the nest.

Woodpeckers have been known to drill into nest boxes with their long, sharp bills, or simply reach inside the boxes to steal the nestlings. Enclosed nest boxes for birds such as tits can be protected by backing the nest hole with a metal plate drilled with a similar-sized hole.

RATS, MICE AND SQUIRRELS

Food left on the ground encourages rats and mice, which will take every opportunity to steal and eat birds' eggs. The rodents are attracted to surplus food, so don't put out too much at any one time. If you store bird food outdoors do so in a strong, sealed container. This will also help to prevent the food from being spoiled by moisture.

Above: *A grey squirrel displays the acrobatic skills that make it a menace at bird tables. Feeders that are enclosed by a stout wire cage can help thwart such raids.*

The grey squirrel causes problems for songbirds both in North America and now in parts of Europe, where it was introduced in the 1800s. With their keen intelligence, acrobatic skills and sharp teeth and claws, these rodents are trouble on bird feeders and tables. Mounting tables on smooth, slippery posts, which can be made from plastic drainpipes, will prevent squirrels and also cats and rats from clambering up to steal food. A number of squirrel-resistant feeders can also be purchased nowadays. These usually consist of a feeder enclosed by a strong wire cage designed to admit small birds but exclude squirrels. However, these rodents are very destructive, and have been known to bear away the whole feeder, in order to attack it at their leisure! Some bird-lovers resort to providing the squirrels with their own supply of nuts in the hope they will leave bird feeders alone.

Grey squirrels not only steal birds' food but also raid nest boxes to steal eggs and young birds. A metal plate around the entrance hole will help to prevent squirrels from enlarging the hole by gnawing. Tree-mounted boxes can be fitted with smooth protective collars of plastic projecting from the entrance hole, or be mounted on a slippery backplate. Some people build an internal ledge underneath the entrance hole, so that the nestlings have somewhere to hide should a predator trespass.

CATS

The biggest threat to garden birds is not wild mammals but the domestic cat. In the UK, the cat population exceeds 12 million, of which at least 1.5 million are feral cats living in the wild and hunting for survival. Scientists estimate that between 27 million and 75 million birds are killed by cats each year in the UK alone. Since the higher figure only represents each cat killing a bird every other month or so, it is credible. Unlike magpies and squirrels, cats kill adult birds, which is more likely to have an impact on bird populations.

If you have a cat, fit it with a safe elasticated collar with a bell attached to alert the birds to its presence, or keep it inside while the birds are at their morning feed. Alternatively, a pet dog let out at the same time will help to deter visiting cats. To prevent cats from killing in your garden, position feeders and bird tables out in the open, where felines cannot use the cover of shrubs to stalk their prey. Make sure nest boxes are sited in places cats cannot reach. You can also put chicken wire or nylon mesh around a box, as long as there is room for the birds to get in and out.

PROTECTION FOR WILD BIRDS

Most countries have organizations that are involved with the protection and conservation of wild birds, and are happy to answer queries. Contact local groups for information about the birds in your area.

In many areas including Britain, European Union countries and North

Above: *Mice and even rats can be surprisingly adept at raiding food sources high above the ground with the help of a nearby shrub or tree.*

America, it is against the law to kill, injure or capture wild birds, or to remove or destroy their eggs. Contact your local police or a conservation organization, such as the RSPB in the UK, if you see or suspect someone is killing or trapping wild birds or stealing eggs.

Below: *The domestic cat's natural agility and hunting instincts make it a formidable predator. Fitting a bell may alert birds to the cat's presence before harm is done.*

NEST BOXES

In recent years, nest boxes have become a familiar sight in our gardens, chiefly because people like to see birds raising their young. Nest boxes have proved extremely valuable for a variety of birds because they provide alternative, artificial nesting sites for many species.

Before you erect a nest box, decide what type of bird you are trying to help. Different species have different needs (see overleaf for the types of box and what birds they are intended for). Choosing the wrong type of box or putting it up in an inappropriate place may mean that it is not used. A box ideally needs to be in place by the start of the breeding season, and that usually means late winter. However, there is never a wrong time of year to put one up, and they often provide winter shelter. A box used as shelter is more likely to be used for nesting next season.

READY-MADE BOXES

There has been a rapid increase in the range of commercially produced bird boxes, and numerous designs are now available to suit a range of garden birds from martins and swifts, tawny owls and wrens, to starlings, sparrows and tits. Small-scale specialist producers of bird boxes can be found on the Internet.

The best designs are usually solid and simple. In general, beware fussy, overly ornate boxes, as they can be useless.

Below: *Swallows usually build mud nests under the eaves of houses. This adult has been induced to nest in a whimsical box.*

Above: *The sight of a parent bird, such as this bluebird, feeding a brood of chicks in the backyard is wonderfully rewarding.*

Above: *Doves roost in dovecotes with ledged entrances. However, in general, an outside ledge can attract predators.*

If you are buying a box, it needs to be waterproof, but it must have a drainage hole in the bottom to allow any water that blows or seeps in to escape. If there's any standing water, it will make the box cold, might lead to disease, and will increase the chances of rotting the box. For the same reason, make sure that the base of the box is inside the sides, and not fixed to the bottom, or water will seep straight into the base. The lid must fit tightly, preferably with a hooked catch to prevent predators, such as squirrels or cats, from getting in and eating the chicks. Boxes with a perch under the entrance hole should be regarded with caution, as they can be used by predatory squirrels to stand on. Lastly, avoid using any boxes that have been heavily treated with preservative. The fumes will be offputting to birds, and could prove poisonous to the adults or chicks.

When you buy bird boxes, read the instructions regarding their positioning to maximize the chances of birds taking up residence. The best brands may also offer advice on how you can improve your garden planting to suit particular species. Buying a bird box from a reputable supplier might be the simplest route, but you can make and personalize your own, as we show in this book.

Opposite: *This ready-made birdhouse has been transformed with a lick of paint, and the additions of a finial, made from an offcut of wood, and a perch, made from a sturdy twig.*

DIFFERENT TYPES OF NEST BOX

There is no standard design for a bird box. What birds really need is a secure and weatherproof home, safe from predators.

Do remember, though, that different bird species have different preferences regarding the type and location of a box.

Front-hole box

Open-fronted box

Communal box

Nesting shelf or ledge

Enclosed box with a front hole

This style of nest box has a small, usually circular entrance hole. An enclosed box will suit many species, including chickadees, titmice, tits, bluebirds, wrens, nuthatches, house finches and woodpeckers. The size of the box and the size and shape of the entrance hole varies with the species you intend to attract. Small birds, such as tits, titmice and chickadees, need relatively small boxes with round holes about 2.8cm (1⅛in) wide, while larger birds, such as woodpeckers and owls, need larger boxes with holes that are 6cm (2¼in) or more across.

Enclosed box with an open front

Many birds, including European robins, wrens, wagtails and thrushes, prefer this design, and the opening width varies accordingly, from 4cm (1½in) for wrens to 12cm (4¾in) for flycatchers and thrushes.

Communal box

Birds such as purple martins, starlings and house sparrows form communal nests, often in the eaves of houses. Modern energy efficiency means that many former sites have been sealed off, so the house sparrows often have difficulty in breeding. A communal nest box can help to boost numbers. Attach it as high as possible on the shady side of a building.

Nesting shelf or ledge

Song sparrows, American and European robins, mourning doves and phoebes will use an enclosure with an entirely open front – also called a roosting box – for nesting. Barn swallows, blue jays, and cardinals also roost in this style of box.

Martin box

Swallows and house martins can have difficulty finding nest sites, and the smooth walls of modern buildings often cause nests to fall, sometimes with the young inside. Near roads, vibration caused by heavy vehicles may also shake nests loose. Artificial nests, made of a wood and cement mix, are sometimes supplied attached to an artificial overhang and ready for immediate use.

Owl box

These vary considerably in their design and are often more of a tube rather than a box. Smaller owl boxes are sometimes used by other large birds as they are often at least three times the size of a standard bird box. While there are many designs, all need a well-drained floor and easy access for cleaning at the end of the season, and are best placed in a large tree in the lower to mid canopy.

Treecreeper box

Treecreepers build nests that have contact with the trunks of thick-barked trees such as oak (*Quercus*), alder (*Alnus*), poplar (*Populus*) or pine (*Pinus*), and so the boxes must be open at the back. They are fixed to the tree using wire attached to each side or with wooden blocks. The entrance holes face downwards and are located at the side of the box.

Duck box

Usually large and square, these are attached to poles sunk in water or on an island in a pond to keep predators away. The rectangular entrance is reached via a ramplike ladder.

Martin box

Owl box

Treecreeper box

Duck box

Once you have bought your bird box, it is very easy to customize it with a splash of paint (check that all wood treatments are non-toxic, and only paint or varnish the exterior of nest boxes), or by adding features such as finials or perches. You can also increase the size of the hole to attract larger birds, such as woodpeckers.

HOME-MADE BOXES
As an alternative to buying a box, it can be rewarding to make your own – see the different types and ideas on pages 122–151. Paint or varnish should be dry before the box is fixed, and as noted above, don't paint or varnish interiors of nesting boxes.

ROOSTS
Most birds sleep at night, with their beaks hidden under one shoulder, their heads tucked in and their feathers puffed up to keep them warm. They need regular roosting places that are protected from the elements and from predators. Birds will often use nest boxes for this purpose, so don't despair if your house or box has not been selected for a nest site – it is still probably being used as a roost or shelter, so it will be doing an important job, and possibly saving birds' lives in severe weather conditions, including icy temperatures and storms.

SITING NEST BOXES
When choosing sites for your birdhouse and other accessories, there are several points to bear in mind. Will birds be left in peace there? It's not a good idea to erect a table, nest box or birdbath where children play or where the pet cat tends to prowl. Birds must have shelter nearby to which they can flee if danger threatens.

Place nest boxes so that they are protected from the prevailing wind, rain and strong sunlight, preferably giving it a shady aspect or wall that faces away from the strong midday or afternoon sun. Try to ensure that the birds have a fairly clear flight path to and from the nest, and try to angle the box slightly downwards to help exclude rain and give more shelter to the occupants. If you put a box on a tree, notice which side of the trunk has more algae growing. This will be the wet side, so place the box on the opposite side.

Be careful not to damage the tree by banging nails into it; securing devices are available for this purpose. Boxes don't

Above: *A post-mounted dovecote provides a sheltering place for pigeons, and also makes an attractive addition to the garden. Choose a site that is protected from prevailing winds, rain and too much sun.*

have to be rigidly mounted, as long as they are secure. Boxes that hang from a wire work well and may offer better protection from predators such as cats and squirrels. Although boxes can be fixed at 1.8m (6ft) above ground, they can be placed higher than this, and a height of 3.7m (12ft) or more will defeat many predators.

The best time of year to put up nest boxes is in the autumn. They can then act as roosts during the winter and be ready for early spring when the birds start choosing their breeding sites. During the winter you can insulate them with cotton, straw or wood shavings for roosting birds, but remember to remove this padding before nesting begins in the spring.

If birds do nest in your boxes, don't be tempted to sneak a look – the shock may cause the mother to abandon her brood or the young chicks to leave their nest prematurely, and it can even be illegal. The best help you can give nesting birds is to leave them undisturbed.

There may also be natural possibilities already in your garden that, with a little thought, can be turned into good nest sites. Birds may nest in an old shed that has had the door left purposely ajar, or make their homes in a hole in the eaves of a house or outbuilding.

Above: *Take care that nest boxes are mounted high enough on trees so that there is no danger of animals, such as cats, reaching the box, especially when there is a ledge attached to the outside.*

AVOIDING AGGRESSION
To discourage fighting, don't overdo the number of boxes you set up in your garden. Robins, tits and titmice can be very territorial and aggressive with other members of their own species. A bird's territory is a fixed area that it will defend for either feeding or breeding or both. If a bird does not manage to establish its territory it will be unable to nest or breed, and may even die of hunger. The gestures birds make to communicate with each other are known as displays: a bird will puff up its feathers, raise its wings and point its beak at its rival to look menacing. To show submission, a bird will crouch down and sleek its feathers in. Fights most commonly occur when a newcomer arrives in the territory of an established group, and the stranger's status needs to be evaluated. Occasionally, birds will fight to the death.

MAINTAINING NEST BOXES
Inspect the box in late summer or early autumn, and remove any nest material or other debris, then clean it (see pages 58–59). You could add some clean straw if you want small birds to use it over winter. Finally, provide nesting materials such as string, cloth, wool, dried grass or even excess hair from your cat or dog.

BIRD FEEDERS

Many species of garden birds have suffered quite serious declines in recent years. By providing food and water you will help the local bird population to remain fit and healthy, so that the birds are more likely to breed successfully when the mating season comes around.

Even a well-stocked garden can be an unforgiving place for birds as winter draws in. Late autumn or fall marks the time when many birds will visit your garden, seeking supplies of food. However, feeding can be beneficial throughout the year, especially in spring when the young are born and adults must find additional food.

There is a possible argument that by supplementing birds' diets with extra food, you are maintaining a falsely high population of birds in your garden. However, this is counterbalanced by the fact that it helps some species to survive when their natural habitats have been reduced by human activities.

Different species of birds have different feeding habits. Hanging food is ideal for members of the tit family, placed high enough up so that cats can't get at it.

Above: *Feeders are available in a wide range of shapes and sizes, and make attractive additions to the garden.*

Above: *In the wild, hummingbirds sip nectar from flowers. They visit backyards to drink sugary liquids from special feeders.*

DIFFERENT TYPES OF FEEDER

By using a wide range of bird feeders, you can provide a greater variety of food items. In doing this, you will increase the chances of more species visiting your garden.

Bird feeder table
Tables are excellent for a wide range of small garden birds and also for larger birds that perch or stand in order to eat their food. Food placed on the table supplies birds in the critical winter season, in spring when birds are nesting, and throughout the year.

Glass/Perspex feeder
These types of feeders are usually filled with mixed seed, which is made accessible to birds through a series of small hoppers in the side.

Half a coconut
A sliced coconut is a excellent way of providing food for small, clinging birds like tits. It can be filled with suet or seeds.

Squirrel-proof feeder
To discourage squirrels, make bird food inaccessible. This type of feeder has a cage to protect the seed.

Wire feeder
These are mostly for peanuts, and are useful because they prevent birds from choking on whole nuts.

Perspex feeder

Half a coconut

Squirrel-proof feeder

Wire feeder

If the food is too exposed, however, the birds may be in danger from sparrowhawks, unless there is nearby cover, such as trees and hedges. Trees, large shrubs or even a dead branch firmly planted in the ground can act as a support for feeders. Wherever you site it, securely attach your feeders to the branches using thin, pliable wire.

TYPES OF FEEDER

Pet and garden suppliers stock a huge range of feeders for different types of nuts or seeds. These are useful, as seeds are otherwise easily scattered and blown away. Some of the feeders that are readily available are squirrel-proof. Mesh feeders are designed to dispense nuts, while feeders made of plastic tubing are intended for offering seeds.

There are also feeders that are designed to be stuck on to a window. Provided you don't mind the birds making a mess of your window and walls, these will enable you to study your avian visitors at close proximity.

As an alternative to buying feeders, you could try making your own, using the ideas given later in this book (see pages 100–117).

BIRD TABLES

Ideally, a bird table should be placed approximately 2–3m (6½–10ft) from a bush or tree, which can provide safety for birds in case of danger, and at least 5m (16½ft) from the house. Many birds are nervous of open sites, but equally they can have accidents flying into house windows, and may be scared away by the movement of people inside the house. Window stickers featuring birds of prey are available which, when stuck to the window panes, indicate the presence of an otherwise invisible surface and will deter smaller birds from flying too close to the house.

A bird table gives you a clear view of feeding birds, and offers the birds some protection against predators and the elements. Use wood that has not been treated with wood preservative if you are making your own table. A roof will keep the food and the birds dry. If you don't make a roof, drill a few holes in the floor of the table for drainage. A small lip around the edge of the food table can prevent lighter food items from being blown away by wind. The bird table must be cleaned from time to time and any food that is past its best

Above: *Hanging feeders offer an easy challenge to species with natural acrobatic abilities, such as tits.*

should be removed. An adequate supply of water should be provided all year round, but this can be as simple as a bowl of water placed on the surface of the table, or a separate facility.

Above: *Ground feeders need to be in an open area so that predators cannot creep up on the birds using them.*

GROUND STATIONS

Some birds, such as dunnocks, song thrushes, grackles, thrushes and American robins, prefer to use ground feeders. Pheasants, finches, sparrows, buntings and turtle doves may also be attracted to ground feeding stations – a wooden or plastic hopper secured to a strong base.

Place a ground feeder slightly away from a bird table or other feeder, so that the food is not contaminated by droppings from the birds above.

HANGING FEEDERS

Some species, such as tits, chickadees and titmice that are adapted to feeding in trees will benefit from a more challenging feeder. Blue and great tits can also cling upside-down from various types of hanging feeders, and these may be joined by siskins and nuthatches.

Many types of feeder are available, or you can make or adapt your own, using the projects shown later in this book. In addition, some foods are also suitable for hanging without the need for a feeder, for example, peanuts in their shells, half coconuts, popcorn garlands and also fat cakes on strings.

Left: *Many types of bird tables can be purchased or constructed. Roofed ones like this will keep birds – and the food provided for them – dry in wet weather, as well as looking attractive.*

BIRD PONDS AND BIRDBATHS

Birds get most of the water that they require from their food, but they still need supplies to supplement this. Seed-eaters, for example, need plenty of drinking water to compensate for the lack of moisture in their diet. That said, the main purpose of providing water for birds is not for drinking but for bathing.

Birds need a constant supply of water, for both bathing and drinking. It is essential for them to keep their feathers in good condition not only for flight but for insulation during the long and bitter nights of winter, and baths are as important in winter as in summer. Some birds, such as blue tits, may drink more in winter because the seasonal diet of dry nuts is not sufficient to hydrate them. Seed-eating birds in general require more water to counterbalance the drier nature of their food.

Most birds drink by dipping their beaks into the water, then tilting their heads back, though pigeons are able to suck water up through their bills. Because birds don't sweat, they need another way to keep cool: they lose moisture by opening their mouths and panting.

Ponds, of course, provide water all year round for bathing and drinking, and will also attract many other types of wildlife to your garden. An alternative is birdbaths, which not only serve a useful purpose to the birds, but add a point of interest to any garden. Fountains, or any form of dripping

Below: *Like all birds, sparrows benefit from a dip. Seed-eaters like these need plenty of drinking water too.*

Above: *A traditional stone and mosaic birdbath makes an atmospheric addition to any garden, as well as benefiting birds.*

water, make ponds and baths even more enticing to birds as well as appealing to human visitors.

Whatever the birdbath, make sure that it has either sloping sides or a ramp if the sides are steep, so that birds can easily walk in and out, and small animals do not

Above: *Water can be provided for birds in small gardens by hanging up bowls or attaching containers or troughs to a wall.*

become trapped. Don't forget to keep the birdbath clean and filled with fresh water, and crack any ice that forms on the surface in winter. It is important never to put antifreeze or salt into the water, as this can kill birds.

MAINTAINING BIRDBATHS

Situate your birdbath in a shady spot. An open place is alright as long as there is cover reasonably close at hand to provide safety from predators. The bath needs to have gently sloping sides, which will make it easy for small birds to use, but it should also be deep enough in the middle to allow a larger bird such as a blackbird or pigeon to take a full dunk.

Since the birdbath will not contain any oxygenating plants, algae will quickly form and make the water smell unless the birdbath is regularly cleaned out and scrubbed. It is best to do this daily in hot weather, before adding fresh water.

If your birdbath has a smooth surface, put some sand or gravel in it to give the birds a secure footing, and place a large stone in the middle for them to alight on.

HOW TO FEED BIRDS

The simplest way to attract birds to your garden, or even window box, is to put out food for them, particularly during the months of winter when natural foods become much scarcer. However, you may provide appropriate food for garden birds throughout the year, which will be better for them.

Whatever feeding method you decide upon, be consistent. A wasted journey to an empty bird table uses a bird's precious energy supply, especially as winter progresses and food becomes more difficult to find. Ideally, feed birds twice a day in winter: once in the early morning and again in the early afternoon.

In spring and summer, feeding can still be helpful, but do follow rules for safety and hygiene. Do not use peanuts unless they are in a mesh container; this will prevent the larger pieces, which can choke baby birds, from being removed. In summer, avoid fat cakes; the fat will melt and become very messy, and can also glue birds' beaks together.

DAILY RITUALS

Birds wake up just before dawn, when they sing with great gusto. This dawn chorus involves many different species and lasts about half an hour, heralding the daylight.

Breakfast is the best time to observe birds' behaviour, as they often quarrel over food. You will soon start to notice their pecking order. The first birds to visit the garden may be blackbirds and thrushes, who come to scan the lawn in search of worms and soft grubs. They hunt quietly and carefully, pausing between hops and watching for their prey. Starlings, who arrive later, appear to stab here and there at the ground until they find a tasty morsel.

Birds have two important daily activities. The first is to find and eat food, which is done throughout the day; the second is to take care of their feathers. These must be kept in perfect condition for both flight and insulation. After bathing comes preening. Birds collect fatty oil from the preen gland at their rump and smear it over the feathers before stroking them back into place. This keeps them looking glossy.

WHAT TO FEED WHEN

Birds will quickly come to depend on your support, so once you have enticed them into the garden, you need to make sure that they continue to thrive. It is important

Above: *When snow covers the ground, small birds are at risk of dying from hypothermia. Foods such as sunflower and peanut hearts can be vital food sources.*

to maintain supplies of food and water through the winter. Birds will appreciate fresh food on the table early in the morning, or at least at a regular time. If you go away, fill your feeder and leave fat balls to sustain the birds until your return.

Birds need food with a high fat and carbohydrate content, as they may lose up to 10 per cent of their body weight overnight in bad weather, so suet, cheese, bacon rinds and dripping will help them build up energy reserves. Crows, starlings, tits, titmice and woodpeckers are particularly attracted to bacon rind, fat and cheese.

The shape of a bird's beak roughly indicates its diet. Finches have hard, thick beaks that are designed to crack and crush. They feed mostly on grain and seed. Robins, warblers and wrens, with their slender, soft beaks, eat caterpillars, grubs and other insects. Gulls, starlings and blackbirds have general-purpose bills,

Above: *Seed balls and strings of nuts are a welcome supplement to the meagre diet that is available to many birds in winter. Remember to provide a supply of water.*

which allow them to eat a bit of everything. Whatever the species, they all enjoy culinary variety, and kitchen scraps are always welcome.

Bread is the food most commonly put out for birds, but it is not particularly good for them. If you do give it, soak it first in water or, even better, fat. In fact any dried foods – especially fruits – should be soaked. Never give birds desiccated/shredded coconut or uncooked rice. These swell up in their stomachs and can kill. Kitchen leftovers such as baked potatoes and spaghetti are good: they are soft enough for birds to eat but difficult for them to pick up whole to fly away with. Keep windfall apples and pears in storage until winter, when they will be most welcome on the bird table. Don't worry if birds don't visit your feeder immediately – it may take up to two weeks for a bird table to be accepted by the neighbourhood bird population.

WHAT TO FEED BIRDS

As warm-blooded or endothermic animals, birds have to expend considerable energy maintaining an even body temperature. This process is particularly costly in terms of energy in cold weather, so when temperatures drop towards freezing point, providing food for birds is especially important.

Birds, like many wild creatures, enjoy a range of foods, many of which are easy to obtain. Leftovers are a valuable but variable commodity, so don't rely on them. Seed is useful and can be supplemented with such items as pinhead oatmeal or porridge oats, soaked sultanas, shredded suet and toasted breadcrumbs. Other popular items for the bird table are cracked corn, canned corn and fresh fruit, broken into pieces.

The wider the range of food types that can be left in different positions and types of feeder, the better. Whatever you decide to place out for the birds, make sure that you stick to natural foods, rather than chemically altered or processed items, such as margarine. Keep food fresh – only leave out enough for a day or two – and never allow food or feeding debris to accumulate because it can rapidly spread disease.

FAT PRODUCTS

The best types of base for fat cakes are lamb and beef fats, either in natural form or as processed suet. Because these are hard, they do not melt too readily in warm weather, which can potentially glue birds' beaks together. Specialist manufacturers add enticements to their fat cakes but you can easily make your own at home with a mixture of seeds, fruits and nuts following the recipes on pages 98–103.

LIVE FOOD

Some birds, for example robins, can benefit from supplies of live food such as waxworms and mealworms particularly during the late winter period when food is scarce. However, avoid offering mealworms during the breeding period. This is because these beetle larvae have a hard outer coating called chitin, which cannot be digested by young blue tits for example, and so they will starve as a consequence if fed mealworms by their parents.

A newer arrival on the live food scene, known as calciworms or black soldier fly larvae, are a better option, especially as they are available in a small size and will also be a valuable source of calcium, as their name suggests. They can be bought from some pet stores (especially those offering reptiles) or by mail order. Limited amounts should be placed in special feeding containers with curved sides, to prevent them escaping.

SEEDS AND GRAINS

Use best-quality seeds from a reliable source, not sweepings or waste seeds, which are not nutritious. Black sunflower seeds rather than the striped variety are the favoured food of many species. Their skins are the thinnest of all sunflower varieties, making them easy for the birds to open. All types of sunflower seeds are safe for young birds to eat, so they may be offered all year round. Canary seeds, melon seeds, hemp seeds, small wheat, kibbled and flaked maize, corn kernels and oatmeal are all good sources of nutrition. The mixture of seeds can be fine-tuned to attract particular species of birds to your garden.

UNSALTED PEANUTS

Buy only high-quality 'safe nuts', marked as such by the Bird Food Standards Association or a similar reputable body, to ensure that the nuts are free from lethal toxins. Whole peanuts are best avoided during the nesting season because of the danger they pose to nestlings. They should be chopped, if left on a table, or placed in a mesh peanut feeder from which adult birds can take only small fragments.

Below: *A live feeder will serve to attract insectivorous birds and some that enjoy a more general diet, such as starlings.*

Above: *Half a coconut filled with seeds and melted fat is a good way of providing supplementary food for small, clinging birds.*

Below: *A string of peanuts provides nutrition and can also look attractive if hung in a well-chosen site such as this.*

COMMON BIRD FOODS

The variety of seed and other food supplements that are commonly available in the shops for birds has increased vastly in the last few years. All have their own merits and will be preferred by different types of birds. Trial and error will show what goes down best with the feathered population in your local area, but here are some ideas.

Mixed seed
Consists of various seed types for a wide range of birds, but can be of variable quality.

Black sunflower seed
More commonly known as the 'oil sunflower', this seed – as its name suggests – is rich in oil and ideal for winter-feeding a range of garden birds.

Striped sunflower seed
This type of seed has a lower oil content than the black variety, and is useful in the spring when natural foods become more abundant.

Niger
Sometimes called thistle seed, this tiny black birdseed, cultivated in Asia and Africa, is high in calories and oil content, and is quickly devoured, especially by finches of various types.

Grain
Consists of any commercially grown crops in the grass family, including wheat, millet, maize and oats.

Bread
This is eaten by many species. Brown bread is best, but whatever type you offer, make sure that it has been thoroughly soaked to avoid the danger of it swelling in birds' stomachs.

Dried and fresh fruit
Always popular, dried fruit should be soaked as for bread. Fresh fruits, especially pears and apples, are enjoyed by blackcaps and thrushes. These fruits are particularly useful in winter.

Half-coconut
Hanging on a string, a half-coconut offers good value for money and provides delightful entertainment when acrobatic tits and titmice come to feed. Once the flesh has been stripped, the shell can be filled with bird pudding – a mixture of nuts, seeds and melted fat.

Fat ball
A ball of suet into which other dried foodstuffs have been incorporated. It is usually hung in nets or special feeders.

Suet cake
The block type of suet food contains a mixture of seeds that provides a balanced diet for many species. It is ideal for feeding birds when you are away, although the fat content can sometimes attract scavenging mammals, such as rats, to a table.

Fruit suet treats
Mainly for bird tables or feeders, this suet-based cake is best made with moist, dried fruit and peanut granules, and is popular with larger birds.

Dried mealworms
These freeze-dried grubs are an excellent source of protein for carnivorous birds (see 'Live food').

Peanuts
In their shells, peanuts can be strung on thread or wire, but don't use multistranded thread as birds may get their feet caught in this. Do ensure the nuts are fresh – mouldy ones produce a toxin that kills many garden birds.

Hazelnuts
Wedged into tree bark, hazelnuts will appeal to nuthatches, which will enjoy hammering them open.

Cheese
Grated cheese is a popular food, especially with robins.

Leftovers
Household foods such as hard-boiled eggs, baked potatoes, uncooked pastry and stale cake and biscuits are all widely available choices that birds will enjoy. Feel free to experiment, taking care not to offer dehydrated, spicy or very salty foods, as these can be dangerous.

Grit for digestion
Although not actually foodstuffs, grit, sand and gravel aid digestion, particularly for seed-eaters.

Mixed seed

Black sunflower seeds

Niger

Dried fruit

Fresh fruit

Fat ball

Suet cake

Fruit suet treats

Dried mealworms

Peanuts

Cheese

Leftovers

HYGIENE MATTERS

Feeding the wild birds that visit your garden and providing them with nesting facilities should help to boost their numbers, but note that it is very important not just to offer safe, suitable food, but also to ensure a high level of hygiene, so as to minimize the risk of diseases being spread.

Especially during the cold winter months, when food is harder for to find, birds will be attracted in larger numbers to tables and feeders in gardens. Providing food and fresh water will assist their survival through this difficult stage of the year. However it is also very important to be careful about aspects of hygiene to ensure that you are not inadvertently spreading disease through the local wild bird population at the same time. Birds visiting the bird table can easily contaminate the food with their droppings, and this can then get picked up by other individuals. Even if the bird removes the husk of the seed before swallowing the kernel, there is still the potential for harmful microbes to spread by this route, entering its mouth.

PREVENTION OF DISEASES
In order to minimize the risk of the seed being soiled in the first place, buy some small heavyweight containers that can be used as seed receptacles, to be placed on the bird table. The food is less likely to be

Below: The greenfinch population in the UK suffered badly from trichomoniasis during the early years of the century, and subsequent investigations revealed that this infection could be spread via bird tables.

Above: *Birds congregate on bird tables, particularly in winter, increasing the likelihood of any illnesses being spread. Great tits* (Parus major) *and Eurasian blue tits* (Cyanistes caeruleus) *are seen here.*

soiled if it is served in small pots raised off the surface of the table than if it is simply scattered all over the area with the birds hopping around on it.

Using pots on the surface will make it much easier to keep the surface of the bird table clean. Ideally, the top of the table should have a smooth surface that allows it to be wiped over easily with a cloth and a special pet-safe disinfectant, following the instructions for use carefully. Aim to develop a routine for cleaning the bird table on a regular basis, probably twice a week. Get a bucket and a pair of gloves kept just for this purpose, as well as a brush for cleaning the food and water bowl. Afterwards, always rinse off the top of the bird table and the containers with clean water, and allow the food bowl to dry thoroughly before refilling it. Don't forget to wash other feeders regularly as well.

Although dry seed can be stored for many months, if the seed on the bird table becomes wet, it will soon start to sprout, and it may also turn mouldy, which will be harmful to the birds. This is why it is recommended only to provide sufficient food that will last about a day or so at a time, especially if the weather is likely to be wet. A roofed bird table offers some protection from the weather.

POTENTIAL KILLERS
While changes in the consistency and appearance of the seed are likely to be obvious if it becomes damp and mouldy, the invisible risk posed by contaminated drinking water can be even greater in some ways. This is particularly due to a microscopic parasite known as *Trichomonas*. This can affect a wide range of birds, with pigeons and doves as well as finches being amongst the most vulnerable groups. The parasites develop at the back of the mouth and in the throat, and can spread further down the digestive tract, making it very hard for the bird to swallow. It will then regurgitate seed that it has attempted to eat, and if another bird eats this soon afterwards, it may acquire the infection as a result. Desiccation kills the parasite outside the body, but it can still survive in drinking water, which becomes another hazard.

A significant bacterial disease that can be spread via droppings contaminating food on bird tables is yersiniosis. This

Above: *Rats are attracted to bird tables to steal food. They may even be able to climb up on to the table itself.*

Above: *Clean out the nest box and treat it for mites – but only in the winter, when the birds have abandoned it.*

disease is responsible for what is sometimes called 'going light', which simply refers to chronic weight loss. Unfortunately, the bird tends to have a greater appetite as its weight declines. An infected individual will therefore spend longer on the bird table, pecking around here while obviously weakened, with its feathers held slightly away from its body, which gives it a fluffed-up appearance.

Yersiniosis is one of a number of diseases that can also be spread by rodents. It is therefore very important not to overload the bird table with food, as any spilt on to the floor will inevitably draw these pests to feed here regularly. Rats may even manage to climb the bird table for this purpose. This is why it is advisable to use gloves when stripping down and cleaning the bird table, in case the surface has been contaminated by rodents. Since they tend to be nocturnal in their feeding habits, you may not actually see rats in the vicinity, but keep a close watch for their droppings as a tell-tale sign.

THE DANGER AT NESTING SITES

It is not just the bird table where good hygiene is important. Birds in the wild often tend to move nest sites between clutches

Right: *If you have a separate birthbath, make sure the water is replenished regularly, and the birdbath is kept clean.*

of eggs, and this is a good way of avoiding any build-up of parasites in their immediate surroundings. However, they may often be drawn back repeatedly to nest sites that you provide in the garden, where natural opportunities to nest may be more limited. Unfortunately, there are various external parasites, notably red mite (*Dermanyssus gallinae*), which can then prove to be a particular hazard as a result. Normally small and inconspicuous enough to be invisible to the human eye, this parasite gains its characteristic red colour by its gruesome habit of sucking the blood of birds in the

nest, and can even transmit blood parasites as it feeds. These mites will multiply rapidly, to the extent that the developing chicks in the nest may suffer from anaemia caused by a shortage of blood, which can stunt their development and even prove fatal. In addition, red mites are remarkably durable. They can easily live in the crevices of a nest box from one year to the next, being able to overwinter without feeding. Then when the nest box is occupied again, their numbers surge quickly once more.

TACKLING THE PROBLEM

What is required – in the depths of winter, when the nest box is not being occupied, otherwise you may be breaking the law by disturbing it – is to clean the box out thoroughly, and use one of the special mite-killing preparations that are marketed for canaries and other pet birds. These are available in both liquid form, being added to water being used to wash the box out, and also as a spray, which needs to be concentrated into the cracks around the interior of the nest box. This is where the mites localize out of sight, before emerging under cover of darkness to indulge in their vampire-like feeding habits.

It is worth spraying the box at the recommended intervals with the mite-killing preparation over the winter, so that any remaining mites will have been eliminated before the birds return here to breed again in the spring. Do not remove the box though, because it may be used for roosting purposes, especially if the weather turns very harsh.

A WILD GARDEN FOR BIRDS

Wild gardens offer the closest substitute to a natural habitat for birds and, if designed properly, can also be very attractive. However, a wild garden should not be thought of as a low-maintenance option and allowed to become completely chaotic. Regular maintenance will still be required.

Wild gardens differ from other styles of 'wildlife' garden primarily because they use only native plants. It is perhaps because of this that more traditional gardeners have sometimes derided them, regarding them as little more than weed patches. But many native plants are not only supremely beautiful, they are also well adapted to the site and soil conditions of the area. In addition, many provide cover for birds, and foods such as seeds and berries.

Thankfully, recent years have seen a reversal of this view of gardening, with native plants now being commonly seen within an ornamental setting. With a little imagination they can form an immensely attractive display. Native plants offer the reassurance that they are excellent choices for local birds as they will have evolved to suit each other. Avoid plants that are known to be invasive – there are always less troublesome alternatives.

Below: *Wildflower areas are more accessible if paths are mown through. Several species of butterfly will lay their eggs alongside the mown paths, producing caterpillars that feed young birds.*

Above: *Wild gardens provide food for seed-eaters such as cardinals, house finches, tufted titmice, sparrows and this dunnock.*

MAINTENANCE

Always choose a range of plants that will flower and also provide foods such as seeds and berries over as long a period as possible. When it comes to maintenance, most native plant species are no different from other garden plants. However, here

Above: *In dappled shade areas, a mass of spring bulbs such as wild garlic offers a welcome early supply of nectar for insects.*

the general effect can be somewhat untidy. Autumn or fall plant debris harbours many overwintering insects that are eaten by birds. Those dead flowers in the borders are often a rich source of seed for birds in winter. The real difference in making a wild garden is that you will have created a refuge for birds and a host of other creatures using a rich diversity of native plants, many of which are becoming increasingly rare in the wild.

Below: *Butterflies are attracted to wild backyards, where they feed on nectar from flowers. Michaelmas daisies (purple asters) provide late-season sustenance.*

WILD GARDEN

A design for a wild garden has to be as well thought out as a formal design. Care should be taken to include as many different habitats as possible, especially wildflower meadows and deciduous trees that support myriad insects to feed birds. Short-cut grass areas are kept to a minimum. Deadwood is allowed to remain to harbour more insect food for birds.

Large deciduous trees provide cover and nest sites

Nectar-rich border attracts insects to feed birds

Lacewing hotel attracts predators of aphids

Hedging links all areas of the garden

Bird table ideally sited close to the house as kitchen scraps are put out daily

Ground feeder to attract birds

Shrubs offer cover and nesting areas for birds

Bird box on shady side of tree

Pond surrounded by vegetation will entice visiting birds

Bog gardens provide cover for aquatic birds and other wildlife

Large log piles offer homes for invertebrates that are eaten by birds

Compost heaps offer homes to reptiles and many insects

Wildflower meadows are fantastic for insects and the birds that feed on them

Standing deadwood offers a habitat for many invertebrates that feed birds

Mown paths allow access around the garden

Various different types of bird feeders will encourage more species to feed

Bird hide to observe the wildlife visiting the feeders

Above: *Water lilies are helpful walkways for moorhens and a landing pad for damselflies, dragonflies and frogs.*

Right: *Allowing short grass to regenerate can result in areas of cow parsley (Queen Anne's lace), offering seeds for birds.*

A BIRD BORDER

Winter is the period of the year when birds most need our help. A border planted with birds in mind can be a real lifeline at this time, providing a diverse array of foods, including seeds, berries and even the odd overwintering insect among the vegetation. The border will also provide colour throughout the year.

A bird border doesn't have to be wild or overgrown, but can look attractive all year round. There are few absolute rights or wrongs when you plan one, but growing a wide variety of plants to attract wildlife in general will offer garden birds food and shelter, helping them both survive winter and feed their hungry fledglings the following spring. Think of your bird border as a roadside café, a place where birds can feed and rest before moving on.

CHOOSING A SITE
Some species of birds are much more sensitive to disturbance than others, particularly during the nesting season. For this reason it is usually best to set aside a quiet area for a bird border. The ideal backdrop might be a hedge or line of berry-bearing shrubs. If you are planting against a fence or wall, clothing it with climbing plants and shrubs can turn it into a 'living boundary' which may well provide cover and nesting sites. Bird borders can be made on any scale with even a small one proving useful, although the more space and diversity you can devote to such a feature, the more birds will benefit.

Below: *The song thrush (*Turdus philomelos*) is a bird species that is carnivorous in the summer but switches to berries and seed during the dormant winter months.*

CHOOSING THE RIGHT SPECIES
Depending on where you live, it is often best to include a range of native plants in your border, and you should try to include as many different kinds as possible. In the example shown opposite, a formal backdrop has been created by using a hedge made of yew (*Taxus baccata*),

Below: *Evening primrose (*Oenothera biennis*) flowers attract a range of insects, providing food for birds. Finches also eat the seeds.*

Above: *Barberry (*Berberis thunbergii*) is an ideal plant to include in a bird border, offering nestlings protection from predators in spring, and a crop of autumn berries.*

although beech (*Fagus sylvatica*), holly (*Ilex aquifolium*) and hornbeam (*Carpinus betulus*) are equally effective, all providing good shelter for birds. If space permits, try a less formal hedge of native shrubs, pruned on only one side in alternate years to provide an excellent source of food and nectar, as well as nesting and shelter.

Trees are also extremely useful, although large forest species – such as oak (*Quercus*) – are often too large for most gardens. If choosing trees for a town garden, make sure you use smaller examples like the ones shown in this design. Mountain ash (*Sorbus aucuparia*), holly (*Ilex aquifolium*) and the crab apple (*Malus* 'Red Sentinel') will provide perches and shelter, and are an excellent food source when in fruit.

A range of shrubs will provide cover from predators and the worst of the weather. Native species might come top of the list, but it is equally important to consider a range of evergreen and deciduous types to give variety and hiding

places in winter. The barberry (*Berberis thunbergii atropurpurea*) is an attractive semi-evergreen whose thorny branches offer protection to smaller birds from the likes of cats. Firethorn (*Pyracantha coccinea*) offers similar protective cover for larger birds, and both have berries that can be eaten over winter. The Oregon grape (*Mahonia aquifolium*) is a slightly shorter, evergreen, prickly leaved shrub with berries that ripen in summer, while both elder (*Sambucus nigra*) and blackcurrant (*Ribes nigrum*) are deciduous species that attract many insects and bear summer berries.

Ideally, in addition to these woody plants, you should aim to plant a range of annual and herbaceous plants. Natives are very useful but, if you want a more ornamental look, choose a range of showier species that will attract insects in spring and summer, and later produce good seed heads to help feed small birds. Lastly, you might want to leave some space in your border for a birdbath and feeders, to provide food when natural sources run low.

Above: *The Eurasian jay (*Garrulus glandarius*) is an occasional visitor to the urban garden. It will take a range of foods, including insects, seed and fruits.*

Above: *The downy woodpecker (*Picoides pubescens*) usually feeds on wood grubs and other insects, but occasionally eats fruit in winter.*

BIRD BORDER

A good bird border needs to provide a range of food throughout the seasons. The plants featured here are chosen to either attract insects or bear fruit in the summer, or to be rich in seeds and/or fruit in the winter months. There is also a range of trees, shrubs and smaller herbaceous plants. Adapt the selection for your locality.

1 *Polygonum bistorta* – Common bistort
2 *Artemisia vulgaris* – Mugwort
3 *Helianthus annuus* – Sunflower
4 *Sorbus aucuparia* – Rowan
5 *Berberis thunbergii atropurpurea* – Barberry
6 *Achillea millefolium* – Common yarrow
7 *Oenothera biennis* – Evening primrose

8 *Lavandula angustifolia* – English lavender
9 *Ribes nigrum* – Blackcurrant
10 *Sambucus nigra* – Elderberry
11 *Pyracantha coccinea* – Firethorn
12 *Ilex aquifolium* – Holly
13 *Angelica sylvestris* – Wild angelica
14 *Amaranthus caudatus* – Love-lies-bleeding

15 *Myosotis arvensis* – Field forget-me-not
16 *Mahonia aquifolium* – Oregon grape
17 *Malus* 'Red Sentinel' – Crab apple
18 *Taxus baccata* – Yew
19 *Dipsacus fullonum* – Teasel
20 *Solidago virgaurea* – Golden rod
21 *Lunaria annua* – Honesty
22 *Viburnum opulus* – Guelder rose
23 *Tanacetum vulgare* – Tansy
24 *Melissa officinalis* – Lemon balm
25 *Ribes uva-crispa* – Gooseberry
26 *Cotoneaster horizontalis* – Herringbone cotoneaster
27 *Fragaria vesca* – Wild strawberry

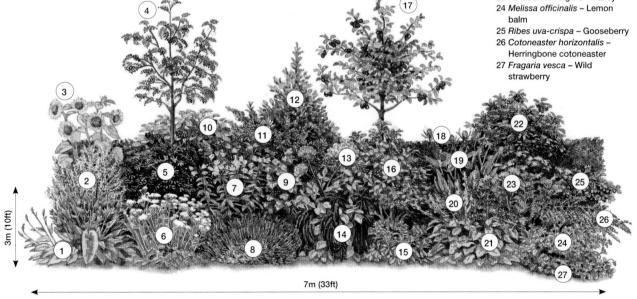

3m (10ft)

7m (33ft)

LAWNS FOR BIRDS

In many gardens, grassy areas all too often consist of manicured lawns, which are of only limited benefit to birds. With just a few changes to the way we maintain our lawns, however, we can transform them into superb wildlife habitats. Simply allowing the grass to grow slightly longer can attract more invertebrates.

The commonest use of grass in the domestic garden is in a lawn. These often carefully tended features mimic grassland in certain respects but, in many ways, the traditional lawn is quite different from its wild counterpart. In its close-cropped, well-tended state, a lawn might look good to humans but as a habitat for birds it doesn't offer much. Changing a lawn from what is effectively a green desert into a thriving habitat often involves little more than reducing the amount of mowing you do, and outlawing the use of fertilizers, pesticides and weedkillers. This will have an almost immediate benefit for birds and other wildlife, although it may take some years before the full effects appear. However, time saved maintaining the lawn can be spent more usefully elsewhere.

THE IMPORTANCE OF LONG-GRASS AREAS

There is a simple truth where grass in your garden is concerned. If a lawn is less frequently mown and not walked on wherever possible, it soon becomes richer in invertebrates that are eaten by birds. Indeed, long-grass habitats are some of the most useful undisturbed areas in the garden and are very simple to provide. Where space is limited they may be restricted to strips of uncut grass alongside a hedge, or around the base of a tree. However, if space allows they can form

more extensive areas. Whatever the size of a long-grass area, they are an important, sheltered habitat and may provide cover for birds and a range of other creatures. Insects such as bumblebees or other wild bees often like to nest in longer grass, while grasshoppers or the caterpillars of moths will feed on the grass leaves, and small creatures such as spiders and beetles move in to eat them. All these species provide food for invertebrate-eating birds, while seed-eaters such as finches, pigeons, cardinals, titmice, dunnocks and sparrows may also search the area for food.

Below: *Field poppies are still a fairly common sight in pastureland. Sparrows and dunnocks feed on the seeds.*

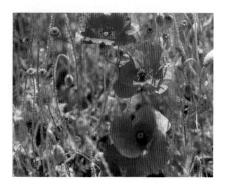

Above: *Spring and summer are the most spectacular times for wildflowers if they are allowed to grow alongside or in place of a manicured lawn.*

WILDFLOWER MEADOWS

Lawns that are converted into a meadow can be an important refuge for declining wildflowers, and are an excellent habitat for many insects and spiders that are eaten by birds. Lawns which face the sun are especially useful, attracting solitary bees and butterflies, and plants such as clover, knapweed, trefoil, various vetches, poppies, coneflowers and rudbeckia which all provide food enjoyed by both bugs and birds.

GARDEN GRASSLANDS

In nature, grassland is a rich and varied habitat that is moulded by the effects of geography, climate, soil and, in many cases, human intervention. Choosing the right type of grassland for your needs will depend on all these factors. Where you live will automatically decide the first three, but the last factor is mostly your choice, and depends on what you want in the garden.

It is possible to try to establish all the types of grassland in miniature in a

Below: *Pigeons and doves are seed-eaters that may find rich pickings in long grass. Other birds feast on insects that lurk there.*

Above: *Lawns provide good hunting grounds for birds that feed on invertebrates such as snails and earthworms, including this blackbird (*Turdus merula*).*

domestic garden setting, to benefit birds, but note that they need to be situated carefully and cut during the summer months, when they are not that attractive. Also note that they can be hard to establish on lawns that have been previously well fertilized.

Short grass or downland turf is most commonly seen in temperate regions. In nature, it is usually the result of grazing sheep, and the consequent short-cropped turf contains a multitude of flower species. It is the closest model to the modern garden lawn, and can be maintained by regular (if infrequent) cutting by a mower on a high setting.

Below: *The hummingbird hawkmoth (*Macroglossum stellatarum*) is preyed on by various birds.*

Above: *Some wildflowers, such as this northern marsh orchid (*Dactylorhiza purpurella*), are especially showy, and attract many insects to gardens.*

Hay meadows are a traditional way of managing grassland. The long grass frequently harbours many species of wildflower during spring and early summer, creating an extremely pretty artificial habitat. Wildflower seeds are eaten by birds such as finches. Traditional forms of management often resulted in poor soil that reduced the vigour of the grasses and favoured the growth of wildflowers. Sadly, modern intensive agriculture has

seen a severe decline in these habitats and consequently in many wildflower species which benefit birds.

Wet meadows or flood meadows are largely similar to hay meadows, except that they are subject to seasonal flooding, usually in winter, and consequently harbour different species of birds.

Prairie is a term used to describe the vast areas of flower-rich grassland that once clothed North America, and is similar to the European steppe. The soils in these wild habitats are often richer than those found in artificial meadows, and they are full of flowering plants that yield seed for birds. Many are now familiar plants. The effect is relatively easy to establish in most gardens because it depends on rich soil.

Marginal grassland is a term used to describe those remnants of grassland plant communities that survive on field margins, roadsides or waste ground. These areas are often a last, vital refuge for grassland birds and also native flower species and their dependent wildlife that were formerly common in the area. The same effect can be created in your garden by leaving a wild grassy area at the base of a hedge. In terms of maintenance, all you need to do is cut the grass back every year or two, preferably in late winter.

Below: *Even when you intend to let grass grow, short-cut paths allow access and creates vegetation of different heights which will benefit insects. Some insects lay their eggs by paths, a food source for birds.*

PLANTING A WILDFLOWER MEADOW

Any area of long grass is a valuable habitat, providing cover for birds, insects and other wildlife. Wildflower meadows and flowery lawns are actually easier to make than you might think. You can add wildflowers by re-seeding an area or by planting pot-grown plants into existing grass.

The first step in transforming an existing lawn is to think about what you want it for, and how much you want to change. If it is important to keep the same amount of lawn, the simplest approach may be to change to wildlife-friendly maintenance. Alternatively, reduce the area of short cut lawn to a minimum, with wildflowers.

CHANGING AN EXISTING GARDEN LAWN

Assuming that you intend to keep some lawn, the simplest change is to let flowering plants colonize it. Reduce the frequency of cutting, and stop fertilizing, using pesticides and weedkillers, and watering it. The initial effect may be hard to see, but low-growing, broad-leaved plants will soon begin to get a foothold. Even allowing areas on a clover-rich lawn to have a flowering break for a week or two will help the bees.

MAKING A WILDFLOWER LAWN

Most grassland wildflowers grow best in full sun and open spaces with minimal root competition from trees, so choose your site accordingly. New lawns are best grown from seed that can either be bought ready mixed or you can mix your own. Ideally, the mix will produce about 60–80 per cent grass coverage, with the remainder being wildflower. The seed mix is sown sparingly – to avoid the grasses out-competing the wildflowers – at a rate of about 15g/m^2 (½oz per sq yd), or less.

You can make an existing lawn richer in flowering plants that will benefit birds by over-seeding in autumn or fall with a mix of wildflower seed. To over-seed an area, you should cut the grass as low as possible and rake away the debris, leaving bare patches of soil. The seed is mixed with some fine, dry sand, thinly sown over the bare patches and then raked in lightly.

The results from over-seeding can be quite variable, and many gardeners prefer to plant out pot-grown wildflowers directly into an existing lawn. Mow the lawn early in

PREPARING THE GROUND AND SOWING A WILDFLOWER MEADOW

1 Start the project by marking out the area you intend to convert to a wildflower meadow. It is best to use a rope or hose to establish flowing lines and curves.

2 Once you have finalized where the edge of the meadow is to be, cut the line in the existing turf using a half-moon edging iron, following the line made by the rope.

3 Lift the existing turf, digging deep enough to remove all grass plants. Plants growing in wildflower meadows prefer nutrient-poor substrate and little topsoil.

4 Once the turf has been lifted and removed, lightly cultivate the whole area with a fork, before raking it to produce a light, crumbly seed bed ready for sowing.

5 Mix the wildflower seed into the grass seed prior to sowing. This will make it easier to distribute evenly. Lightly sow the mix at a rate of 15g/m^2 (½oz per sq yd).

6 The grass and wildlflower seedlings will soon emerge, and the light sowing rate ensures that the grass does not swamp the less vigorous wildflowers as they develop.

the season and scrape or use bare patches for planting into. Arrange the young plants in groups of three to nine for the best effect and maximum chances of success. Once planted, the lawn can be mown on a high setting every two to three weeks in the first year to reduce the competition from grasses. The following year, the lawn can be mown less.

MOWING LONG GRASS
The amount of time and effort a bird-friendly lawn needs will vary. Shorter lawns need little change to their maintenance because the basic method of mowing remains the same, albeit less frequent.

Long grass is trickier, not least because it can be a fire hazard during dry weather. Always site an area of long grass at least 6m (20ft) away from buildings or other combustible items. A buffer zone of conventional lawn can be made more attractive by cutting the first strip of lawn next to the tall grass on the highest mower setting, and reducing this by one setting on each consecutive strip so that the longer grass blends in gradually.

Mowing a margin between long grass and features such as flowerbeds means that the grass will not collapse on to them following rain or storms. If you have a large lawn, mow a path through it so you can watch ground-feeding birds and other wildlife without having to trample on the tall grass. Frequently mow areas you want to keep as paths to keep the grass low.

Hay and water meadows are usually best cut after they have stopped flowering, though if space allows you can try leaving some areas of long grass uncut until late winter to provide shelter for birds and hibernation sites for insects. When you do cut the grass, remove all the clippings, after letting them lie for a day to let any wildlife escape.

PLANTING WILDFLOWERS IN EXISTING GRASS
1 Set out small wildflower plants grown in pots, and, once positioned, cut out and remove a plug of turf before planting.

2 The wildflower plants, once planted into the turf, have a head start and are able to compete with the surrounding grass plants.

TOP PLANTS FOR A WILDFLOWER MEADOW (UK)
Choosing flowers for a wildflower lawn will depend on which species are native to, or will succeed best in, your area. Below are some suggestions for plants that will benefit birds by providing seed and supporting insects, depending on location.

SHORTER GRASS
Cowslip (*Primula veris*) An ideal plant for areas of grass that are cut somewhat infrequently. Suited for hedge bottoms, it produces copious nectar that attracts insects and insect-eating birds in late spring.

Harebell (*Campanula rotundifolia*) The diminutive harebell is widespread in the wild, being found across much of the northern hemisphere. It is ideal for dry sites where its flowers attract bees and insect-eating birds.

Red clover (*Trifolium pratense*) A pea family member with round, red flower-heads that produce copious nectar for bees. Often included in agricultural mixes of grass seed because of its ability to fix nitrogen in the soil and enhance grass growth.

LONG GRASS
Field scabious (*Knautia arvensis*) A nectar-rich meadow flower with pretty blue-mauve pincushions on branching stems throughout summer and well into autumn, when its seed is often eaten by birds.

Ox-eye daisy (*Leucanthemum vulgare*) This pretty perennial produces an abundance of yellow-centred, white daisy flowers in summer, and later, seeds for birds. Many daisy flowers – including coneflowers (*Echinacea*) and asters – are suited to long grass.

Queen Anne's lace/cow parsley (*Daucus carota*) This wild ancestor of the cultivated carrot has dainty flowers in summer – an excellent source of food for hoverflies, butterflies and other insects that feed birds.

TOP PLANTS FOR A PRAIRIE-TYPE MEADOW (US)
For a pretty, low-maintenance prairie-type meadow, a mixture of native, European, and Asian species produces good results. The flowering plants listed below provide colour, shelter and food for birds and insects. Some native grasses are also listed.

FLOWERING PLANTS
Black-eyed Susan (*Rudbeckia* species) The many types of rudbeckia produce long-lasting, yellow, daisy-like flowers.

California poppy (*Eschscholzia californica*) This perennial produces yellow to orange flowers from February to September, and later fruits containing numerous small black seeds.

Coreopsis (*Coreopsis* species) Plains coreopsis and lanceleaf coreopsis both yield attractive yellow or red flowers.

Purple aster/Michaelmas daisy (*Symphyotrichum novi-belgii*) Flowers have purple petals and yellow centres.

Purple coneflower (*Echinacea purpurea*) Produces lavender or purple flowers with red-orange, cone-shape centres.

Queen Anne's lace/Wild carrot (*Daucus carota*) This pretty plant has a delicate filigree head of dainty flowers in summer – an excellent source of food for insects.

GRASSES
Little bluestem (*Schizacyrium scoparius*) This grass reaches a height of up to 90cm (3ft) tall, and turns an attractive orange colour in fall.

Broomsedge (*Andropogon virginicus*) Reaches a similar height to little bluestem and also turns orange in fall. These two species may be seeded together or separately.

Sheep fescue (*Festuca ovina*) This grass reaches a maximum height of about 60cm (2ft) tall, and has an attractive bluish colour all year.

HEDGEROWS FOR BIRDS

Widely used as boundaries and dividing features in landscapes for centuries, hedges are important habitats for birds and many other creatures. Properly managed, they provide shelter and food for birds and other wildlife, and are home to once common and often beautiful wildflower species.

A hedge can be defined as a boundary of closely planted woody shrubs or trees. The earliest known use of the word dates back to Anglo-Saxon times. The Anglo-Saxons used hedges as a way of defining ownership of land, but their hedges were not the same as those we know today, being more like a rough fence, and often containing as much deadwood as living material. They used many species that benefit birds, such as hawthorn (*Crataegus monogyna*) – haw also means 'hedge' in Old Saxon – and briar roses.

In centuries past, people exerted less pressure on wildlife and hedges were just another place for birds and other animals to shelter and forage. With increased land clearance, intensified agriculture and a growing population, however, habitats have dwindled and hedges have become an important refuge for many native species. In this way ancient agricultural hedges are a tangible link with the wildlife that once inhabited the wooded edge and open spaces, containing a rich variety of birds and other animal life and a multitude of plant species, both woody and herbaceous. Hedges are often a prime habitat in their own right.

Below: *Hedges are often rich in seed- and berry-producing shrubs that provide an ideal food source for overwintering birds.*

THREATS TO TRADITIONAL HEDGEROWS
The intensification of agriculture in recent decades, coupled with the introduction of large machinery, has meant that many areas that were once traditionally managed using hedgerows as part of the rural landscape have now been transformed beyond recognition.

Machines work more efficiently in large fields, and hedges were seen as taking up valuable land that could produce crops. In addition, hedges in North America contained a lot of barberry (*Berberis*), and this was identified as the alternative host species of the wheat rust (*Puccinia graminis*), which is a serious fungal disease of commerically grown wheat.

The net effect of this was that farmers on both sides of the Atlantic were encouraged to remove hedges and in doing so this rich and vital habitat was removed from the landscape. In the case of European hedges, the rich legacy of over a thousand years was lost in some cases, and it left birds and other wildlife in a precarious position. Gardens became one of the few places where hedges remained common, and as such they are an invaluable resource for birds.

Above: *Even where a more formal effect is required, you can choose a hedging that benefits birds, for example this hornbeam.*

GARDEN HEDGES AND WILDLIFE
The modern approach to hedges, especially in backyard settings, has been to cultivate a tight-cropped and controlled shape with many closely planted

Below: *Hedgerow species such as hawthorn have abundant spring blossom that attracts insects and in turn birds.*

specimens of the same species. But while highly decorative, these have limited appeal to wildlife. Some birds are able to find shelter in the dense growth, but the range of species is limited, as is the likelihood of finding much food.

The answer often lies in planting a mixed, native hedge. Remember that a mosaic of plant species will favour a wider range of wildlife. Choose plants that provide food in the form of nectar-rich flowers and berries for overwintering birds. Hawthorn (*Crataegus*), wild roses (*Rosa*), holly (*Ilex*), hazel (*Corylus*) and elder (*Sambucus*) are good all-round choices.

TYPES OF HEDGE
Hedges are quite diverse, partly as a result of their function but also because of how they are maintained.

Mixed hedges Quite simply, a mixed hedge is one where the intention is to grow a range of species and provide a habitat that has the maximum species diversity. This type of hedge is most like a natural wooded edge.

Single-species hedges These hedges are common, especially in gardens, where their intention is to provide a consistent backdrop or feature. They can be useful for birds provided that a suitable species is chosen.

Formal hedges Found in highly manicured gardens and cut with a smooth face, the high frequency of their cutting and general absence of flowers or fruits mean that formal hedges are less useful for birds.

Informal hedges As the name suggests, these are hedges where the cutting regime does not entail frequent cuts or a smooth face or finish. They can be planted as single- or mixed-species hedges.

Dead hedges These barriers consist of dead branches and twigs that are firmly staked in place. Climbers are allowed to ramble through them and provide excellent shelter for birds.

You could also try planting shrubs such as barberry, cotoneaster and pyracantha, which produce lots of berries for the birds.

Resident birds may also appreciate hedges for shelter and also breeding, which is why wildlife hedges can't be trimmed in the nesting season, from early spring to late summer. Human impact can be further lessened by cutting back (not too tightly) only one side of the hedge on alternate years. Ideally, hedges should be pruned in late winter so that birds can take advantage of the insects, fruits and buds during the cold months, and again in summer and autumn.

Hedgerows are especially important because, as with woodlands and open fields, they can provide corridors for

Above: *Informal mixed hedges are the kind most likely to attract birds such as chiffchaffs (*Phylloscopus collybita*), which may build their nests near the hedge base.*

wildlife, allowing species to disperse and move from one habitat to another. In the larger landscape setting, plants also find it difficult to spread across open fields, and 'travelling' along the base of a hedge is their only realistic option.

Always allow the bottom of your hedge – the portion where the base of the hedge adjoins another habitat – to become overgrown with grasses and flowers. The bottom is characteristically the dampest and most fertile area, and often proves to be the part richest in wildlife.

Below: *The bases of hedgerows often provide a refuge for woodland flowers. This area is also rich in birds and other wildlife that find cover here.*

Below: *Honeysuckle (*Lonicera periclymenum*) is a good example of a hedgerow climber that is useful for birds and moths, and is also ideal as an ornamental plant.*

PLANTING A WILDLIFE HEDGE

Wildlife hedges are a real boost to a bird-friendly garden. The best usually consist of mixed plant species that provide nesting sites and year-round cover for birds. They may also produce flowers and berries. Single-species hedges provide less variety, but may still be useful if managed properly.

When deciding what sort of hedge will most benefit birds and other wildlife, you must also consider your own needs. If the hedge is also to provide security or a barrier, or if you need a certain height, then check the plants' possible dimensions. Also note that a wildlife hedge will not be frequently pruned, and can grow both tall and wide in a single season.

The most bird-friendly hedge includes a range of four or five species. The exact species will vary considerably according to the conditions, but any plants chosen should always be compatible in their maintenance requirements when grown together as a hedge.

CHOOSING HEDGE PLANTS

Start by taking a walk around your neighbourhood, looking at the hedges and seeing what plants are growing well. Try to choose at least half of your plants from locally indigenous species because they'll often be most valuable to native birds. If possible, when looking at other hedges growing locally, make notes about the

Above: *Some grosbeaks are birds of hedges and wooded edges. They benefit gardeners by eating insect pests.*

range and types of wildlife they attract. A single-species hedge can be very useful, if only because all the plants will have similar maintenance requirements. For plants that both flower and set fruit, you could try fuchsia, escallonia, elder or barberry, all of which attract birds. Traditional agricultural hedges mainly consist of up to 80 per cent of one species, such as hawthorn, but will usually also contain other trees and shrubs. This creates a variety of blossom, berries and scent with a range of niches that make such a hedge the best choice for birds. If you have a large garden, this type of hedge may be appropriate, but for a typical suburban neighbourhood, a single-species hedge may be more aesthetically pleasing.

PREPARATION AND PLANTING

When planting a wildlife hedge, prepare the soil beforehand. Dig a trench at least 50cm (20in) wide, and mix plenty of organic compost and a general fertilizer at around 50g per m^2 (2oz per sq yd). Refill the trench and allow it to settle for a couple of weeks before planting. Hedges are usually planted as either single rows of plants, about 30cm (1ft) apart, or as staggered, double rows

SETTING OUT AND PLANTING A HEDGE

1 Start by levelling your previously prepared ground, using a rake to ensure that there are no rises and dips on the row.

2 Consolidate the ground to make sure there are no void spaces by lightly treading the area with a flat foot rather than a heel.

3 Rake the ground level, either with a rake or uing the back of a fork. It is always best to start planting into level ground.

4 Using a spade to make a planting pit, slide the roots down into the hole, ensuring all are covered.

5 Using the heel of your boot, make sure the plant is firmly planted, with no air spaces around the stem.

6 Use guards to protect the stems from rabbits. These also shelter the young plants from the wind.

with the same distance between the plants and rows. When planting, peg out a line of string to keep the hedge straight. Species such as beech (*Fagus*) and hawthorn (*Crataegus*) are best planted at a 45-degree angle to encourage thick growth at the base.

To stimulate dense, twiggy growth, trim off one-half to two-thirds of the total height of the hedge and then, for the first two or three years, remove at least half of the new growth during the winter period. Mulch the base of the rows annually, and apply an organic feed just before you do this.

MAINTAINING YOUR HEDGE

Once established, trim your hedge every second or third year, but avoid doing so when birds are nesting. The ideal time is in late winter, making nuts and berries available to birds for the longest possible period. Try cutting opposite faces of the hedge in alternate years where space is restricted, or if a slightly more formal shape is desired, because this will produce some flowers and fruit each year.

The best shape for a wildlife hedge is an 'A' shape because the sloping sides allow light and rain to reach the bottom of the hedge. An established hedge, say four to five years old, can be enhanced by planting climbers that benefit birds, such as honeysuckle, roses and clematis. Take care, though, as planting climbers before the hedge is well established can result in the hedge being overwhelmed and strangled. You can also plant hedgerow wildflowers at the base to provide extra cover for birds.

CUTTING A HEDGE

1 Once the hedge begins to outgrow its setting, it must be cut. This should be done before or after nesting time.

2 Set out a line of canes every couple of metres (7ft) to mark the line you want to cut, to produce a good face.

3 Before cutting the top, set out a string line to mark the desired height and ensure a straight line is maintained.

4 Even for neater wildlife hedges, the finished cut should not be too tight; aim to preserve a somewhat informal look to the shape.

TOP HEDGE PLANTS FOR BIRDS

Any hedge has potential as a wildlife habitat, but the species described here are among the most useful plants to attract the widest range of birds.

Alder buckthorn (*Rhamnus frangula*) A thornless tree with five-petalled, green-white flowers, this is visited by many insects that are hunted by birds. The flowers are followed by red berries that turn black in autumn and are eaten by birds.

Blackthorn (*Prunus spinosa*) Also known as sloe, the flowers of this thorny plant attract early bees and butterflies, while the leaves support caterpillars that feed nestlings. It doesn't like heavy shade but withstands strong winds.

Blue mist (*Caryopteris clandonensis*) This shrub, growing to 1.2m (4ft), bears blue flowers that attract bees.

Chokecherry (*Prunus virginiana*) This tree, growing to 6m (20ft), produces clusters of white flowers and black fruit.

False indigo (*Amorpha fruticosa*) This shrub, growing to 2.4m (8ft), has delicate foliage and clusters of purple flowers. A favourite with insects, mostly in the western USA.

Fernbush (*Chamaebatiaria millefolium*) A dry-tolerant shrub up to 2.4m (8ft), it attracts bees and insect-eating birds in the western USA.

Golden currant (*Ribes aureum*) This attractive shrub, growing to 1.8m (6ft), has fragrant yellow blossoms. It is a good understorey plant for moist areas.

Gooseberry (*Ribes leptanthum*) This understorey shrub, which grows to 1.5m (5ft), flowers in early spring. The summer fruits are enjoyed by many different birds.

Hazel (*Corylus avellana*) Also called hazelnut or cobnut, hazel supports woodpeckers and at least 70 insect species, and squirrels and small rodents, which are attracted to the nuts.

Mulberry (*Morus* species) This tree, growing to 15m (49ft), has glossy foliage, and produces multiple sweet berries that attract birds and wildlife.

New Mexico locust (*Robinia neomexicana*) This thorny shrub, growing to 3m (10ft), produces large clusters of magenta blossoms. It is native to the south-west USA.

Russian sage (*Perovskia atriplicifolia*) A silvery-grey shrub, growing to 1.2m (4ft), bearing purple flower spikes throughout the summer, which attract insects and insect-eating birds.

Silver buffaloberry (*Shepherdia argentea*) This large shrub, growing to 3m (10ft), is an excellent hedge plant that yields bright berries in autumn.

Sweet briar (*Rosa rubiginosa*) Also known as the eglantine rose, the leaves and stems of this European species have a brownish-red tint. The pink flowers that appear from late spring to early summer give way to bright red hips that are enjoyed by birds.

Wayfaring tree (*Viburnum lantana*) This small shrub is naturally found on chalk and limestone soils. It sports bright red berries in autumn or fall that ripen to black, which sustain birds. These are preceded by clusters of scented white flowers in late spring and early summer.

Alder buckthorn   Blackthorn   Hazel   Sweet briar

WOODED AREAS FOR BIRDS

Wooded areas provide a rich and varied natural habitat for birds and other wildlife species. Woodland varies greatly, depending on location and the tree species, and the way in which it has been managed. If space allows, a small wooded area in your garden can benefit many kinds of birds.

Vast areas of the Earth's surface are still covered with trees. Natural, undisturbed woodlands are one of the most diverse habitats found anywhere on the planet. There are many types of woodlands, and each harbours a different community of birds and other wildlife. If you are able to

Below: *Even a small tree is of great benefit to birds and wildlife in your garden, especially when long grass is allowed to grow underneath, as here.*

plant a tree or few in your garden, it will appeal and be of benefit to many birds.

Almost all woodlands can be divided vertically into a series of layers called storeys, which contain different plant species. The tallest and most dominant trees form the topmost layer, called the canopy. The canopy can either be closed, in the case of dense woodland, or more open, with sunlight penetrating between the trees. Beneath the canopy is a layer of less dominant tree species, called the

Above: *American redstarts (*Setophaga ruticilla*) are seen in wooded backyards in the USA, where they are common, preferring second-growth woodland.*

understorey, and beneath that is a layer of smaller, woody plants and immature trees called the shrub layer. The ground layer, sometimes called the forest floor, is covered to a greater or lesser extent with a herbacious layer. The soil is continuously enriched by the decomposing leaves, shed from the trees either throughout the year, in the case of evergreens, or in autumn in the case of deciduous trees.

Below: *Fallen leaves and seed coats form layers on woodland floors, where they break down and release nutrients.*

Above: *Taking a long time to die, trees often become full of deadwood, which in turn provides a habitat for invertebrates.*

Above: *Species such as tawny owls (Strix aluco) inhabit coniferous forests, which are well adapted to colder climates.*

TYPES OF WOODLAND

Broad-leaved deciduous woodlands contain a greater variety of birds than any other wooded area found outside the tropics. The trees here mostly lose their leaves in autumn in order to survive harsh winter weather. They are dominated by trees with wide, flat leaves. There is considerable variation between broad-leaved woodlands in different locations in respect of the birds and other wildlife they contain.

Coniferous woodlands grow naturally in northern parts of North America, Europe and Asia. The trees here are mostly adapted to a cold, harsh climate and a short growing season. Coniferous woodlands are less productive in terms of birds than deciduous woodlands, but nonetheless support species such as woodpeckers, owls and crossbills.

Temperate rainforests grow in areas with warm summers and cool winters, and can vary enormously in the kinds of plant life they contain. In some, conifers dominate, while others are characterized by broad-leaved evergreens. These are mostly restricted to coastal areas in the north-west Pacific, south-western South America, New Zealand and Tasmania. However, small, isolated pockets of temperate rainforest grow in Ireland and Scotland. Despite their relative rarity, these are amazingly diverse natural habitats and home to some of the world's most massive trees.

TRADITIONAL MANAGEMENT

In many areas where woodland once formed extensive cover, much has now been removed and the vast majority that remains has long been managed by people. Despite the loss of ancient 'wildwoods', the remaining managed woodlands prove to be excellent habitats for birds, whose exact nature depends on the system of management employed.

Coppicing is a traditional method of woodland management, by which young tree stems are cut down to 30cm (1ft) or less from ground level to encourage the production of new shoots. This is done repeatedly through the life of the tree and results in a habitat that transforms from a clearing into a woodland habitat. Many familiar woodland birds, such as jays and woodpeckers, are well adapted to coppiced woodlands. Pollarding is a similar system but involves cutting the branches from a tree stem 2m (6ft) or so above ground level. Pollarding was mostly practised in wood-pastures and grazing areas where cutting above head height protected the new shoots from being damaged by browsing animals.

THE BEST WOODLAND FOR BIRDS

The ability of woodland to support birds and other wildlife varies considerably. The age of a woodland and the variety of plant species it contains have their part to play, as does the way in which it has been managed. Generally, open woodland, especially when deciduous, is more accessible than closed woodland to species that browse and graze, and tends to be richer in ground-level plants.

The woodland floor is often rich in species that feed on decaying plant matter. Deadwood is also important for many insect species that live in rotting wood and feed many types of birds. Where the greatest concentrations of wildlife occur will vary greatly according to the type of woodland, but the richest areas always tend to be those that border other habitats, for example at woodland margins. The latter is the easiest to recreate in a garden.

Below: *Chaffinches (Fringilla) frequent parks and gardens, but are mainly woodland birds. Their diet includes caterpillars, shoots, seeds and berries.*

CREATING WOODED EDGES

In the wild, the edges where forests and woodlands give way to more open areas are potentially highly productive habitats for birds, offering a wide range of foods, shelter and also breeding sites. If you have the space, including some trees in your garden creates a fantastic bird-friendly habitat.

Woodland is most diverse at its edges, either in the treetops of the upper canopy, where there is plenty of light, or where it meets another habitat. The exact nature of this edge is largely dependent on the adjoining habitat, whether grass, cultivated land, marsh or water. The woodland produces an abundance of growth which leads to a rich organic layer deposited over the soil that produces very fertile ground. More directly, birds benefit from the shelter and fruits and seeds offered by the trees.

Of course, most gardens, even large ones, do not have room for an area of naturalized woodland, but you may be able to accommodate a group of several small or medium-sized trees, which will support insects and provide food and perches for birds.

Above: *Nuthatches (Sittidae) are woodland birds, feeding on seeds and insects. The white-breasted variety is sometimes seen in wooded backyards and gardens.*

SITING A WOODED EDGE
A wooded edge is easier to recreate in a garden than you might think. Even if space is limited, shrub borders fulfil some of the role of a wooded edge, and, if managed correctly, hedges can also attract wooded-edge species.

Choose a strip along an edge of the garden facing the sunniest direction. This means you'll minimize shade on the rest of the garden while the wooded-edge border gets the benefit of sunshine, which will widen its appeal to a greater range of species. Alternatively, make it face the afternoon sun. This will, of course, cast shade on your garden in the morning, but this need not be a problem. The plants often benefit most from the afternoon sun, especially in the cooler seasons.

When choosing a site, don't forget to discuss your plans with your neighbours, whose gardens may be affected by shade. A wall or a fence is the ideal back boundary for your wooded edge because it can provide support for some of the climbing plants that benefit birds.

Left: *In this large garden, there are several layers to the planting: a border at the front with tall flowering plants which attract insects, then shrubs and smaller trees, and at the back, a single large canopy tree – an oak.*

Above: *Pileated woodpeckers (*Dryocopus pileatus*) will visit some gardens in the USA, especially those with a wooded edge.*

PLANTING AND MAINTAINING A WOODED EDGE

Plant a wooded edge so that there is a general increase in height from the front to the back of the area or border, thereby allowing light to reach all the plants. The tall plants at the back are called the 'canopy edge' plants. In a narrow border, you will need around one canopy tree for about every 5m (17ft). Choose smallish, sun-loving woodland trees, particularly those that bear berries to feed birds. The plants in front of this are the shrub layer, with the herbaceous layer forming the smallest layer at the front. Growing under the canopy trees, these layers can include both sun-loving and shade-tolerant plants because the canopy trees cast very little shade on the border. There is always room for variety, though, and many smaller, more shade-loving plants, such as early perennials and bulbs, can easily be planted among the taller woody plant species.

Managing a wooded edge area in your garden takes far less time and work than you might imagine. Once planted, you just need to keep the area well watered and clear of weeds until everything is established. You should also keep an eye on the border for the next few years, making sure that no one plant is dominating and smothering the others. Eventually, though, the area should need little or no maintenance.

Right: *Where trees and shrubs give way to grassland and wildflower meadow, such as in this informal wooded edge, the mosaic of different habitats is naturally rich in plants and birds.*

TOP TREES FOR BIRDS

If you have the space, trees are a valuable feature for birds, and by choosing the species carefully, you can greatly enhance the wildlife potential of a garden.

Apples and crab apples (*Malus sylvestris*) These are a familiar fixture in many gardens. The older varieties are best, supporting diverse insects on the leaves and stems. The buds are eaten by some birds, as is the fruit. The tree is of most use to birds if left largely unpruned.

Pine (*Pinus sylvestris*) Pines are among the best conifers for birds, offering a source of seeds that are taken by many species. The dense crowns are used by nesting birds such as owls. These trees are an excellent choice for dry soils, although they eventually grow quite tall.

Red mulberry (*Morus rubra*) The mulberry produces berries throughout the summer that are eaten by at least 40 different bird species. It makes an ideal tree for moist, fertile soils. Keep it clear of paths and patios as the fruit can be messy.

Rowan (*Sorbus aucuparia*) A medium-sized tree that is well suited for the smaller garden, with numerous closely related species and cultivars. Birds visit rowan trees but rarely make them a permanent habitat. Insects love the flowers, while birds, especially thrushes, often feed on the attractive, bright red berries.

Southern beech (*Nothofagus alpina*) A fast-growing and, eventually, quite large forest tree, only worth growing in a big garden. In many places it supports a variety of species that feed on the nuts and live in the tree, especially in the gnarled bark of older specimens.

Sugar maple (*Acer saccharum*) This fruits between early summer and autumn/fall in North America. It attracts birds, such as pileated woodpeckers, as well as insects. The leaves provide spectacular colour, from yellow through orange to deep red.

Pine   Rowan   Southern beech   Sugar maple

PLANTING TREES AND SHRUBS

Trees and shrubs form the essential framework of any garden, providing cover for a variety of birds, as well as nesting sites that are well above the ground and safe from ground-dwelling predators. The secret to success in planting lies in careful ground preparation, stock selection and planting.

When selecting plants, always choose trees and shrubs that are vigorous, healthy and suitable for the site conditions or intended usage. They should be free from any obvious signs of damage, pests or disease. If you are buying bare-rooted stock, make sure that the roots never dry out before planting, and keep them covered at all times – even a couple of minutes left exposed to cold or drying winds can cause a lot of damage. You should plant them as soon as possible; if the soil is frozen or waterlogged, plant them in a temporary bed of compost, at a 45-degree angle (this is called heeling in), and keep them moist until you are in a position to be able to plant them out.

PREPARING THE GROUND

Despite what is written in many books and guides, organic additives such as compost can be a mixed blessing if they are incorporated into soil at planting time. An enhanced soil mix does improve the soil but also causes the plants to become 'lazy'. Quite simply, the roots like compost better than the surrounding soil and circle round as if in a pot, resulting in an unstable 'corkscrew' growth pattern known as girdling. Avoid this by applying organic matter across the surface after planting. This creates more natural conditions and encourages insects including beetles. Apply fertilizers only if really needed, after planting but before mulching.

WHEN TO PLANT

Plant deciduous species during early winter, when they are dormant. Evergreens, on the other hand, tend to do well if planted either in early autumn or late spring. Trees and shrubs growing in containers can

PLANTING AND STAKING TREES AND SHRUBS

1 Container-grown trees and shrubs should be watered an hour before you plant them. Soak really dry ones overnight.

2 Clear any weeds and cut any suckers coming from the roots as these may slow the tree or shrub's top and root growth.

3 Once you remove the pot, tease out any encircling roots to encourage root spread in the soil and to prevent root-balling.

4 Dig the planting pit and ensure that it is deep enough for the root-ball. Check by lying a spade or fork on its side.

5 Backfill the pit, firming the soil with a heel every 8cm (3in) to make sure it is well planted and contains no large air pockets.

6 Drive the stake in at an angle to avoid damaging the roots. Face the stake into the prevailing wind for stronger root growth.

7 Secure the stem of the tree or shrub using a tie, nailed on to prevent movement. Choose one with a spacer.

8 The amount of time the tree or shrub should be staked varies. However long, the tie must be checked and loosened.

Above: *Trees and shrubs, once established, provide ideal habitats for birds, while flower beds attract insects and provide cover.*

Above right: *Greenfinches (Chloris chloris) nest in small colonies in dense vegetation. About half a dozen pairs may nest together.*

be planted throughout most of the year, provided that the ground is kept sufficiently moist, although they too will generally establish best in the cooler months. Never plant when the soil is frozen, excessively dry or waterlogged, as this may damage the roots and lower stem.

Make planting holes big enough, allowing a quarter to a third of the diameter again of the root spread. Check that the plant is at the same depth as it was before.

STAKING AND PROTECTION

Large shrubs and trees require staking to prevent them blowing over in their first season. Smaller, more vulnerable stock is protected by putting it in a tree or shrub shelter that helps stems thicken, promotes rapid upward growth and protects plants from rodents and sometimes deer attack.

MULCHING TREES

Young trees growing in grass are often slow to establish due to competition from the surrounding plants. Remove the turf around the tree. Create a cleared circle around the stem of the tree that is 1m (3ft) in diameter. Water the ground, then apply an even layer of mulch to a depth of about 5cm (2in) on the cleared circle.

TOP WOODED EDGE PLANTS FOR BIRDS

Wooded edges are naturally rich in flowering and fruit-bearing species, many of which provide a vital food resource for a variety of visiting birds.

CANOPY PLANTS

Apples and crab apples (*Malus*) Deciduous, small, shrubby, spring-flowering tree with abundant round, fleshy, apple-like fruits that follow large, cup-shaped, white, pink-flushed flowers that attract bees. These trees are a great food source for many different insects and birds.

Rowan (*Sorbus*) This group includes the familiar rowan tree or mountain ash *Sorbus aucuparia*, which becomes heavily laden with bright red berries that are enjoyed by birds in late summer and early autumn. A versatile genus with many species and cultivars.

Box elder (*Acer negundo*) A small, usually fast-growing and fairly short-lived maple native to North America, whose winged seeds are sometimes eaten by birds and other animals. Its sugary sap is sometimes eaten by squirrels and songbirds.

SHRUB LAYER

Rose (*Rosa*) Roses can be extremely attractive shrubs. If possible, plant a wild species and choose single flowers over double types as these are best for visiting insects. The hips that follow the flowers are often eaten by birds. If possible, plant a wild species and choose single flowers over double.

Rubus An important group of bird-friendly shrubs that includes the common blackberry (*Rubus fruticosus*). Care should be taken when choosing this as it can quite easily become very invasive. Many other species and cultivars are good garden specimens.

Viburnum An extremely varied group of plants that includes a wide range of species and hybrids, with good wildlife value and an attractive appearance. Choose varieties with berries, such as the guelder rose (*Viburnum opulus*) to provide food for birds.

Crab apple

Rowan

Rose

Viburnum

PONDS FOR BIRDS

A wildlife garden would not be complete without a pond, which provides a bathing and drinking site for birds and a habitat for many other creatures. With its aesthetic appeal, a pond makes a worthy addition to any design, but where space is limited, even the smallest patch of water can be useful.

The term 'pond' is surprisingly vague, there being no clear distinction between a large pond and a small lake. The average garden pond is relatively small, but a well-designed pond can attract a greater variety of wildlife than any other single feature in the garden. Ponds also provide a unique visual focus, and have a restful quality that is hard to match.

WILDLIFE VALUE
A pond offers not only a drinking and bathing site for birds, but also a breeding site for amphibians and for a whole host of insects, such as dragonflies, that spend part of their life here. In addition, it is the sole habitat for a range of other creatures, from water snails that spend their life

Below: *An area of water can be an attractive garden feature, which results in a surprisingly diverse habitat for birds and other creatures.*

Above: *Birds like this jay* (Garrulus glandarius) *are often drawn to ponds to drink, especially in summer. A rock edging provides a useful perch.*

Above: *This female blackbird* (Turdus merula) *is collecting mud from the edges of a small garden pond for her nest-building purposes.*

PLANTS FOR WETLANDS
Natural wetlands contain both open water and wet ground, with different plant species living on the margins and in deep water.

Marginal or emergent plants
Plants that have roots and sometimes stems that grow in shallow water, but with shoots, leaves and flowers above the water surface.

Oxygenators These important plants live beneath the surface and enrich the water with oxygen.

Water lilies and deep-water aquatics The roots of these plants are submerged, the leaves are on the surface, and the flowers are either on or above the surface.

Free-floating plants The leaves and stems are free-floating on the water surface. The roots are submerged and the flowers grow on or just above the water.

Bog plants These are plants that prefer to grow in permanently wet or waterlogged ground. Some species that flourish on pond margins can also be grown as bog plants.

beneath the water to pond skaters that spend most of their life on the water surface.

Ponds should be shallow at one end to provide a bathing area for birds, and if possible have wet, muddy margins to attract birds needing a drink.

POND PLANTS
Plants are essential to the health of any small area of water, enabling the habitat to achieve a correct water balance and provide surface cover on otherwise open water. Without them the water would, over time, probably start to resemble a thick pea soup, as algae – small, mostly microscopic plant-like organisms – will start to grow prolifically and ultimately colour the water. Plant leaves have the double action of absorbing both carbon dioxide and minerals from the water, which in turn starves the algae. Many natural bodies of still or slow-moving water have extensive cover of floating plants and their sides are also shaded by larger, bank-side or shallows vegetation.

In a garden pond it is easy to recreate this by ensuring that there are plenty of submerged plants, about half of the water surface is covered with foliage, and that the margins have plants in them that are capable of surviving immersion in shallow water. This will keep the water clear and will also make the pond attractive for birds and a host of creatures that are either residents or visitors.

Above: *Pond dipping is a good way to assess what wildlife you have in a pond and check how clear the water is.*

BOG GARDENS
Usually specially constructed areas, bog gardens provide permanently waterlogged soil. They are often made in conjunction with a pond, and can support a range of unusual plants normally found in wetland habitats. Bog gardens are an important element of any mosaic, and can be a vital refuge for aquatic birds, such as coots and moorhens, and also amphibians, which will relish the cool, damp shelter.

POND PLANTINGS
Ideally, a pond profile will include shallow areas as well as deeper water. In the deeper reaches, the vegetation consists of plants able to live permanently underwater or those with roots that send up leaves which float on the surface. Shallow water will support plants capable of tolerating waterlogged conditions, and the remainder are free-floating on the surface.

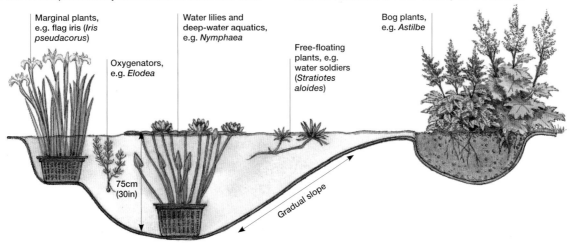

Marginal plants, e.g. flag iris (*Iris pseudacorus*)

Oxygenators, e.g. *Elodea*

Water lilies and deep-water aquatics, e.g. *Nymphaea*

Free-floating plants, e.g. water soldiers (*Stratiotes aloides*)

Bog plants, e.g. *Astilbe*

75cm (30in)

Gradual slope

MAKING A POND

Ponds are a real benefit in a wildlife garden, providing a watering hole for birds and a complete habitat for other wildlife. They are relatively easy to construct, but need to be properly sited and designed to be useful habitats. Care and attention at the planning stage will boost the wildlife potential of your garden.

When choosing a site for your pond, look for an attractive, sunny place, sheltered from the prevailing wind. Try to avoid a site that is shaded by trees because they will cut out light, and their leaves will drop into the water, enriching it with nutrients and organic debris. This promotes green water and blanket algae in the warmer months.

In any garden where a water feature is planned, child safety is of paramount importance. If there is any risk that young children might fall in, consider delaying your plans until they are older. Children love water and the wildlife it attracts, but you should always weigh up the risks.

THE SHAPE AND SIZE OF A POND
As a general rule, 4m² (43sq ft) is the minimum area needed to create a balanced environment, with marginal shelves at least 25cm (10in) wide to support containers of emergent plants. Create the outline using sweeping curves with no sharp bends; a figure-of-eight or a kidney shape is often the best idea for smaller ponds. Then draw a rough cross-section of the pond to check how much depth you will get for your width. Aim to get at least 60cm (2ft) and ideally 90cm (3ft) or more in the deeper

Above: *Even a small garden pond may attract a kingfisher foraging for fish and molluscs, perhaps to feed its young.*

reaches to benefit a range of wildlife. The slopes should drop at a rate of one-third of the equivalent distance travelled across the top to assure stability.

CHOOSING A LINER
For small ponds, moulded or fibreglass pools can be used but are limited in terms of design, and don't look very natural.

A flexible liner, such as butyl rubber, is generally considered the best (if most expensive) option, although UV stabilized PVC can be a cheaper alternative. Both these materials are prone to puncture, for example by the sharp beaks of herons, and care must be taken to line the hole with soft sand and/or an underlay, such as old carpet (made of natural fibres), to avoid this. The liners are easy to lay, and can also be used when creating bog gardens.

HIDING THE EDGE
Both flexible and rigid liners need to be hidden if you want to promote a natural effect. There are many ways of doing this.

A cobbled edge is easily achieved by setting some large stones or cobbles into a bed of sand/cement laid on the liner, both below and above the eventual water surface on a shallow slope. The stones form a firm base, and other stones can be piled between, with the gaps providing sheltering space for small animals, while also providing a gently sloping 'beach' for birds to approach and drink.

A drystone wall, or alternatively a loose rock pile set on a mortar base on the liner, just below the water, can act as a retaining

CREATING DRINKING SHALLOWS

1 The shallow areas of ponds are important to allow birds to drink, but they can become muddy traps for smaller creatures and offer little protection or shelter for visitors.

2 Start by placing some larger stones or rounded rocks both in the shallow water and on the bank, arranging them in small groups of varying sizes to create a natural-looking effect.

3 Once the larger stones have been placed, the spaces between them should be filled with round cobblestones to create both shallow stony pools and drier beach areas.

4 The finished effect is very ornamental, and the strong shoreline provides hiding places for smaller creatures as well as a basking area and safe drinking site for birds.

wall for nearby planting, with the niches between the stones providing shelter for amphibians. Walls or rock features are best placed at the back of the pond so that they create a reflection on the water surface.

A planted edge is also an option with a 'planting pocket' being built on the liner. This involves running the liner about 10cm

(4in) above maximum water level, and then burying it in the soil around the edge. It provides a simple and natural effect, with the overhanging plants hiding the edge, but the liner will show when the water level drops, and there is always the added danger of damaging a flexible liner when mowing or gardening near the pond

Concrete or stone slabs laid on a sand/ cement bed over the edge of the liner are a somewhat formal solution, but are very practical if you want to view the water up close. Try to avoid this all the way around, though, as very small animals, such as young frogs, may have difficulty climbing in and out over the stone edge.

PUTTING IN A BUTYL LINER FOR A POND

1 Start by marking out the outside edge of the pond using stakes or canes, and then mark out the locations of any shallow margins with spray paint.

2 Once marked out, begin digging the pond, starting with the deeper areas first, before digging out the margins and finalizing the edge of the pond.

3 Once you have excavated all of the pond to the required depth, establish the slopes on the side of the pond and the planting shelves within it.

4 To gain nicely smooth sides to the excavated pit, line the whole of the base and sloping sites with graded stone-free sand, fabric or old carpet.

5 Carefully lift the liner over the pit. Don't drag it because sharp stones may puncture it. Secure the corners using bricks or stones and start to fill the pond with water.

6 As the liner fills with water, it will mould to the shape you have excavated. Once the pond is nearly full, cut the edge of the liner, leaving a generous overlap.

7 As the water level continues to rise, fold the liner to create an even finish and avoid any unsightly creases across the pond bottom or sloping sides.

8 Once the water is almost up to the top, bury the edges of the liner by cutting and then lifting the turf edges of the pond and laying it under the cut turf.

9 The new pond can now be filled to the brim, then planted with various wetland species. Shallows can be created using stones of varying sizes.

PLANTING A POND

Naturally occurring ponds and wetlands are rich in plant life, much of which is specially adapted to grow in waterlogged ground, shallow water or even under the surface. By including a range of these plants, you will greatly improve the look of your water feature and also its value for birds and other wildlife.

Surprisingly, new ponds can seem initially quite stark and lifeless. Plants provide the magic to bring them to life and, once surrounded by vegetation, the whole feature becomes more attractive both to us and to birds and other wildlife.

To create a natural look, you could put a layer of soil on top of the liner for plants to root into, and creatures to hide in. This has the disadvantage, however, of introducing nutrients that can cause algal growth, and often means that you must be prepared to cull the plants regularly because aquatic plants can spread rapidly and choke the pond. Most people minimize the problem by using special aquatic plant containers that curtail excessive growth. Most pond plants are perfectly happy in clay loam. Provided you ensure that the soil used is free of pesticides or pollutants most heavy types are fine, but the best idea is to buy a proprietary brand.

When planting pots in a pond, the soil needs to be firmed down more than usual, and it is a good idea to spread gravel and/ or cobbles on top of the soil to keep the container stable. The best time for planting is late spring as the water warms up. Don't shock plants by plunging them straight into icy water.

Above: *Water lilies, such as this* Nymphaea alba, *are a beautiful addition to any garden pond. Frogs are often seen on the leaves.*

PLANTS THAT ARE BEST AVOIDED

These plants can become invasive in a garden pond and, if they escape into the wild, can become a severe problem. (Some may even be banned by law, depending where you live. If these plants are already in the pond, they should be disposed of carefully to prevent their spread either here or elsewhere.)

- Duckweed (*Lemna*)
- Australian swamp stonecrop (*Crassula helmsii*)
- Fairy moss (*Azolla filiculoides*)
- Floating pennywort (*Hydrocotyle ranunculoides*)
- Curly waterweed (*Lagarosiphon major*)
- Parrot's feather (*Myriophyllum aquaticum*)
- Kariba weed (*Salvinia*)
- Water fern (*Azolla*)
- Water hyacinth (*Eichhornia crassipes*) – a particularly invasive species
- Water lettuce (*Pistia stratiotes*)

CHOOSING POND PLANTS

There are three different types of plant that you need to attract wildlife. All are essential to a healthy pond because they constitute the range of habitats needed to support a diverse wildlife community.

Oxygenators spend the whole year submerged. These plants supply a steady infusion of oxygen, which is needed by the aquatic creatures that breathe through their gills. Oxygenators often grow densely and serve as egg-laying sites, nurseries and cover for many aquatic animals.

The second type of pond plant are deep-water aquatics, which have roots

FILLING A POND BASKET AND PLANTING IT UP

1 Pond plants are best planted in specially made crates. These are lined on the base with gravel and filled with specially formulated compost.

2 Once the base is covered with stones and soil, put your plants in the crate. Fill around the remaining gaps with more of the aquatic compost mix.

3 When the compost is up to the height of the top of your plant root-ball, dress the compost surface with more gravel to help keep it in place.

4 The pond plants should quickly establish in their new surroundings and will soon send up new shoots and flowers above the surface.

RENOVATING A BOG GARDEN

1 Thoroughly weed the bog garden, taking special care to remove all the roots of any persistent perennial weeds or unwanted plants.

2 Retain any useful specimens and dig in some organic matter to enrich the soil. Take a note of bare areas to calculate numbers of new plants needed.

3 Dig over the whole area to be planted, then set out the new plants and decide the best arrangement before planting them in their final positions.

4 Once the area is planted, give the garden a thorough watering to help the plants settle in. Note all species planted in case replacements are needed.

and stems in the deeper reaches, but with floating leaves and flowers. They are especially important because they help to shade the water from too much sunlight in summer. Too much light entering the water can cause algae to become a problem, and ideally you need to cover about half the surface of the pond with these plants. Water lilies (*Nymphaea*) are a big favourite, being very decorative, relatively easy to grow and available in a wide range of colours and sizes. Other plants are also available, and you must ensure that the species chosen are not too vigorous for your pond size. A few species are entirely free-floating and include duckweed (*Lemna*), water fern (*Azolla*) and water hyacinth (*Eichhornia crassipes*), but they can be invasive and are best avoided.

The third class of aquatic plants, marginal or emergent plants grow in shallow water at the edge of the pond and offer shade and cover for birds and other animals, while greatly enhancing the visual appeal. Dragonflies lay their eggs here, and their nymphs crawl out of the water and then pupate.

PLANTING BOG GARDENS

Bog gardens mimic areas of marshy ground found in wetlands. They provide ideal cover for amphibians as the soil in these areas is always wet. The need for permanently wet ground means they are lined in a similar way to a garden pond.

Many species of marginal plants are equally at home in a bog garden, and careful planting in such situations can help hide the division where the water stops and the bog garden starts, thereby enhancing its look.

TOP PLANTS FOR WILDLIFE PONDS

There are various types of wetland plants; the suggestions here are split into categories to make it easy to select the correct plants for different areas of the pond or bog garden, although some may be dual function. Not all will be available or suitable for your region; your choice will be influenced by local climate and weather conditions, particularly in terms of overwintering.

MARGINAL AND EMERGENT PLANTS

Arrow arums (*Peltandra*)
Arrowhead (*Sagittaria*)
Blue flag (*Iris versicolor*)
Bulrush (*Scirpus*)
Buttonbush (*Cephalanthus occidentalis*)
Cardinal flower (*Lobelia cardinalis*)
Cattail (Typhaceae)
Flowering rush (*Butomus umbellatus*)
Forget-me-not (*Myosotis scorpiodes*)

Joe-pye weed (*Eupatorium dubium*)
Marsh marigold (*Caltha palustris*)
Pickerelweed (*Pontedaria cordata*)
Smartweed (*Polygonum*)
Spike rush (*Eleocharis*)
Sweet flag (*Acorus* species)
Water forget-me-not (*Myosotis palustris*)
Watermint (*Mentha aquatica*)
Yellow flag (*Iris pseudacorus*)

OXYGENATORS AND SUBMERGED PLANTS

Curled weed (*Potamogeton crispus*)
Hornwort (*Ceratophyllum demersum*)
Milfoil (*Myriophyllum spicatum*)

Pondweed (*Elodea* spp.)
Water celery (*Vallisneria americana*)
Water starwort (*Callitriche stagnalis*)
Waterweed (*Elodea canadensis*)

FLOATING AND FLOATING-LEAVED PLANTS

Broad-leaved pondweed (*Potamogeton natans*)
Frogbit (*Hydrocharis morsus-ranae*)

Water chestnut (*Trapa natans*)
Water hawthorn (*Aponogeton distachyos*)
Water soldier (*Stratiotes aloides*)

WATER LILIES/DEEP-WATER AQUATICS

Floating heart (*Nymphoides peltata*)
Golden club (*Orontium aquaticum*)

Japanese pond lily (*Nuphar japonica*)
Water lily (*Nymphaea alba*)

ATTRACTING INSECT-EATING BIRDS

Insects offer a rich source of protein for birds and their young. Insectivorous birds are a familiar sight in gardens particularly in summer, when their activities help to control pests. Many of the species seen are summer migrants that visit to feast upon the abundance of insect life that appears at this time.

Insects and small invertebrates constitute an important food source for birds and particularly their young, especially in regions where insects are most plentiful. Swallows, martins and swifts pursue their insect meals while flying, often swooping down in pursuit, while woodpeckers can sometimes be seen – and more often heard – making holes in wood to find grubs. Even the flocks of starlings that walk across your lawn are systematically searching for insects.

INSECT-EATERS

Typical species Swallows, swifts, martins, wrens, woodpeckers, warblers, nuthatches, flycatchers.

Garden benefits Insect-eaters benefit gardeners by eating many pests. Incoming migrants help tackle the rocketing summer population.

Migratory species For insectivorous birds, with their high mobility, migration is the rule rather than the exception. For some, such as swallows and swifts, the journey covers thousands of miles.

Natural diet Insectivorous birds will often take a range of invertebrates. Because they gain most of their moisture from these, they drink less frequently than seed-eaters.

Resident species Very few insectivores remain as residents in higher latitudes. Those that do – mostly small birds such as the wren – are very susceptible to cold and therefore limited to mild regions.

Supplementary diet Mealworms are an excellent supplement and can be offered in a simple dish or a specialist feeder. In addition, many food suppliers now provide dried food for insectivores.

HABITAT PREFERENCES

While some birds are entirely insectivorous, others, including many common songbird species, eat insects only when raising young. Some of these feed their offspring an entirely insect diet, although only a small percentage of their own food is insects. Some larger birds also eat insects as part of their diet when these are plentiful but revert to other foods at other times of the year. This habit has the obvious advantage that they do not have to change their preferred habitat and can remain in a garden all year. The swallow, on the other hand, is a well-known example of a species that feeds only on insects and so must make radical shifts in its habitat preferences within a single season by migrating vast distances to follow seasonal 'gluts' of its prey in different countries.

FEEDING STRATEGIES

Although there are many different species of insect-eating birds, they often adopt similar strategies for catching their prey. Most have fine, narrow beaks, although even this can vary greatly according to

Below: *Barn swallows (*Hirundo rustica*) migrate vast distances to follow seasonal abundances of insects.*

Above: *Wrens (*Troglodytes*) are among the smallest of garden birds, but are voracious predators of insects in the summer months.*

species. Ecologists therefore tend to divide insectivorous birds according to their hunting habits, or guilds. These guilds consist of groups of species that, although not necessarily closely related, behave in similar ways. Leaf-gleaners, such as warblers, pick insects off leaves, whereas bark-gleaners, such as nuthatches, pick them off tree trunks. Woodpeckers are wood- and bark-probers because of their ability to dig out their prey from within the trunk or branch.

The air-salliers, including flycatchers, sit on a perch waiting for their prey to pass,

THREATS

Pesticides Increased use of pesticides in both urban and rural settings means that insects are now relatively scarce. Many surviving insects carry small traces of poison which can accumulate in the bodies of insect-eating birds.

Predation Small birds are vulnerable to predation from larger species, both birds and mammals. Domestic cats are a big danger in urban gardens, and both squirrels and large birds, such as magpies, will take eggs and the young in the breeding season.

Territory If food becomes scarce, small birds are generally less able to compete with larger birds and become seasonal insectivores. Many need larger territories as a result, and the effort of defending this may use a lot of energy.

Urbanization Insect-eating birds often find it difficult to find enough food in very built-up areas. The lack of suitable vegetation means that insect prey is often relatively scarce. Vehicular pollution in the environment can also limit insect populations.

Above: *Several species of woodpecker may visit gardens, all of which prefer to feed on wood-boring grubs.*

whereupon they fly out and catch insects on the wing. The final guild includes swallows, martins and swifts – gleaners of aerial plankton. These eat a large number of small insects while on the wing. In reality, however, most birds opt for more than one strategy, particularly if food becomes scarce. Most insectivorous birds consume several different kinds of insect, often switching their preferences through the season according to the abundance of species available.

MIGRATORY SPECIES
Birds that feed exclusively on insects often face seasonal food shortages if they remain in one place, and that's why they travel in search of food. Swallows and flycatchers in north-western Europe fly south in autumn to spend winter in Africa, and those in northern parts of North America fly south to southern parts of the continent or in Central or South America. It is easy to see why they do so because the cold, dark months offer little reward in terms of insects. What is less easy to understand is why they should return. The simple answer is that countries in high or low latitudes have a large seasonal glut of insects in summer.

The birds move around, so that it's always summer, and there's always plenty of food.

Migrating insect-eating birds also prosper because there are often not many resident insectivorous birds in their summer feeding grounds. This means that the migrants have an abundant food supply without facing competition from too many residents. Furthermore, feeding and raising their young in high or low latitudes means that they can use the longer hours of daylight to gather plenty of food, so they can potentially raise more young. A final advantage for migratory birds is that they avoid specialist predators trying to feed on them, because few of their predators make the same migratory journey.

Below: *Milkweed (*Asclepias*) attracts insects, such as bees and butterflies, which become food for birds.*

**PLANTS TO ATTRACT
INSECT-EATING BIRDS**
Baccharis (*Baccharis* species)
Buckthorn (*Rhamnus californica*)
Elderberry (*Sambucus mexicana*)
Evening primrose (*Oenothera biennis*)
Fern-leaved yarrow (*Achillea filipendula*)
Flowering rush (*Butomus umbellatus*)
Golden rod (*Solidago virgaurea*)
Honesty (*Lunaria annua*)
Lavender (*Lavandula angustifolia*)
Lemon balm (*Melissa officinalis*)
Monkeyflower (*Mimulus* species)
Sage (*Salvia* species)
Tansy (*Tanacetum vulgare*)
Wild lilac (*Ceanothus* species)
Willow (*Salix* species)
Yarrow (*Achillea* species)

Sage

Wild lilac

ATTRACTING SEED-EATING BIRDS

Seed-eaters include some of the most engaging of garden birds. Changes in agriculture have caused a decline in these birds, many of which were once very common. Fortunately, the increasing popularity of garden feeders has thrown the birds a lifeline, and many now prosper in a domestic setting.

The majority of birds using garden feeders will be seed-eaters for at least part of the year. However, comparatively few species are exclusively seed-eating, since most seed-eating birds hunt nutritious insects when they are feeding and raising their young. The main problem with being a seed-eater is that the majority of seeds ripen in summer and autumn/fall. By the following spring, seed is in short supply and the birds must switch to a substitute food during winter or face a shortage. Feeding seed-eating species therefore helps them to survive this period, and ensures that they will be in peak condition, ready for the breeding season in spring.

HABITAT PREFERENCES

Recent years have seen a serious decline in many formerly common seed-eating birds. Intensification of agriculture has borne most of the blame, although the seed-eaters' numbers were probably artificially high, previously, as they had prospered under traditional agricultural practices. If that sounds puzzling, note that large flocks of seed-eaters were often seen feeding on

Above: *Although they have a variable diet, titmice and tits (above) are largely dependent on seeds during winter.*

winter stubble before moving on to land that was ploughed in late winter to find weed seed that had been thrown on to the surface. Before the later widespread use of herbicides, crops had many weeds that left seed in the soil. It was these weeds that the seed-eating birds depended on, and modern agricultural efficiency has

Above: *Goldfinches eat mostly seeds but will sometimes consume buds, sap and occasionally insects through a season.*

largely removed them. A second problem is that seed-eaters can no longer feed on spilt grain in the stubble because fields are now ploughed soon after the autumn harvest.

Another traditional agricultural habitat that has declined is the hay meadow. Many were rich in plant species, but it is actually how they are managed that is important. In fact meadows do not have to have a great variety of plants to be useful food sources for birds, but those that contain dandelion, sorrel, thistles and poppies are especially helpful for seed-eating birds in summer.

Ironically, housing developments on former farmland may yet help save some of these birds. Domestic gardens and the habit of feeding seed-eating birds has meant a reprieve for some species. It is not the same for all birds, however. The house sparrow, introduced from Europe and now found in many cities in North America, was first attracted to towns when the only form of transportation was horse-drawn. The sparrows fed on the grain spilt in the streets and lived around the stables, common all over the city. The arrival of the car saw the decline in their numbers across much of their original range, although they remain a pest in areas where they were introduced.

SEED-EATERS

Typical species Finches including linnets, goldfinches and house finches, buntings, sparrows, tits, titmice, pigeons, doves, dunnocks and cardinals.

Garden benefits Seed-eating birds are beneficial when they switch to hunting insects to feed their young. Foraging seed from the soil in winter also helps to reduce weed growth the next season.

Natural diet Seed-eating birds eat a range of seed, including grain, nuts and sunflowers. They will switch their preferences as a season progresses according to the availability of food.

Resident species Resident breeding populations of seed-eating birds are

extremely dependent on the availability of food, and almost all non-migratory species will move between breeding and wintering areas in order to forage.

Migratory species Bramblings, buntings, siskins and other finches migrate in short hops in search of food. Their movements may largely depend on the availability of food.

Supplementary diet Many seed-eating birds are choosy about what they eat, and prefer oil-rich, high-energy food. The best includes black sunflower hearts (seed with the husks removed), white proso millet, niger (thistle) and good-quality peanuts, including peanuts in their shells.

PLANTS TO ATTRACT SEED-EATING BIRDS

Amaranth (*Amaranthus caudatus*)
Baccharis (*Baccharis* species)
Bunchgrasses (various genera)
Dandelion (*Taraxacum officinale*)
Fat hen (*Chenopodium album*)
Field forget-me-not (*Myosotis arvensis*)
Knapweed (*Centaurea* species)
Millet (*Panicum miliaceum*)
Oak (*Quercus* species)
Red clover (*Trifolium pratense*)
Sage (*Salvia* species)
Sunflower (*Helianthus annuus*)
Teasel (*Dipsacus fullonum*)
Wild lilac (*Ceanothus* species)

Sunflower   Red clover

Always try to provide as much natural food as possible to ensure that you preserve birds' natural behaviour patterns. Plants such as sunflowers, and a patch of wildflowers that includes thistles, tickseeds, coreopsis, goldenrod, knapweed and teasel will help to attract seed-eaters.

Traditionally, feeding birds was limited to the winter, but recent evidence suggests that serious shortages are experienced in summer by many species when they are rearing their families. Summer feeding

Below: Knapweed is a common perennial weed with attractive flowers. The seeds are eaten by species such as finches.

with sunflower hearts and other seed can help the birds to lay more eggs and rear a healthier brood. However, note that not all commercial bird foods are formulated to meet all nutritional needs of seed-eaters.

FEEDING STRATEGIES

The seed-feeders generally have short, thick, strong beaks that are good for crushing or cracking open seed. They can take some time to learn which foods are safe or good for them to eat. They often have an instinctive wariness about any change in their habitat, and you will need to be patient when you try to feed them. Seed-eaters prefer their natural food sources, and when they come to the garden for the first time they may not actually recognize supplementary foods.

Try offering black sunflower, white proso millet, niger (thistle) and peanuts, but remember that most of these foods are supplements and can't always meet all of the birds' nutritional needs. Gradually add variety once they become accustomed to feeding at the site. They will soon overcome their caution and start to experiment.

Seed-eaters are naturally more gregarious in winter, probably because of their tendency to form large flocks at this time. This helps them locate food and feed more efficiently than when alone, and also makes them less vulnerable to predators.

MIGRATORY SPECIES

Seed-eaters tend to be resident species, however buntings, such as corn, snow, indigo and painted buntings, and finches such as siskins and pine siskins do migrate

Below: Cardinals have a variable diet through the seasons but depend heavily upon small seeds during winter.

Above: Dandelions are generally regarded as weeds by gardeners but their seed is an ideal food for smaller seed-eating birds.

in search of food, moving to areas where the climate is milder and food more accessible. These winter migrants return to their breeding grounds in spring, although in some populations, for example goldfinches, only part of the population migrates. Other species simply move to lower ground.

THREATS

Competition Winter is a time when birds naturally flock, and this can cause aggression and tension. Birds at a winter feeder are forced together, and confrontation is likely. Try to spread food around, and for aggressive species such as robins, you should put food out separately to avoid conflict.

Habitat loss Intensification of farming has meant that many species of once common birds are in serious decline due to loss of habitat and food sources. Oil-rich wildflower seed is vital for these species, with many now remaining abundant only in gardens.

Herbicides Weedkillers have been used with increasing regularity in many countries, both to control crop weeds and also to improve the look of the garden. However, letting some weeds flourish is vital for the survival of foraging seed-eaters.

Predation The seed-eaters' habit of feeding on the ground makes them vulnerable to attack by cats, especially where the latter can hide and wait under garden bushes.

ATTRACTING FRUIT-EATING BIRDS

Fruit is an abundant and nutritious source of natural food, and one that many bird species have learned to exploit. In cooler climes, fruit tends to be a seasonal bounty, and so most fruit-eaters in these regions alternate their diet, eating other foods when fruit is not available.

Berries grow on a wide variety of plants including trees, bushes, climbing plants and even some herbaceous and ground-cover plants. When they are ripe, birds often descend on them and can clear a bush in a matter of hours, with some species, such as thrushes, warblers and orioles switching almost totally to a fruit diet from late summer into autumn.

ROLE IN GARDENS

Birds and berries are a remarkable example of how plants and animals have evolved together, with one exploiting the other. The fleshy pulp of a berry is surprisingly nutrient-rich, and contains a good deal of starchy carbohydrate or sugars that conceal and protect the seed within. Most berries are also full of vitamins. The trade-off is simple. Birds benefit from the nutrients contained in the soft flesh. The berry-bearing plant benefits as birds spread its seed in their droppings.

The major limitation for most birds with a fruit diet, however, is that it is not available for enough of the year. Late winter to midsummer is a time when there is precious little fruit around, so birds must find an alternative. Most fruit-eaters switch

Below: *A blackbird (*Turdus merula*) feasts on the fruit of a crab apple (*Malus sylvestris*). This fruit is a favourite of many birds.*

FRUIT-EATERS

Typical species Blackbirds, thrushes, starlings, waxwings, blackcaps, catbirds, thrushes, sparrows, finches, waxwings, titmice, vireos, orioles and woodpeckers.

Garden benefits Play an important role in dispersing seed, but are most useful in summer when they switch to insect-eating and thus help to control pests.

Natural diet Fruit rarely provides all of any bird's diet for the whole year, but it does form an important part of some species' diet from midsummer into winter.

Migratory species While there are fewer migrant fruit-eaters, many bird species that move short distances in winter will eat fruit in winter. Waxwings, on the other hand, are unpredictable in their movements but travel long distances in search of food.

Resident species Birds often widen their territories to forage, and may even defend fruit sources. Many species flock together in winter and adopt a methodical feeding approach that is different to their summer behaviour.

Supplementary diet Fruit-eating birds will quite happily take substitutes for fruit, provided they are able to recognize what it is. Pieces of broken apple and dried raisins may prove popular, and specialist suppliers now sell dried fruit especially for these birds.

to eating insects or other protein-rich foods in summer. Even when fruit is plentiful, many fruit specialists still supplement their diet with insects or other animal protein to ensure that they maintain a balanced diet.

HABITAT PREFERENCES

Fruit availability varies according to the season and, in most temperate climates, is available from midsummer until late winter. The fruit of the guelder rose or European cranberrybush (*Viburnum opulus*) or currants (*Ribes*) are quite short-lived and, if not consumed immediately, will fall from the plant and rot. However, the fruit of the cotoneaster and holly (*Ilex*) remains on the plant for months, being a vital food reserve for much of the winter.

Choose a range of plants that produce fruit over a long period. Remember that most species of fruit-eating birds have their favourites that they will take first, and that some fruit will remain on the plant for a long time. Early fruiting bushes, such as currants and wild strawberries, are just as important as the late berries, and even a small garden can accommodate some of these plants.

FEEDING STRATEGIES

Fruit is extremely important for many songbirds that switch from a summer invertebrate diet to a winter one based on berries. This is especially important when cold weather arrives and frozen ground

Below: *The scarlet berries of the rowan tree (*Sorbus aucuparia*) provide sustenance for many species of birds in autumn.*

Above: *Elderberry is an excellent source of berries in midsummer, enjoyed by blackbirds, thrushes, catbirds and titmice.*

THREATS

Competition Even if there is plenty of food at the start of winter, harsh weather may force the birds to eat more of it and shorten the supply. In addition, migrants moving into the area compete for resources and visiting flocks may even strip an area clean.

Habitat loss Changes to the countryside caused by agriculture have meant that many native berrying shrubs have been destroyed, particularly when hedgerows are removed from field margins, and bird numbers often fall as a consequence.

Poor fruit years In some years the amount of fruit that sets on a tree or shrub will be considerably less than usual, mainly because the weather has damaged blossom or deterred pollinators. Shortages may occur the following winter.

Predation The tendency to seasonal fruit-eating among many bird species often attracts them to settled areas where domestic cats are common predators. Ironically, the very shrubs they are feeding on often give cover to these ambush specialists.

prevents resident species foraging for worms, grubs or fallen seed. It is at these times of year, when food is short, that nourishing fruit is most vital.

Some birds tend to descend en masse to take berries when ripe. Starlings, for example, are highly systematic in their approach, methodically stripping bushes and trees from the top down. They also drop far fewer berries than other birds, and leave bushes picked clean. Thrushes, on the other hand, are well known for their tendency to defend their territory, and will often defend a berrying tree or shrub against all-comers. This acts as a pantry that will see them through the winter, and if hard times do not materialize the birds gain a great advantage in having food to the end of winter, enabling them to nest early.

MIGRATORY SPECIES

As with most bird species, harsh winter weather is often a trigger for berry-eaters to move south. While most only move short distances, a few species cover much greater distances. The movements of berry-feeding birds are always inextricably linked to the availability of the fruit itself. Possibly the most famous migratory berry-eaters

are the waxwings. In both Europe and North America, these beautiful birds leave their forest homes and move to warmer climes, often descending on gardens to feast on berries. They are communal feeders, with individuals eating up to 500 berries each day, and in Holland they are called *pestvogel*, meaning 'invasion bird', due to their habit of appearing suddenly and clearing all the fruit.

Flocks of some berry-eating birds show a high degree of co-operation when they feed. On trees or shrubs where slender twigs hold a supply of berries that only one bird can reach at a time, flock members have occasionally been observed lining up along the twig and passing berries from beak to beak so that each bird gets to eat.

PLANTS TO ATTRACT FRUIT-EATING BIRDS

Blackcurrants and gooseberries (*Ribes* species)
Buckthorn (*Rhamnus californica*)
Elder (*Sambucus* species)
Herringbone cotoneaster (*Cotoneaster horizontalis*)
Holly (*Ilex aquifolium*)
Guelder rose (*Viburnum opulus*)
Mezereon (*Daphne mezereum*)
Oregon grape (*Mahonia aquifolium*)
Rowan (*Sorbus aucuparia*)
Wild strawberry (*Fragaria vesca*)
Wax myrtle (*Myrica californica*)
Wild grape (*Vitis californica*)

Holly   Rowan

Below: *The small berries of the blackcurrant (*Ribes nigrum*) are popular with birds such as blackbirds as well as people.*

Below: *Though migratory, the availability of food in gardens means some blackcap warblers (*Sylvia atricapilla*) can overwinter.*

ATTRACTING OMNIVOROUS BIRDS

The need to survive has driven the majority of resident garden birds to adopt an omnivorous diet, which allows them to exploit various foods as they become available. It is a highly successful strategy, and the chief reason behind the success of many species in colonizing our towns and gardens.

Birds that eat anything digestible/edible are known as omnivores. This is not to say that an omnivorous bird will eat any item of food that is put in front of it, and in most cases omnivores have specific feeding needs that may vary seasonally or perhaps in response to local variations in their habitat. In fact the vast majority of birds tend to be somewhat omnivorous, although the tendency is usually most pronounced when their normal food source is in short supply.

Being an omnivore is usually the most successful survival strategy in rapidly changing environments, or in places subject to extreme seasonal variation. It is also noteworthy that many larger birds are omnivores because their body size makes specialization difficult unless their habitat – and therefore food supply – is very consistent all year round.

In time, successful omnivorous species can become very numerous. Members of the crow family, such as magpies and jays, will eat smaller birds and immature chicks, among other foods. This results in an unusually high number of these large birds.

Above: *Chaffinches (*Fringilla coelebs*) have a very wide range. Their varied diet has contributed to their success.*

Above: *A familiar sight in many European gardens, blue tits (*Cyanistes caeruleus*) exploit numerous food sources.*

HABITAT PREFERENCES
The changing seasons bring times of alternate plenty and shortage for birds with highly specialized diets. Eating many different foods is usually a much more successful strategy. Because omnivores will eat both plant and animal matter, they survive well in many environments and often prove highly adaptable. Some, like the gull, have no problem adapting to living near humans and now commonly scavenge in landfill sites and city streets. This ought not to be so surprising because modern cities are similar in many ways to tall, rocky cliffs, and as the gulls often nest or roost on top of tall buildings, safe from predators, it is only natural that they should feed nearby.

As habitats change, those creatures that best adapt to them tend to prosper. Urban bird populations have changed over time, and pigeons have now reached epidemic proportions in many cities. Surprisingly, garden birds can be quite urban in their distribution, with higher densities in towns than in the surrounding countryside. The most common species of these urbanized populations are often omnivores, and the garden is an ideal habitat.

FEEDING STRATEGIES
Being omnivorous has obvious advantages, but various foods often require adaptations to the digestive system. Some omnivorous bird species lengthen the digestive tract

OMNIVORES
Typical species Corvids including jays, crows and magpies, also thrushes, tits, finches, starlings and gulls.

Garden benefits Omnivores can be a mixed blessing in the garden, particularly if you have a vegetable patch. On the other hand, their varied diet includes many garden pests.

Resident species Resident omnivores often face a bleak prospect during winter. Food shortages, exacerbated by resident competitors and incoming winter migrants, means that there is a naturally high mortality rate.

Migratory species The vast majority of omnivores are able to avoid the necessity of migrating vast distances, but many – including members of the thrush family – just travel short distances to escape harsh winter weather, and often take up temporary residence in gardens.

Natural diet Many omnivores have set patterns regarding exactly what and when they will eat. These species are often insect-eaters in the summer months, for example, before their digestive tracts adapt for their winter diet of berries and seed.

Supplementary diet Omnivores should be provided with a varied diet. Numerous mixes exist, and the best idea is to provide a full range of food types, including grain, small seeds, suet, fruit and even some live food.

**PLANTS TO ATTRACT
OMNIVOROUS BIRDS**
Blackthorn (*Prunus spinosa*)
Bramble (*Rubus fruticosus*)
California fuchsia (*Epilobium* species)
Currants and gooseberries (*Ribes* species)
Evening primrose (*Oenothera biennis*)
Hawthorn (*Crataegus monogyna*)
Honeysuckle (*Lonicera* species)
Ivy (*Hedera helix*)
Juneberry (*Amelanchier lamarkii*)
Manzanita (*Arctostaphylos* species)
Monkeyflower (*Mimulus* species)
Penstemon (*Penstemon* species)
Sage (*Salvia* species)

Gooseberry   Honeysuckle

in winter to get more out of relatively poor-quality food. This allows them to be mostly vegetarian in winter, switching to an insectivorous diet in summer.

The beaks of omnivorous birds are usually relatively long and unspecialized, although this can vary considerably according to their evolutionary history. For example, in some parts of Europe, there are now populations of feral ring-necked parakeets (*Psittacula krameri*)

Below: *Ivy (*Hedera helix*) berries are eaten by many species including pigeons, doves, jays, thrushes and waxwings.*

derived from escaped cage birds. These are more omnivorous than the original wild populations in Asia that eat fruit, berries, nuts and seed. This is likely to be a result of their foraging in domestic gardens where different types of food are left out on bird tables. It is this ability to adapt, learn new tricks and exploit unfamiliar food sources that differentiates omnivores from other birds with more restrictive diets.

MIGRATORY SPECIES
Omnivores, like most birds, will migrate if food becomes scarce. They rarely undertake the huge journeys so characteristic of insectivores, however, with starlings or European robins simply travelling a few hundred miles and, even when they do migrate, it will not always be the whole population that does so. In fact the most likely migrants in a normally resident bird population are invariably the females and young. Many common species move from one area to another, while others simply move into the towns from the countryside. Some species regarded as non-migratory will sometimes move large distances when faced with harsh winter conditions, and because these newcomers look just like the residents, their arrival often goes largely unnoticed.

Robins, thrushes, skylarks and blackbirds in the UK and corvids and towhees in North America all tend to undertake short flights to warmer areas. Some species, such as blackbirds, change their habits and distribution over the year,

Below: *Corvids, such as the black-billed magpie (*Pica hudsonia*), are adaptable in their feeding habits.*

Above: *The sweet, edible fruits of juneberry* (Amelanchier) *mature in midsummer and are eaten by a wide variety of birds.*

raising families and feeding in gardens and backyards during the spring and summer, where they can raise up to three broods. After the breeding season, they must 'feed up' for the coming winter, and move out into the surrounding countryside to do so.

THREATS
Competition Omnivores are adaptable and able to exploit new situations, but this brings them into contact with new competitors. Some urban birds are highly aggressive, and often chase away newcomers.

Disease Any increase in population raises the chances of disease spread. Omnivorous birds often congregate where there is a food source, and disease becomes more prevalent than for birds following a solitary life.

Habitat changes As changing habitats favour certain incoming species, others are less favoured and some omnivorous birds that were formerly common in cities – such as the raven in London – are now scarce or absent, having been unable to adapt to modern city life.

Predation All birds face predators in either the garden or their natural habitats, but they are usually numerous enough to cope with any losses. In gardens, cats are usually the main threat, although other birds (including birds of prey) can also take their toll.

PLANTING GUIDE FOR BIRDS

The species listed below are just a small selection of the many varieties that can be planted to attract birds. Your choice will depend on your location, personal preference and the space available, soil type and the position, whether in sun or shade. A good rule is to choose the widest variety of plants possible.

TREES

The trees listed here provide foods such as fruits or insects, and also make good nesting sites for birds. If space allows, large trees such as oaks and maples will support a wealth of insect life.

Crab apple *Malus sylvestris*
Height: 10m (33ft). Spread: 10m (33ft). This small woodland tree grows in fertile, well-drained soil in gardens. It prefers full sun or partial shade. In late spring this deciduous tree produces white flowers. In autumn it bears red fruits which are eaten by birds such as finches and thrushes. The cultivated apple (*Malus domestica*) is also highly attractive to birds.

False acacia *Robinia pseudoacacia*
Height: 25m (80ft). Spread: 15m (50ft). This quick-growing tree is a native of North America, where it is also called the black locust. It needs a sunny position, and will grow in poor soil, but not waterlogged ground. Scented, drooping white flowers appear in late spring or early summer. This deciduous tree with dark-green leaves attracts seed-eaters such as finches.

Below: *Waxwings (shown here) and fieldfares are among the birds that feast on rowan berries during the autumn period.*

Above: *The crab apple is often found growing wild in hedgerows and along wooded edges.*

Mountain ash (Rowan) *Sorbus aucuparia*
Height: 15m (50ft). Spread: 8m (26ft). This small deciduous tree has delicate, frond-like leaves. It requires light, moist soil which can be acidic, and prefers full sun or partial shade. In autumn the rowan produces small scarlet berries which provide food for many birds. The whitebeam (*Sorbus aria*) and wild service tree (*S. torminalis*) are related.

Lodgepole pine *Pinus contorta*
Height: 15–25m (50–80ft). The lodgepole pine is native to North America, as are the Monterey pine (*P. radiata*) and black pine (*P. nigra*). These evergreen conifers have needle-like leaves and bear cones that ripen in their second year. All three prefer full sun and moist soil. The dense evergreen foliage provides shelter for nesting birds, while the cones provide food for seed-eaters.

European bird cherry *Prunus padus*
Height:15m (50ft). Spread: 10m (33ft). The bird cherry is a small deciduous tree which produces white scented flowers in spring. Its black cherries are eaten by birds such as finches in autumn. It prefers full sun and needs well-drained soil. Many *Prunus*

Above: *The English oak is renowned for supporting larger numbers of invertebrates than any other European tree.*

species attract birds, including the wild black cherry (*P. serotina*), the choke cherry (*P. virginiana*) and the cultivated plum (*Prunus domestica*).

English oak *Quercus robur*
Height: 30–40m (100–133ft). Spread: 25m (83ft). This large deciduous tree is suited only to large gardens. It requires well-drained soil and is a slow-grower. The oak supports a huge range of insects whose caterpillars provide food for nesting birds. It produces acorns in autumn. Relatives include the fast-growing red oak (*Quercus rubra*), and live oaks, which have evergreen leaves.

Black maple *Acer nigrum*
Height: 20m (65ft). Spread: 8m (25ft). This native of North America is now also grown in European gardens. The leaves of this deciduous tree turn bright orange in autumn/fall. It needs sun or partial shade and fertile, well-drained soil. Winged fruits and insects living on the tree provide food for birds. Relatives include the Cappadocian maple (*A. cappadocicum*), red maple (*A. rubrum*), the silver maple (*A. saccharinum*) and the sugar maple (*A. saccharum*).

SHRUBS

Seed-bearing shrubs will attract birds such as sparrows, buntings and finches, while berry-bearers nourish thrushes, warblers, orioles and vireos. Dense shrubs provide cover and safe nesting sites.

Barberry *Berberis vulgaris*

Height: 2m (6ft). Spread: 3m (10ft).
This evergreen shrub bears scarlet berries that are eaten by many birds. Sharp spines make it a good hedging plant. It grows in sun or partial shade in most well-drained soils. *Berberis thunbergii* grows in similar conditions, but is deciduous, with leaves that turn orange in autumn or fall. This produces pale flowers in spring, followed by bright red berries in autumn.

Guelder rose (European cranberrybush, Viburnum) *Viburnum opulus*

Height: 4m (12ft). Spread: 4m (12ft).
This deciduous shrub produces white flowers in spring and red berries in autumn. It requires sun or semi-shade and well-drained soil. Relatives include Laurustinus (*V. tinus*) which bears white flowers and black fruits. Black haw (*V. prunifolium*) is popular with birds, as are nannyberry (*V. lentago*) and arrow-wood (*V. dentatum*).

Hawthorn (May) *Crataegus monogyna*

Height: 10m (30ft). Spread: 8m (25ft).
This deciduous, spiny bush prefers sun but will tolerate shade. Its white blossoms are attractive in spring. The crimson berries are eaten by birds such as starlings, tits, titmice and thrushes in autumn. Dense foliage provides good cover.

Below: *Hawthorn is often found growing wild in hedges. Many birds eat the berries, and wood pigeons eat the leaves.*

Above: *Tits, titmice, warblers and cuckoos are among the species that harvest caterpillars and insects from buddleja.*

Pyracantha (Firethorn) *Pyracantha coccinea*

Height: 2m (7ft). Spread: 2m (7ft).
This evergreen shrub is sometimes grown as a hedge or along a wall. It grows in sun or partial shade and any well-drained soil. It has dark-green leaves and produces white flowers and clusters of scarlet berries. The dense, spiny foliage provides safe nesting sites for birds, while thrushes, pigeons and other species eat the berries.

Common elder (Black elderberry) *Sambucus nigra*

Height: 10m (30ft).
This deciduous shrub does well in partial shade. It provides good cover for nesting birds. The pale blossoms of early summer are followed by drooping clusters of small black berries which attract birds. The American elderberry (*S. canadensis*) and red-berried elder (*S. racemosa*) are also popular with many birds.

Cotoneaster *Cotoneaster microphyllus*

Height: 1m (3ft 4in). Spread: 2m (7ft).
This evergreen shrub has rigid, drooping branches. The dense foliage provides safe nesting sites for birds, while in autumn, the berries are eaten by species such as thrushes. It prefers full sun. A relative known as rock- or wall-spray (*C. horizontalis*) provides similar attractions for birds and will grow along walls, banks or the ground.

Dogwood *Cornus sanguinea*

Height: 4m (13ft). Spread: 3m (10ft).
The bright red stems of this deciduous shrub provide colour in winter. It needs sun and grows well in chalky soil. The small black berries are eaten by birds in autumn/fall. Many *Cornus* species are attractive to birds, including Siberian dogwood (*C. alba*), the red osier (*C. stolonifera*), and flowering dogwood (*C. florida*), a small tree.

Buddleja (Orange eye butterflybush) *Buddleja davidii*

Height: 5m (15ft). Spread: 5m (15ft).
This sprawling deciduous shrub requires full sun and well-drained soil. In midsummer it produces drooping spikes of scented lilac flowers which attract butterflies. In turn the insect life attracts insect-eaters such as tits and warblers. Prune it severely in spring.

Serviceberry (Juneberry) *Amelanchier lamarckii*

Height: 6m (20ft). Spread: 3m (10ft).
The green or tawny leaves of this deciduous shrub turn red or orange in autumn, providing a blaze of colour. It needs full sun or semi-shade and prefers slightly acidic soil. The berry clusters are eaten by many types of birds. Related species such as *A. arborea* and *A. canadensis* are also popular with birds.

Dog rose *Rosa canina*

Height: 3m (10ft).
This deciduous rambling shrub grows wild in some woods and rows of hedges. It prefers sun and fertile soil. The pale pink flowers open in summer, following by juicy red hips that are eaten by many birds. Many species of cultivated shrub roses, such as *Rosa rugosa*, also attract insects, insect-eaters and fruit-eating birds.

Below: *Dog rose flowers give off a delicate scent. Blackbirds and thrushes are among the birds that eat the fruit.*

Above: *Honeysuckle has a sweet scent. The fruit can feed birds such as this hen house finch (*Haemorhous mexicanus*).*

Above: *Blackberry plants flourish on waste ground. The berries feed wood pigeons, crows, starlings and finches.*

Above: *Virginia creeper is an ornamental climber, particularly in autumn. It can be grown up buildings and walls.*

CREEPERS AND CLIMBERS

Leafy climbers offer sheltered nesting sites for birds. Some species provide foods such as autumn berries, nectar, or a wealth of insects to eat.

Honeysuckle (Woodbine)
Lonicera periclymenum
Height: 7m (23ft).
This deciduous climber grows well up garden walls. It requires sun or partial shade and fertile, well-drained soil. The sweet-scented pink or yellow flowers attract insects and insect-eaters, while some types of birds sip the nectar. The red berries are enjoyed by warblers and finches. The Amur honeysuckle (*L. maakii*) is also attractive to birds.

Blackberry (Bramble) *Rubus fruticosus*
Height: 3m (10ft). Spread: 3m (10ft).
This prickly deciduous climber runs wild in hedgerows and on waste ground. It grows in either sun or partial shade. Small white flowers in summer are followed by black fruits that are enjoyed by birds and people. Other *Rubus* species such as dewberry (*R. caesius*), cloudberry (*R. chamaemorus*) and raspberry (*R. idaeus*) produce edible fruits.

Virginia creeper
Parthenocissus quinquefolia
Height: 15m (50ft) or more.
This fast-growing, deciduous climber clings to walls with its tendrils. Its foliage

provides cover for nesting birds. The leaves turn crimson or purple in autumn, when the plant also produces dark-blue berries which are eaten by crows and thrushes. This creeper grows best in sun or semi-shade in fertile, well-drained soil.

Grape vine *Vitis vinifera*
Height: 30m (100ft).
This woody, deciduous climber is grown for its juicy green or purple fruits, which are enjoyed by birds and humans. The vine's green, scented flowers open in early summer. It needs full sun or semi-shade and fertile, well-drained soil, and can be grown against walls and trellises.

Below: *The grape vine can be a useful screening plant when grown up a trellis. There are hundreds of varieties.*

HERBACEOUS PLANTS

Flowering plants provide foods such as seeds and insects and their caterpillars. Some attract slugs, snails and other invertebrates which also feed some types of birds. As with other types of plants, old-fashioned and native plants should predominate, but non-native species can play an important role, too.

Sunflower *Helianthus annuus*
Height: 3m (10ft). Spread: 60cm (2ft).
This native of North America grows wild on wasteland. A leggy annual, the long green stem bears a single large, deep-yellow flower with a massive seedhead. The seeds

Below: *Many birds, including this lesser goldfinch (*Spinus psaltria*), enjoy eating the seeds of sunflowers.*

feed doves, nuthatches, crows and other birds. The plant requires full sun and fertile, moist but well-drained soil. It may need to be staked when in bloom.

Michaelmas daisy (Purple aster)
Symphyotrichum novi-belgii
Height: 1m (3ft 4in). Spread: 50cm (20in).
This North American plant grows wild. A tall perennial, it has branching stems and likes sun or partial shade and fertile, well-drained soil. Purple, daisy-like flowers with yellow centres appear in autumn. These attract insects such as bees and butterflies. The seeds also provide food. Many other asters are also popular with birds.

Cornflower *Centaurea cyanus*
Height: 1m (3ft 4in). Spread: 30cm (1ft).
This tall perennial has slim, grey-green leaves. It requires a sunny position and fertile, well-drained soil. The flowers appear in late autumn – most commonly deep blue, but also pink, red, purple or white. These attract insects which feed birds. Cornflower seeds are eaten by tits, titmice, finches and members of the crow family.

Yarrow *Achillea millefolium*
Height: 60cm (2ft). Spread: 60cm (2ft).
This perennial herb grows wild in hedgerows, grasslands and meadows. With its delicate, frond-like leaves, it needs

Below: *Insect-eaters feed on aphids attracted to the yarrow. Sparrows, finches, tits and titmice eat the seeds.*

full sun and moist, well-drained soil. It produces pale flowers in summer or autumn. These attract insects which provide food for birds, as do the seeds.

Dill *Anethum graveolens*
Height: 90cm (3ft).
This slender plant is often found on waste ground. It prefers full sun and sandy soil. The seeds are used in cooking, so it makes a good kitchen-garden plant. The tall stems support flattened clusters of yellow flowers in late summer. The seeds provide food for birds, while slugs attracted to the dill plants feed species such as thrushes.

Marigold *Calendula officinalis*
Height: 60cm (2ft). Spread: 30cm (1ft).
This quick-growing plant with light-green, scented leaves is often found growing wild on waste ground. It requires a sunny position but will grow in any well-drained soil. Cultivated varieties bear yellow or orange, daisy-like blooms from spring to autumn. The plant attracts insects and slugs which provide a source of food for invertebrate-eating birds.

Foxglove *Digitalis purpurea*
Height: 1–1.5m (3–5ft). Spread: 60cm (2ft).
This tall, upright plant grows wild in woods and heathland. It grows best in semi-shade and needs moist, well-drained soil. In summer the foxglove produces tall spikes of bell-shaped flowers which may be purple, pink or white. These attract bees which provide food for insect-eaters. The seeds also nourish birds.

Above: *The many varieties of marigold brighten gardens with their single- or double-headed flowers.*

Coreopsis (Largeflower tickseed)
Coreopsis grandiflora
Height: 45–120cm (1½–4ft).
The many varieties of coreopsis produce bright yellow, daisy-like flowers from early summer to autumn. These long-lasting blooms provide colour and attract insects, which in turn draw insect-eating birds. *Coreopsis* species require full sun and fertile, well-drained soil.

Below: *Foxglove flowers attract bumblebees, which are hunted by flycatchers. Some birds eat the seeds.*

MAKING BIRD FEEDERS, BIRDBATHS AND NEST BOXES

Perhaps it is the opportunity to create a world in miniature, while simultaneously giving nature a helping hand, that is the appeal of crafting your own bird boxes. Nest boxes, feeders and birdbaths can be plain, pretty or fanciful, without affecting their primary function. The greater the choice that you can provide, the better, as this will benefit a wider range of birds, rather than just the more dominant species. Adding more feeding stations will also encourage the shyer birds.

Left: *Although decoratively embellished, this house still retains its practical function, providing a safe, dry site for birds to nest.*

Above: *From rudimentary woodwork to more complex projects, bird-feeder construction can suit every skill level.*

Above: *Simple feeders such as this one look very attractive when filled with foods of different colours and textures.*

Above: *Even unoccupied nest boxes make charming decorative features that enhance a garden setting.*

SWEET TREAT

This pretty hanging 'pudding' heart will look lovely in the garden. You can mould the puddings in any other suitably shaped moulds, or simply in empty yogurt pots (as described overleaf), though these will take longer to set than those in flat moulds. A wreath of berries offers a tempting bird bonus.

YOU WILL NEED
pan
wooden spoon
string
heart-shaped mould
garden wire
wire cutters

TYPICAL FOOD
75g (3oz) lard or white cooking fat
shelled nuts
seeds
berries
raisins
dried cranberries

TYPICAL VISITORS
starlings
tits and titmice
nuthatches
waxwings

Above: *Starlings love sweet foods, but may drive away competing visitors to this treat.*

1 Place the lard or white cooking fat in a pan and slowly melt it over a gentle heat. When the lard has completely melted, stir in a generous mixture of shelled nuts and seeds, and some raisins and cranberries.

3 Thread raisins and cranberries alternately on to a piece of garden wire long enough to surround the heart pudding. Twist the ends together and soak the wreath in water to plump up the fruit.

2 Lay a doubled piece of string in the bottom of a mould and spoon in the nut and seed mixture, embedding the string within. Smooth the top of the pudding and leave it to cool completely.

4 When the pudding is set, turn it out of the mould and tie the string to the twisted ends of the wire so that the heart is suspended in the middle of the wreath. Tie a ribbon over the join to hide it, if you like.

OTHER SWEET TREATS
Hollowed-out fresh fruit containers are a simple way to offer up enticing bird treats. Scoop out fruit halves and fill with a mixture of nuts, seeds and dried fruit, and either muesli/granola or cooked rice. Put them on a bird table or hang them as described above.

Orange sunrise pudding
Prepare a mixture of muesli/granola, fruit, nuts and seeds for the filling. All these ingredients should be fully soaked to rehydrate before mixing. Cut an orange in half, and remove the flesh to create a hollow. Fill with the mixture.

Bejewelled apple
An apple stuffed with colourful, nutritious goodies is a visual as well as a nourishing feast. Hollow out an apple that is past its best. Fill it with a mixture of cooked rice, seeds, rehydrated dried fruit and berries. Make sure the fruit has been thoroughly rehydrated before adding.

FAT TREAT

When the weather gets colder, garden birds keep warm by eating high-energy foods such as this fat, fruit, seed and peanut snack. Hanging the treat will suit acrobatic birds such as tits and titmice. You could use a net bag instead of a pot. Or, simply crumble one on to the bird table, for less agile species.

YOU WILL NEED

pan
wooden spoon
yogurt pot or plastic plant pot
scissors
aluminium foil
garden string or wire

TYPICAL FOOD

about 100g/4oz suet
mixed birdseed
shelled fresh peanuts
raisins

TYPICAL VISITORS

tits and titmice
sparrows
finches
starlings
woodpeckers

Opposite and below: *When hung from a tree, tasty fat treats attract all sorts of birds, such as the Eurasian blue tit (Cyanistes caeruleus). If you have a dog, make sure that the fat treat is positioned high up, well out of your pet's reach, and securely fastened in position. This will also ensure any foxes will not be able to pull it down.*

1 Melt the grated suet in the pan. Keep it on the heat until the suet is melted, and stir until the fat goes clear.

2 Take the pan off the heat. Add birdseed, broken-up peanuts and a few raisins. Stir the mixture, then allow it to cool.

3 If you are using a plant pot, cut out a circle of aluminium foil to fit inside the base of the pot to cover the drainage holes.

4 Twist a length of string to make a thick cord or use some garden wire. Tie a knot at one end.

5 Hold the knot at the bottom of the pot with the string or wire upright. Spoon the fat, seed, peanut and raisin mixture into the pot. When the pot is full, firm the mixture down with the back of the spoon. If you have more mix, repeat with another pot.

6 Stand the pot outside to allow the mixture to cool and set. When it has set and is quite hard, remove the snack from the pot by squeezing the pot sides carefully. Peel off the foil base. Now hang the treat from a branch using the string or wire.

BOUNTY BOWER

In winter, the food you provide can make the difference between life and death for birds. These treats are hung along a rope garland, or they can be tied from a pergola beam or tree branch.

1 Skewer an apple and thread it on to a long piece of garden wire. Wind the end around the base of the apple to prevent it slipping off. Embed sunflower seeds into the flesh of the apple. Hang the wired apples from your garland or along the beam or tree branch.

2 Screw metal eyelets into the base of a selection of pine cones. Thread them with string and tie the cones together in size order. Hang the strings along your 'bower'.

3 Tie a selection of millet bunches with raffia. Using a darning needle and strong thread, thread unshelled peanuts to make long strings. Saw a coconut in half, and drill two holes near the edge of each half. Thread a piece of wire through the holes and twist the ends of the wire together.

4 When the pine seeds have been pecked out of the cones, you can revamp them by filling with peanut butter and dipping in small mixed seeds.

YOU WILL NEED
rope garland (if using)
skewer
garden wire
wire cutters
metal eyelets
string and scissors
raffia
darning needle
strong thread
hacksaw
drill

TYPICAL FOOD
apple
sunflower seeds
pine cones
millet bunches
peanuts in their shells
whole coconut
unsalted, unroasted smooth
    peanut butter
mixed birdseed and niger (thistle)
    seed

TYPICAL VISITORS
goldfinches and grosbeaks
titmice and chickadees
blue jays, hawfinches and grosbeaks

RUSTIC BIRD TABLE

A basic table is one of the simplest ways of dispensing food to birds. One of the advantages is that it can offer many different kinds of food. You can make this attractive rustic table quite simply from two pieces of rough timber, nailed together with battens to strengthen the structure. The lip around the edge is designed to stop nuts and seeds rolling off. String is tied to a hook in each corner to hang the table out of reach of predators. Attach an extra fat treat ball if you like (see page 100).

Above: *Purple finches* (Carpodacus purpureus) *and other finches forage at bird tables in winter. These finches are especially fond of sunflower seeds.*

YOU WILL NEED

rough timber/lumber, 25 x 13 x 1cm
 (10 x 5 x ½in) (cut 2 for base)
battens, 25 x 2.5 x 1cm (10 x 1 x
 ½in) (cut 2 for supporting base)
 and 25 x 5 x 1cm (10 x 2 x ½in)
 (cut 4 for sides)
nails
hammer
wood preservative and brush
4 brass hooks
2m (2yd) sisal string
scissors

TYPICAL FOOD

varied, including seeds and nuts

TYPICAL VISITORS

finches and cardinals
sparrows
juncos
titmice and tits

1 Join together the two pieces of rough timber by positioning them side by side and placing the two narrower battens crossways, underneath, at each end. Nail the battens securely in place to form the bird table base.

2 Nail the four wide lengths of batten around the edges of the table, creating a lip of at least 2.5cm (1in). This will ensure the food is not spilled.

3 Lightly paint all the surfaces of the table with wood preservative. Leave to dry.

4 Screw a brass hook into each corner of the table to attach the sisal string.

5 Cut the sisal string into four equal lengths and tie a small loop in one end of each piece. Attach each loop to a hook, then gather up the strings above the table and tie in a knotted loop for hanging.

COCONUT FEEDER

A plastic tube, made from a recycled bottle, makes a practical seed-dispenser, suspended within a hollowed-out coconut. The half-coconut roof lifts off to the side, allowing you to refill the tube with seeds. Tits are particularly adept at using this kind of feeder, and can be very acrobatic.

Above: *While not as acrobatic as tits, redpolls (*Carduelis flammea*) will also use feeders such as this one. This species is named after the red patch on the forehead, which both sexes posses, though the male's is brighter in hue.*

YOU WILL NEED

2 coconuts
drill
hole saw
knife
hacksaw
florist's wire
twigs
small pliers
4cm (1½in)-diameter straight-sided
 plastic bottle
scissors
string
large bead

TYPICAL FOOD

sunflower seeds
mixed seed

TYPICAL VISITORS

robins and finches
sparrows
tits and titmice
redpolls

1 Drill two small holes in the top of each coconut to drain the milk. On one, cut 5cm (2in) holes on opposite sides, and a third hole on top. Remove the flesh with a knife.

3 Beneath each large circular side hole in the first coconut, drill two tiny holes on either side. These will be used for holding the perches. Drill two further tiny holes on each side for attaching the roof.

5 Remove the top and bottom of a plastic bottle to make a tube. Cut two semicircles at the bottom on opposite sides to allow seeds to spill out. Place the tube inside the coconut by inserting it through the large hole at the top.

2 Saw the second coconut in half. Remove the flesh from one half to form the roof of the feeder. Make a small hole in the top and two holes on each side near the rim.

4 Attach a perch beneath each side hole by threading wire through the small holes and around a twig, twisting to form a cross over the centre. Using pliers, twist the ends together inside the coconut to secure.

6 Attach the roof to the base by threading string through the side holes in the coconuts. Tie a large bead to a doubled piece of string, to act as an inside anchor, and thread the string through the central hole of the roof for hanging the feeder.

BOTTLE FEEDER

This elegant and unusual bird seed feeder keeps the food dry. You will be able to regulate the flow of seed by adjusting the distance of the gap between the bottle neck and the dish. The seeds can be replenished when necessary by unwiring and then reattaching the bottle, or just the tray.

Above: *House sparrows (*Passer domesticus*) are among the most common visitors to seed feeders. In recent years, this species has declined, but putting out seed for birds can help to reverse the trend.*

YOU WILL NEED
bottle
pierced galvanized metal L-shaped
    bracket
hacksaw (if needed)
13cm (5in) tartlet tin/pan with
    removable base
aluminium gauze
old scissors
epoxy resin glue
florist's wire
galvanized wire
pliers

TYPICAL FOOD
black sunflower seeds
striped sunflower seeds
mixed seed

TYPICAL VISITORS
blue tits, great tits and titmice
sparrows
finches and goldfinches
dunnocks
juncos and siskins

1 Measure your chosen bottle against the metal bracket and, if the bracket is too long, cut off the excess metal using a hacksaw. However, it does not matter if a little of the bracket shows above the top.

2 Remove the bottom of the tart tin and use it as a template to cut out a circular piece of aluminium gauze with old scissors. Use epoxy resin glue to stick the gauze into the bottom of the tin.

3 Using florist's wire, attach the tin to the arm of the bracket by wiring through the aluminium gauze. The gap between the bottle neck and the pan should be wide enough to allow seeds to trickle through.

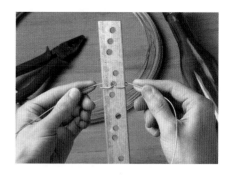

4 Cut a piece of galvanized wire long enough to wrap around the bottle in a criss-cross fashion. Thread both ends of the wire through an appropriate hole positioned near the top of the bracket.

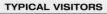

5 Place the bottle in position on the bracket and wrap the wire around it, threading through the bracket. Repeat the process at the neck of the bottle, so that the bottle is held in place by two lots of crossed wire.

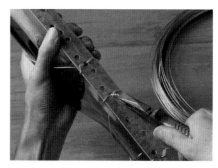

6 Twist the ends of the wire together at the back of the bracket using a pair of pliers. The bottle can be filled with seeds before assembly, but cover the opening while you insert the upturned bottle into the frame.

PALLADIAN BIRD TABLE

This classical-style feeding table looks so elegant and impressive but is relatively simple to make. It will not only attract birds that enjoy eating seeds, fat and scraps, but will also beautify any garden setting. It can be mounted on a pole, hung from a branch or fixed to a wall using a large bracket.

Above: *Virginian cardinals (Cardinalis cardinalis), are among the species attracted to bird tables holding seeds and scraps.*

YOU WILL NEED

1cm (½in) medium-density fibreboard
   (MDF) or exterior-grade plywood
   (for base)
5mm (¼in) medium-density
   fibreboard (MDF) or exterior-grade
   plywood (for steps and roof)
ruler, pencil
saw
wood glue, or glue gun and glue sticks
8 threaded knobs, 3cm (1¼in)
   diameter x 2cm (¾in) deep
4 dowels, 12 x 1.6cm (4¾ x ⅝in)
drill and 3mm (⅛in) bit
exterior-grade filler
fine-grade sandpaper
medium paintbrush
off-white emulsion/latex paint
exterior-grade matt varnish

TYPICAL FOOD

varied, including seeds, fat, scraps

TYPICAL VISITORS

tits, titmice and chickadees
finches and cardinals

1 Mark and cut out all the pieces, following the template on page 240. Assemble the base and steps with wood glue. You could apply hot glue using a glue gun if you possess one.

3 Glue each half of the roof on to the top of the gable triangles. Make sure each roof half overlaps the ceiling by the same amount at the sides and each end.

5 Glue the threaded cupboard knobs in position at each corner mark on the base and the ceiling. Allow to dry thoroughly. Meanwhile drill each end of the dowel columns to accommodate the protruding thread of the knobs.

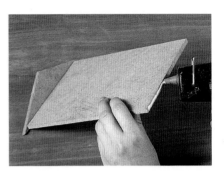

2 Mark the positions of the columns at each corner of the top step and on the underside of the ceiling. Glue the main gable triangles in place on each end of the ceiling piece.

4 Allow enough time for the roof glue to dry thoroughly. Next, glue the decorative gable triangle in place centrally on the face of the front gable.

6 Apply glue to each thread and assemble the dowels to join the base and the roof. Fill any gaps with exterior-grade filler. Rub down with fine-grade sandpaper and paint with off-white emulsion followed by several coats of exterior-grade matt varnish.

SEASIDE-STYLE BIRD TABLE

The decorative details and distressed paintwork of this roofed bird table are reminiscent of seaside architecture, perhaps a pretty beach hut. Suspended on a ready-made stand, you can use plain dowelling to make the supports for the roof, or recycle a broom or the legs from an old piece of furniture.

Above: *Robins (Erithacus rubecula) are among the tamest species to visit gardens, and enjoy feeding from bird tables.*

YOU WILL NEED

2cm (¾in) pine board (for bases)
jigsaw or scroll saw
drill
wood glue
4 screws and screwdriver
fretsaw
sandpaper
4 x 20cm (8in) lengths of 2cm (¾in)
    dowelling or other supports
5mm (¼in) medium-density
    fibreboard (MDF) or exterior-grade
    plywood (for roof)
plated moulding pins
hammer
31cm/12in length of thin dowelling
    (for roof trim)
watercolour paints and brushes
petroleum jelly
white emulsion/latex paint
blowtorch (optional)
satin yacht varnish

TYPICAL FOOD

varied, including kitchen scraps

TYPICAL VISITORS

starlings, sparrows and juncos
robins, finches and thrushes
mockingbirds

1 Using the templates on page 241 as a guide, cut out the base, roof base and roof ends from the pine board with a jigsaw. Drill holes (for the dowelling) in each base corner. Glue and screw the roof ends to the roof base.

3 From the plywood, cut fourteen 31 x 2.5cm (12½ x 1in) slats for the long roof sides. Cut another ten to go over the roof ends; for each, cut a block of five into a matching triangle. Cut out the frills, four 20cm (8in) eave strips, and two finials.

5 Paint with a dilute mixture of cobalt blue and burnt umber watercolour paint. Leave to dry, then smear on a thin layer of petroleum jelly with your fingers. Apply white emulsion paint, and if you like, dry it with a blowtorch to make the paint crack.

2 In the main base, drill a starter hole for the fretsaw and cut out a 7.5cm (3in) hole (to hold the water bowl). Sand the edges. Glue the four dowelling supports in place to link the base and roof base. Leave to dry.

4 Glue the slats across the roof ends and sides and nail in place with the pins. Attach the scalloped frills all around the roof and main base. A piece of cardboard can hold the pins steady while hammering. Glue on the eave strips, finials and top roof trim.

6 To age the paintwork, apply a dilute, equal mixture of yellow ochre and burnt sienna watercolours. Leave to dry, then finish with a coat of satin yacht varnish. Secure your seaside bird table to your chosen stand or support.

RUSTIC FEEDERS

These two feeders in different styles originate from the same basic store-bought model. One has been sanded and given a driftwood-style paint effect, while the other has been camouflaged beneath found objects, including a rusty tin sheet and a short length of plasterer's angle bead.

Above: *With its long, pointed bill, the great spotted woodpecker (*Dendrocopos major*) can easily take nuts from feeders.*

YOU WILL NEED
wooden bird feeders
light grey emulsion/latex paint
medium paintbrushes
sandpaper
clear glue
sand
stub wire
pencil
natural twine
shells, twigs or moss, corks
craft/utility knife or scalpel
thick florist's wire
protective gloves
sheet of old tin
tin snips or saw
glue gun and glue sticks
plasterer's angle bead
black spray paint

TYPICAL FOOD
shelled peanuts

TYPICAL VISITORS
woodpeckers
tits, titmice and finches

1 Paint the first feeder grey and allow to dry. Rub down with sandpaper to give the surface a weathered, driftwood effect. Apply clear glue to the roof and sprinkle sand over it. Twist lengths of stub wire around a pencil and weave natural twine through them to imitate coils of rope.

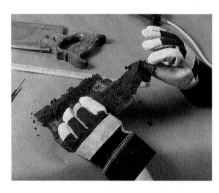

3 For the second feeder, wearing protective gloves, snip pieces of old tin to make a roof. Remove all sharp edges and glue in place. Glue moss around the base.

2 Add natural objects found either in the countryside or on the seashore, such as shells, twigs and moss, to decorate and personalize the feeder. Shells can be attached with glue. Use cut-off corks to seal the feed chambers, and tie a loop of florist's wire to suspend the house.

4 Make the roof ridge from plasterer's angle bead sprayed with black paint. Glue it firmly to the house. Plug the feed holes with corks and suspend with wire as before.

Left and right: *Two very different decorative results can be achieved using the same store-bought feeder as the base. You can experiment with materials and craft techniques to create your own designs.*

GLASS GAZEBO FEEDER

A ready-made glass lantern was the inspiration for this hopper-style feeder, reassembled with additional materials. It makes an attractive feeder, which will shine, jewel-like, among dark foliage.

1 This lantern didn't have all its windows, and so required extra glass to be installed. (You might not need to cut and solder windows, so ignore these steps if that is the case.) The lantern had one 'drawer'; another two are created here. A new base provides a landing platform for the birds.

2 If you are making new windows, measure the areas required and reduce by 5mm (¼in) to allow for the metal borders. Using a chinagraph pencil, mark the measurements on the glass, then cut the pieces out by running a glass cutter in a single pass along a ruler, while pressing firmly. Tap along the score line to break the glass.

YOU WILL NEED
glass lantern
ruler or try-square
thin glass (optional)
chinagraph pencil (optional)
glass cutter (optional)
protective gloves
shiny tin can, washed (for hoppers)
tin snips
flux, solder and soldering iron
fine wire mesh (for platform)

TYPICAL FOOD
shelled peanuts
black sunflower seeds
striped sunflower seeds

TYPICAL VISITORS
tits and titmice
sparrows and juncos
finches and starlings
siskins, redpolls and blue jays

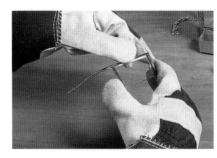

3 Still wearing protective gloves, cut 1cm (½in) strips of metal from a tin can using tin snips. Wrap a strip of metal around each edge of each glass panel. Trim, then smear a small amount of soldering flux on to the adjoining surfaces of each corner joint.

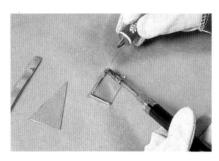

4 Solder the corner joints of each panel. Heat up a joint using a soldering iron and apply solder until it flows between the surfaces to be joined. Remove the heat source. The solder will set in seconds, but the metal will remain hot for some time.

5 Measure the openings for the hopper drawers, and cut and fold sections of tin, using a try-square or ruler to keep the folds straight. Cut out a large base platform from fine wire mesh, then solder the base, panels and hoppers all into place.

CABBAGE PATCH BATH

The leaf pattern embedded in this home-made birdbath suits its surroundings. A supply of fresh drinking water is almost as important for birds as food. Always keep the bath clean and filled up.

1 Cover the ground with a tarpaulin and use a flat board to work on. Wearing gloves, make a smooth dome of moist, sharp sand. Compact with your hands.

2 Lay large outer leaves from a Savoy cabbage over the mould with the undersides facing upwards. Fill in any gaps by overlapping smaller pieces.

3 Prepare the mortar in a bucket with a little water, using a trowel. Wearing gloves, put it over the mould, about 4.5cm (1¾in) thick.

4 Cover well with sheets of clear film and leave to dry. It will take between two to three days to dry, or more if the weather is cold and damp. Check the mortar is hard before moving.

YOU WILL NEED
tarpaulin or piece of plastic sheeting
flat, rigid board
gloves
sharp sand
Savoy cabbage
ready-mix (pre-mixed) mortar,
    5kg (11lb) bag
bucket
trowel
clear film (plastic wrap)
non-toxic sealant

TYPICAL INHABITANTS
blackbirds and sparrows
tits and titmice
finches and siskins

5 Pull off the film and lift the bowl up off the sand mould. Remove the leaves. Finally, paint the interior with a non-toxic sealant, leaving it to dry thoroughly. This will prevent unsightly algae colonizing the concrete, making it safer for the birds too.

NESTING MATERIALS DISPENSER

This sculptural container will not only look elegant in your garden but will encourage birds to build their nests nearby. At nest-building time, keep the dispenser topped up with nesting materials such as scraps of wool, fur, fabric, straw, feathers and even hair, all of which will be most welcome to garden birds.

Above: *The domed nest of the long-tailed tit (Aegithalos caudatus) is an amazing structure, made of feathers bound together with strands of cobweb. The outside is disguised with lichen to conceal it from predators. Most birds build the basic nest structure using tough plant fibres such as twigs, leaves and dry grass. The interior is lined with soft, warm materials such as moss, hair and feathers. By providing nesting materials, you will give birds a helping hand to raise their young.*

YOU WILL NEED

chicken wire, approximately 25cm
    (10in) wide
protective gloves
wire cutters
small pliers
thin and thick garden wire
plastic picnic plate
bradawl or awl
coffee jar lid
epoxy resin glue
large beads

TYPICAL VISITORS

finches, warblers and orioles
sparrows and juncos
tits, titmice and chickadees

1 Cut a rectangular piece of chicken wire and roll it into a cylinder. Join the wire along the edges by carefully twisting the cut ends together. Using a pair of pliers, pull the bottom of the cylinder to draw the wires together into a tight roll.

3 Splay out the rim of the container at the top. Twist and bind the bottom with thin green garden wire. Add a bead if liked.

5 Make holes to match the positions of the wires around the edge of a plastic plate using a heated bradawl or awl. Thread the plate, upside down, on to the wires. Glue an upside-down lid on to the plate, to make a container for food or water.

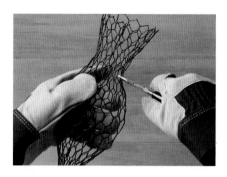

2 Now start to shape the wire into an elegant vase shape. A third of the way from the top, form a neck by squeezing the wires together with the pliers. To create the belly of the container, pull the holes further open to fatten out the shape.

4 Attach four lengths of thicker wire, evenly spaced, around the rim of the container. Loop them through and secure the ends.

6 Connect the four wires to a single wire threaded with a large bead. Twist the wires neatly into position. Now you are ready to hang the dispenser from a tree or large shrub, so that nesting birds can pluck the contents at will.

BIRDBOX MAKEOVERS

Inexpensive ready-made plain boxes can be customized to suit your taste. Paint makes for the simplest transformations – an alpine chalet and a Shaker-style dwelling are created here, along with a leafy hideaway using fabric shapes. Paint each house with primer before you begin, and allow to dry.

YOU WILL NEED
wooden birdhouses
emulsion/latex paints, paintbrushes
exterior-grade matt varnish, brush
pencil, paper and scissors
self-adhesive roof flashing
craft/utility knife, cutting mat
waterproof green canvas
staple gun
waterproofing wax (optional)

TYPICAL INHABITANTS
tits, titmice and chickadees

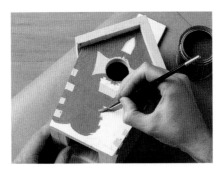

1 To create an alpine chalet, draw the design on the box. Paint the roof, shutters and other details in pale blue. When this is dry, paint the walls of the house in rust red.

2 Add details on the gable, shutters and stonework in white and grey. Paint flowers, grass and leaves along the front and sides in yellow and green. Varnish when dry.

1 To make a Shaker-style dwelling, cut a heart out of paper and position it over the entry hole. Draw around it in pencil and paint the heart rust red.

2 Paint the walls in duck-egg blue using a larger paintbrush. When this layer is dry, paint on little starbursts in rust red using a very fine artist's brush.

3 Cut a piece of roof flashing to fit the birdhouse roof. Cover the roof, folding the edges under the eaves. Protect the paintwork with varnish.

1 To make a leafy hideaway, paint the birdhouse a colour complementary to your green canvas, such as mid-blue, and leave to dry. Cut the canvas into 4cm (1½in) bands and scallop one edge. Staple the bands on to the house, starting at the base and allowing the scallops to overhang.

2 Staple more canvas bands around the front and sides, with each layer overlapping the last. When you reach the entry hole, snip the top of the canvas and glue it down inside. Staple on the next band, then trim back the central scallop to form a few small fronds above the entry hole.

3 Overlay strips on the side of the roof. Cut the top strip double the width, with a scalloped edge along both sides, so that it fits over the roof ridge. Finally, staple bands along the gable ends. Spray the finished house with waterproofing wax, if not using a waterproof fabric.

LAVENDER HIDEAWAY

This pretty and practical makeover takes only a short time using a ready-made birdhouse. Even the heaviest shower pours freely off the lead roof, leaving the occupants warm and dry inside.

1 Paint the birdhouse with lilac emulsion and allow it to dry. Sketch out the decorative design using a pencil. Fill in the sketch using acrylic or watercolour paints. When dry, cover the whole house with several coats of exterior-grade matt varnish.

2 Make a paper pattern for the lead roof, measuring your box (use the template on page 243 as a guide to the shape). Allow 1cm (½in) extra for each side and 3cm (1¼in) extra for the scallops on the front.

YOU WILL NEED
wooden birdhouse
lilac emulsion/latex paint
medium and fine paintbrushes
pencil
acrylic or watercolour paints
exterior-grade matt varnish
paper, scissors
protective gloves
thin sheet lead
tin snips or craft/utility knife
soft hammer or wooden mallet

TYPICAL INHABITANTS
house sparrows and bluebirds
titmice and chickadees
wrens and nuthatches

3 Transfer the design on to a piece of thin sheet lead and cut it out using tin snips or a craft knife. Wear gloves or wash your hands afterwards.

Above: *Nuthatches (Sitta species) are hole-nesters and are well suited to this box.*

4 Hold the lead roof in place and mould to shape by tapping the lead with a soft hammer or wooden mallet until the correct fit is achieved. Turn the 1cm (½in) allowance under at the back and at the eaves to secure the roof in place.

SNUG NESTING BOX

The small, round entrance hole of this box is designed to suit small birds such as tits, titmice, bluebirds, wrens and others. Once birds have taken up residence, they could return annually.

1 The timber used in nest boxes should preferably be of hardwood, such as oak. Softer woods such as pine can also be used, but will start to rot more quickly. Whatever wood you use will last longer if you give the finished box a coat of exterior-grade matt varnish.

2 Measure the dimensions on the timber, referring to the template on page 242, and mark them clearly using a pencil and carpenter's square. Always double-check your measurements before cutting. Mark the names of each section in pencil.

3 Cut the pieces using a sharp carpentry saw and put them to one side. Sand off any splintered edges to the wood.

4 Carefully screw the sections together. Don't use nails as these can cause the wood to split, allowing water into the box.

5 On the front face of the box, make a hole with a 3cm (1¼in) drill bit. Attach the roof, using the rubber strip as a hinge. Varnish and fix the bird box in the garden, choosing a suitable spot out of direct sun and high enough to be out of reach of predators.

YOU WILL NEED

length of timber/lumber, 142 x 15 x
    1–1.5cm (56½ x 6 x ½in)
pencil
ruler
carpenter's square
saw
sandpaper
screws
screwdriver
drill with 3cm (1¼in) drill bit
rubber strip (for hinge)
exterior-grade matt varnish
paintbrush

TYPICAL INHABITANTS

tits, titmice and chickadees
house sparrows and house finches
nuthatches and wrens
starlings – these could use the box if
    you enlarge the entrance hole

FOLK-ART BIRD BOX

This box is simple to make, but with its traditional weathered look, it makes the perfect springtime retreat for blue tits, titmice and other hole-nesters, such as nuthatches, wrens, bluebirds and house sparrows. Mounted on a post in a quiet spot, it should be safe from prowling predators such as cats.

1 Mark and cut out the house pieces on MDF or plywood following the templates on page 243. In the upper centre of the front piece, draw a 3cm (1¼in) circle using compasses (or draw around a lid of that size). Cut out the hole by drilling a pilot hole, then enlarging it with a padsaw. Stick together the front, back, sides, base and the shorter roof piece, using glue and panel pins hammered down flush with the surface.

2 Paint the whole house, including the base and loose roof piece, with blue-grey emulsion paint. When dry, paint the four walls of the house white. When these are dry (about 2–3 hours), distress the surfaces by rubbing with medium-grade sandpaper until the undercoat shows through.

3 Wearing protective gloves, cut a strip of lead the depth of the roof and 5cm (2in) wide, using tin snips. Staple this to the loose roof half. Position the roof halves together, bending the lead to fit, and staple through the lead into the fixed roof half.

4 Drill two small holes just below and to either side of the entrance hole. Bend a piece of copper wire into a flattened loop slightly wider than the distance between the holes. Pass the two ends of the wire through the holes and turn them down just inside the box to hold the perch in place.

Above: *Titmice (Paridae) nest in tree holes and bird boxes. They line their nests with warm materials, such as moss and leaves.*

Above: *The nest box can be adapted with different embellishments. It can be fixed on a pole or hung from a tree.*

YOU WILL NEED

5mm (¼in) medium-density fibreboard (MDF) or exterior-grade plywood
saw
pair of compasses
drill
padsaw
PVA/white glue
panel pins
hammer
emulsion/latex paint: blue and white
medium paintbrush
medium-grade sandpaper
protective gloves
lead sheet, tin snips
staple gun
copper wire and wire cutters

TYPICAL INHABITANTS

tits, titmice and chickadees
nuthatches and wrens
bluebirds
house sparrows

PEBBLE AND THATCH HOUSE

As long as the basic box requirements for birds are fulfilled, the finish is up to you. This one has been given a pebbledash wall and thatched roof treatment. Made for hole-nesters, such as sparrows, tits, titmice, bluebirds, swallows and chickadees, site this box somewhere quiet, so the birds are not disturbed.

Above: *Eastern bluebirds (*Sialia sialis*) benefit from the provision of nest boxes because starlings can take over their nest sites.*

YOU WILL NEED

5mm (¼in) medium-density fibreboard (MDF) or exterior-grade plywood
pencil, ruler
carpenter's square
tenon saw
drill
wood glue
masking tape
craft/utility knife
cutting mat
self-adhesive roof flashing
ready-mixed tile cement
palette knife
aquarium gravel
sisal hanging-basket liner
PVA/white glue
paintbrush
raffia
large-eyed needle
clothes pegs/clothespins
diluted brown watercolour paint
exterior-grade matt varnish
varnish brush

TYPICAL INHABITANTS

sparrows
swallows
bluebirds
tits, titmice and chickadees

1 Following the templates on page 244 mark and cut out the house parts from MDF using a saw. Drill an entry hole in the front wall and, if required, drill a small hole in the back wall for hanging.

2 Glue the base and walls together with wood glue, and then hold the structure in position with strips of masking tape until the glue is quite dry.

3 Using a craft knife and cutting mat, cut a strip of roof flashing the length of the roof ridge and 13cm (5in) wide. Position the two roof pieces, leaving enough of a gap to allow the roof to hinge open. Cover the ridge with the strip of roof flashing.

4 Working on a small area at a time, spread ready-mixed tile cement over the house walls. Embed aquarium gravel firmly into the cement, choosing darker stones to outline the entry hole. Cover the walls of the house completely.

5 Cut a rectangle of sisal 28 x 14cm (11 x 5½in) for the thatch and a strip 15 x 7.5cm (6 x 3in) for the decorative ridge. Coat the undersides with diluted PVA/white glue and leave to dry. Stitch two rows of large cross-stitch in raffia along the sides of the strip, then glue and stitch it across the thatch.

6 Glue the thatch pieces on to the roof. Secure it all in place with clothes pegs/pins and a strip of masking tape until quite dry. To finish, wash the pebbledash sides of the house with brown watercolour and, when the paint is dry, give it a coat of protective varnish.

NESTY NOOK

This cosy home to suit hole-nesters, including wrens and nuthatches, is formed from plastic-coated chicken wire covered with moss. Place the nest in a hidden position, low down in thick undergrowth or even in the bank of a stream beneath overhanging roots, as long as the site is dry.

Above: *Red-breasted nuthatches (Sitta canadensis) usually nest in cavities in pine trees. They smear the nest entrance with pitch to discourage predators. The female lays 5–6 eggs inside. In winter, the birds forage widely. They feed mainly on pine seeds, but will also visit bird tables to take suet and seeds. In summer, their diet includes insects and wood-boring grubs.*

YOU WILL NEED
chicken wire
wire cutters
large leaves
sisal hanging-basket liner
scissors
pliers
hair net
moss
sea grass string
garden wire

TYPICAL INHABITANTS
nuthatches and wrens
tits, titmice and chickadees
sparrows
jackdaws and woodpeckers – these
    will use a nest of this type with
    slightly larger dimensions, placed
    in a high-up position

1 Cut a square of chicken wire measuring about 30cm (12in). Line it with large leaves. Cut a square of hanging basket liner made of sisal to the same size and lay it down on top of the leaves.

3 Pull at the wire structure from the front and back to 'puff' it out and create a larger space inside for the bird to nest.

5 Stuff moss evenly between the nest and the hair net to cover the chicken wire completely. Work on one part at a time until you are satisfied with the look of the whole.

2 Fold the four corners into the centre and join the sides by twisting the ends of the wires together. Leave the centre open. Tuck in the wire ends to ensure that there are no sharp bits poking out.

4 Carefully stretch a hair net over the whole nest structure. Take care to keep the entrance hole clear.

6 To define the entry hole, form a ring of sea grass string and secure it by twisting garden wire around it. Wire it into position, tucking in the wire ends carefully.

HOLLOW LOG NEST BOX

Choose an appealing log for this nest box. Depending on its size, you can adapt it to suit the type of bird you want to attract, from tits to woodpeckers. Mossy logs look beautiful, as do chunks of silver birch. Avoid pieces of wood with knots or branches, as they are difficult to split neatly.

Above: *Place the nest box high in a tree to attract woodpeckers, such as this northern flicker (*Colaptes auratus*). These birds use their short, stiff tails to balance upright on the trunk while they extract grubs from beneath the bark. They usually nest in tree holes excavated with their sharp beaks.*

YOU WILL NEED

2 logs
pencil
ruler
mallet
straight-edged chisel
drill and various drill bits
saw
hammer
nails
garden wire
pliers

TYPICAL INHABITANTS

starlings
woodpeckers
tits and titmice
wrens

1 Mark out a square on the end of one log. Use a mallet and straight-edged chisel to split off the first side, making sure that you work evenly along the line.

2 Repeat this process to remove all four sides of the square. Drill an entrance hole through one of the sides, making a sizeable hole if you want to attract woodpeckers.

3 Saw a 2cm (¾in) slice off one end of the centre of the log to form the base.

4 Using the base piece, reassemble the log by nailing the four sides together.

5 Wrap a length of garden wire around the top of the box, twist the ends to tighten it and hold the sides securely together.

6 Split the second log to make a roof for the nest box. Attach it using one long nail, so that the roof can easily swivel open.

ROCK-A-BYE BIRDIE BOX

This unusual box is a good project for a keen woodworker. Designed to suit small, acrobatic birds such as wrens, tits, titmice and chickadees, the removable roof is covered with flashing to repel rainwater. The box hangs on stout string, though if you have a problem with predators, it would be safer to use greased wire.

Above: *The wren (*Troglodytes *species) is one of the most common breeding birds, but they are not conspicuous.*

YOU WILL NEED

paper, pencil
scissors
5mm (¼in) medium-density fibreboard
    (MDF) or exterior-grade plywood
drill
sandpaper
fretsaw
V-board
length of 2cm (¾in) wide and 5mm
    (¼in) thick D-shaped moulding
tenon saw
wood glue
nails
hammer
scrap wood
exterior-grade matt varnish
paintbrush
self-adhesive roof flashing
craft/utility knife
cutting mat
string or wire

TYPICAL INHABITANTS

tits, titmice and chickadees
wrens

1 Copy the templates on page 244, cut out and use to mark out the shapes for the base and top on thin plywood (two of each, for the back and front). Drill an entry hole in one of the tops, and sand the edges.

3 Glue and then nail the lengths of moulding around the base, with the flat sides facing outwards. You'll find the easiest way of working is to start with the central strip and then work out.

5 Mark a line around the box base, about 5mm (¼in) below the top edge, and trim back the mouldings to this level to allow the roof to overlap the base when it is placed on. Apply a coat of varnish to the box.

2 Cut out the top and base shapes using a fretsaw and V-board. Next, cut the D-shaped moulding into 10cm (4in) lengths to make the curved base surround and 15cm (6in) lengths to make the curved roof.

4 From a piece of scrap wood, make a temporary spacer to hold the two sides of the top in place. Attach the curving roof slats as before, starting from the centre, and allowing for an overlap on each side.

6 Cut a strip of 15cm (6in)-wide roof flashing, long enough to cover the roof, and smooth it over the moulding strips. Hammer the surface if you wish. Attach a length of string or wire for hanging.

POST BOX

Thick wooden stakes can be hollowed out and turned into unusual nest boxes for small birds such as tits, titmice, wrens and nuthatches. The boxes can be sited on their own or form part of a fence. The cover of roof flashing protects the box from the elements and also helps prevent the wood from splitting.

Above: *Great tits (*Parus major*) can be distinguished from their smaller cousins, blue tits (*Parus caeruleus*), by their size, and also by their broad black chest stripe. Another distinguishing feature is the blue-black cap, which extends down as far as the eyes.*

YOU WILL NEED
fence post of 10cm (4in) diameter
drill and 2.5cm (1in) bit
chisel
mallet
self-adhesive roof flashing
craft/utility knife
cutting mat
protective gloves
lead flashing
pair of compasses
pencil
ruler
scrap wood
vice
pliers
nails
hammer

TYPICAL INHABITANTS
tits and titmice
wrens
nuthatches

1 Using a 2.5cm (1in) bit, drill an entry hole into the side of the post 5cm (2in) from the end, then drill out the end to a depth of about 15cm (6in).

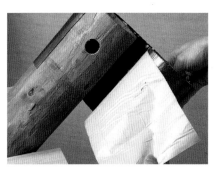

3 Cover the end of the post with self-adhesive roof flashing. Pierce the flashing in the centre of the entry hole and cut back to the edges. Now turn back the flashing inside the hole, but take care not to significantly reduce the size of the entry hole which the birds will use.

5 Wearing gloves, bend the lead to a cone shape. Next, join the seam by squeezing the edges together with pliers. Flatten the seam against the cone.

2 Use a chisel and mallet to remove the waste wood left in the end of the post after drilling. Work to create a roughly circular cavity at least 15cm (6in) deep.

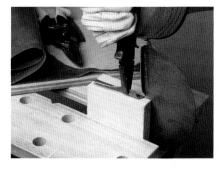

4 Wearing protective gloves, cut out a circle of lead flashing for the lid and remove one quarter of the circle, using the template on page 243 as a guide. Clamp the lead between pieces of scrap wood and fold one inner edge in by 90 degrees. Fold the other edge twice, each at 90 degrees.

6 Attach the cone roof to the post using two nails, but leave one not fully nailed in so that it can be removed to give access to the box when you need to clean it out.

OPEN-FRONTED NEST BOX

Some birds, such as robins and wrens, prefer more open-fronted boxes for nesting. Other species, including spotted flycatchers, pied wagtails, phoebes, blue jays, sparrows and swallows, may also be happy to use them as a nest or roost. This plain construction can be painted and decorated as you like.

Above: *A nest box with a large, square entrance hole as shown in this project will attract robins and wrens. Eastern phoebes* (Sayornis phoebe)*, above, will nest in a similar box with an entirely open front. These nest throughout the east of the Rockies and overwinter in some southern states. They nest on buildings and bridges with ledges and can be tame when breeding. An entirely open-faced box can also attract cardinals, blue jays, barn swallows and song sparrows as a nest or roost.*

YOU WILL NEED
length of 1.5cm (⅝in) pine board
saw
pencil, ruler
wood glue
hammer
nails or panel pins
strip of sacking/burlap or rubber
exterior-grade matt varnish
paintbrush

TYPICAL INHABITANTS
European robins and wrens
American robins, phoebes, blue jays,
  some sparrows and swallows –
  these will also roost in a similar
  box with an entirely open front

1 Cut out the timber using the template given on page 242. Arrange the pieces of wood in position to make sure that they all fit properly.

2 Glue the low front of the box to the base. Give the glue a little time to dry. Now add one of the side pieces of your nest box. Glue it in place carefully.

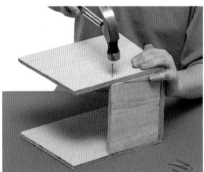

3 Glue on the other side and nail all the pieces together. Position the box on the rear board, and draw round it in pencil.

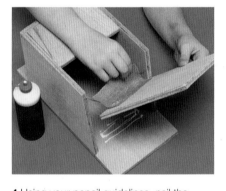

4 Using your pencil guidelines, nail the rear to the box. Add the roof by gluing and nailing on the sacking hinge.

5 Your nest box will last longer if you give it a coat of exterior-grade matt varnish both inside and out. Leave the box overnight to let the varnish dry completely.

6 To position, nail your box to a tree, shed or post, about 2m (7ft) from the ground. Face the box away from any direct sunlight, as this may harm very young birds.

LITTLE LOG CABIN

Designed for small European robins and wrens, who like open-fronted nest boxes where they can build their nest, this log cabin-effect box will blend in well with the natural environment. Position it low down in a well-hidden site, preferably surrounded by thorny shrubbery, and well away from any other birdhouses.

Above: *One of the best-loved garden birds, robins (*Erithacus rubecula*) are actually quite aggressive, defending a feeding territory for much of the year. Robins breed from March to August, fashioning a cup-shaped nest from grass and leaves, and lining it with hair. Females lay 4–6 eggs. Both parents help to feed the young and may raise two broods within a season.*

YOU WILL NEED

sticks – newly-cut hazelwood from
    coppiced woodland is best, as
    the stems can be cut to length
ruler
pencil
tenon saw
bench hook
hammer
short, fine nails or sturdy panel pins
10cm (4in) square plastic tray,
    washed
piece of grassy turf/sod

TYPICAL INHABITANTS

European robins
wrens and goldfinches
American robins, swallows and
    sparrows – these may use this
    box as a roost

1 Select evenly sized, straight sticks and cut them to length, using a tenon saw and bench hook. You will need 4 sturdy uprights 15cm (6in) long, 10 sticks to make the base 12cm (4½in) long, and about 50 sticks for the sides, 10cm (4in) long.

3 Attach the two sides by nailing more sticks across the back. You may need to brace the structure. Work from bottom to top, hammering nails into the uprights at an angle, to keep the structure strong.

5 Build up the top of the box by adding two more of the shorter sticks to each side, on top of the existing pieces. Gently nail the new sticks on top of the walls.

2 Construct the first side by nailing 10cm (4in) lengths to two of the uprights. Use short, fine nails or sturdy panel pins. Nail on the two end sticks first to make a rectangle frame, then fill in with other sticks. Repeat to make the other side.

4 Turn the box over. Attach one stick at the top of the front, then leave a gap of about 5cm (2in) for the entrance hole before completing the rest of the front. Use the 12cm (4½in) sticks to make the base.

6 Fit the tray into the top so that it rests on the uprights, or so that the lip rests on top of the walls. Cut a piece of turf/sod to fit and place it in the tray to make the roof.

DUPLEX LIVING

This elegant ridged birdhouse is divided into two. With an entry hole at each end, it is made to suit pairs of larger birds, such as starlings, jackdaws or purple martins, which live in colonies.

1 Using the templates on page 245, mark and cut out the pieces for the birdhouse, adapting the pitch of the roof to fit your tile. Drill and saw an entry hole in each end.

2 Sand all the surfaces. Glue and then nail the base to the sides. Next, measure and mark the centre line of the box and glue the dividing wall in position.

3 Glue and nail each end piece to the sides. Paint the outside of the birdhouse and leave it to dry thoroughly, then varnish.

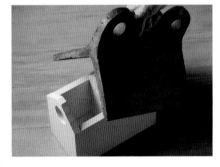

4 Place the ridge tile in position on top of the birdhouse. This house can be erected on a post or simply placed at medium height in a quiet location.

Below: *Starlings* (Sturnus vulgaris) *are gregarious birds that feed and roost in flocks. This box will suit two pairs of birds.*

YOU WILL NEED

length of 2cm (¾ in) pine board
pencil, ruler
tenon saw
drill
hole saw
sandpaper
wood glue
galvanized nails
hammer
paint, paintbrush
exterior-grade matt varnish
ridge tile

TYPICAL INHABITANTS

starlings or purple martins
jackdaws

SCALLOPED SHELTER

This little nest designed for martins and swallows is made of papier-mâché. It is easily replaced each season, though the chicken wire container will last longer. Attach it to the wall with two cup hooks, in a dry place under the eaves. The scallop shell is purely decorative.

Above: *Barn swallows (Hirundo rustica) originally nested on rocky ledges, but now they mostly nest under the eaves of buildings, using mud for the nest itself. They are found in most parts of the world.*

YOU WILL NEED
newspaper
bowl of water
plastic bowl
wallpaper paste
brush
scissors
corrugated cardboard
pencil
masking tape
acrylic paints
paintbrush
chicken wire
protective gloves
wire cutters
small pliers
drill
scallop shell
florist's wire

TYPICAL INHABITANTS
martins
swallows
tits and titmice

1 To make the papier-mâché, tear a newspaper into small squares and soak it in water. Cover one half of a plastic bowl with a layer of wet, unpasted pieces of paper. The pieces should slightly overlap.

2 Brush wallpaper paste liberally over the first layer and add more pieces, pasting each layer, until you have built up about six layers. Leave it to dry out in a warm place such as an airing cupboard.

3 When the papier-mâché is completely dry, remove it from the plastic bowl and trim the rough edges to make a neat half-bowl shape. Now cut out a semicircle of corrugated cardboard, which will form the backing for the nest.

4 Attach the cardboard to the papier-mâché bowl shape using masking tape, then reinforce the structure by adding a few layers of pasted paper over the back and edges. Leave the nest in a warm place to dry out thoroughly.

5 Paint the nest in variegated muddy tones. Cut a piece of chicken wire using wire cutters. Wrap it around the nest and join the wire ends together at the sides.

6 Squeeze the chicken wire with the pliers to shape it to the form. Drill two small holes in the top of the scallop shell and one at the bottom, and wire it on to the frame.

SWIFT NURSERY

Swifts build their nests in wall crevices, under the eaves of houses or in tunnel-shaped boxes. Although they will sometimes take to boxes with front-facing access holes, an entrance hole underneath is better, as it prevents house sparrows and starlings taking over the box.

Above: *Swifts* (Apus apus) *spend almost their entire lives on the wing, but touch down to nest, often high up on walls.*

1 Using the templates on page 246, mark and cut out all the pieces for the box, except the front, from pine board. Include the three battens. Make a paper pattern to mark the curved entry hole at one end of the base and cut it out using a fretsaw.

2 Glue and nail the base to the back of the box, fix the sides in place and add the top batten. Cut the tongue-and-groove board into 15cm (6in) lengths. Glue and nail these along the front of the box, extending down from the batten to overhang the base.

YOU WILL NEED

length of 2cm (¾in) pine board
pencil, ruler
tenon saw
paper
scissors
fretsaw
wood glue
hammer
nails
2cm (¾in) tongue-and-groove
   pine board
drill
piece of scrap wood
sandpaper
emulsion/latex paint
exterior-grade matt varnish
paintbrushes
self-adhesive roof flashing
craft/utility knife
cutting mat

TYPICAL INHABITANTS

swifts

3 Allow the glue time to dry. Next, drill a 1.5cm (⅝in) decorative hole at each joint, placing a piece of scrap timber behind the tongue-and-groove to prevent it splitting. Now trim the lower edge of each board to form a chevron shape. Drill two holes in the back of the box for fixing to a wall. Sand and paint the box, then leave to dry. Paint the outside with protective varnish.

4 Mark positions for the two roof battens on the underside of the roof and fix them on with glue and short nails. Paint the underside of the roof black. Cover the top of the roof with strips of self-adhesive flashing and fit the roof on to the box. Overlap the last strip of flashing to the back of the box. Finally, fix the box securely on to a wall.

DOVECOTE

This beautiful structure will make a comfortable roost for up to half a dozen doves or pigeons, but it could be adapted to accommodate more birds by increasing the number of tiers. The dovecote is probably best sited on the side of a building, but it can also be mounted on a stout post.

Above: *Collared doves (*Streptopelia decaocto*) only began to breed in Britain in the 1950s, but are now quite common. Their call is a gentle cooing sound.*

YOU WILL NEED

1cm (½in) and 5mm (¼in) medium-density fibreboard (MDF) or exterior-grade plywood
pencil, ruler
carpenter's square
jigsaw
length of 2cm (¾in) pine board
tenon saw
2 x 4.5cm (¾ x 1¾in) pine batten
sandpaper
wood glue
nails
hammer
drill
screws
screwdriver
paint, paintbrush
self-adhesive roof flashing
craft/utility knife
cutting mat
metal ruler

TYPICAL INHABITANTS

doves and pigeons

1 Using the template on page 247, mark and cut out the back board from 1cm (½in) plywood with a jigsaw. Cut the roof shapes and front arches from 5mm (¼in) plywood.

2 The centre, sides, floors and battens will require 2cm (¾in) pine board. Mark and cut out these pine timber parts, following the templates provided. Sand all the surfaces.

3 Join the sides and centre by gluing and nailing on the front battens. Fit the back battens into the notches cut in the centre piece. Attach by nailing in the centre of the batten and at each end.

4 Drill pilot holes for the screws in the backboard. Attach the backboard to the frame using glue and screws. Paint the frame and the arched fronts and leave to dry. Attach the fronts using glue and nails.

5 Cover the small roof sections with self-adhesive roof flashing. Cover the main roof with horizontal strips of flashing. Start from the bottom of the roof and overlap each section, allowing some overlap on the final piece to attach to the backboard.

6 Using nails, assemble the last parts in the following order: first the small roof sections; then the floors; then the main roof. Attach the dovecote to a wall by screwing through the backboard from the inside. Take care when fixing, as the structure is heavy.

DIRECTORY OF GARDEN BIRDS (UK)

Many people derive pleasure from watching garden birds, and it is a pastime that can be enjoyed without the need for any special equipment, although binoculars and a notebook can add to your understanding. To help you identify the birds that visit your garden, the following pages present illustrations and in-depth profiles of some of the most common British species, the majority of which can be seen in domestic surroundings, and some more occasionally, giving details of their distribution, size, habitat, nests, eggs and food, together with descriptions of their songs and behaviour. There is not space to include all the varieties but you will find plenty of examples to guide you in your bird-spotting adventure.

Left: *The jaunty breast and trusting nature of the robin (*Erithacus rubecula*) make it popular with birdwatchers. It is a member of the thrush family.*

Above: *Chaffinches (*Fringilla coelebs*) usually feed on the ground, pecking at a range of seeds and invertebrates.*

Above: *Tits are the species most likely to visit feeding stations and use nest boxes. This is a coal tit (*Parus ater*).*

Above: *Small, brownish birds such as the chiffchaff (*Phylloscopus collybita*) are often easiest identifed by their songs.*

GARDEN FINCHES

Finches feed mainly on seeds but, by adopting different feeding strategies, they can exploit a variety of food sources without competing with each other. Goldfinches, for example, eat small seeds such as teasel, whereas the hawfinch can crack very tough seeds such as cherry with its strong, stout bill.

CHAFFINCH
Fringilla coelebs

The behaviour of chaffinches changes significantly during the year. These birds can be seen in groups during the winter, but at the onset of spring and the breeding season, cock birds become very territorial, driving away any rivals. While resident chaffinches remain in gardens throughout the year, mainly feeding on the lawn, large groups of migrants seek refuge from harsh winter weather in farmland areas, associating in large flocks.

Chaffinches usually prefer to feed on the ground, hopping and walking along the lawn and flower beds in search of seeds. They seek invertebrates for rearing their chicks.

FACT FILE
Habitat Woodland, parks, gardens.
Nest Cup-shaped, in a tree fork.
Eggs 4–5, light brown or blue with dark, very often smudgy, markings.
Food Seeds, also invertebrates.
Distribution British Isles, western Europe; west of northern Africa and south-western tip. Summer visitor to Scandinavia and eastern Europe.

IDENTIFICATION
• Cock's summer plumage: black band above the bill, grey over head and neck. Cheeks and underparts pinkish. Brown back, two white wing bars. Less brightly coloured in winter.
• Hens: grey cheek patches, dark grey-green upperparts. Buff to grey-white underparts. Young similar to hens.
• Size 16cm (6¼in).

EUROPEAN GOLDFINCH
Carduelis carduelis

Goldfinches are very agile birds, which are able to cling on to narrow stems when feeding. They often congregate in winter in order to feed on stands of thistle heads and teasel in wild corners of the garden. The long, narrow bill enables the birds to prise kernels from seeds. Alder cones are also a favoured food in the winter, and they will also happily take peanuts and seed from bird tables in gardens.

Goldfinches are social by nature, usually mixing in small flocks in areas where food is plentiful, although they are shy when feeding on the ground.

They have a relatively loud, attractive, twittering song that is quite distinctive. Pairs usually prefer to build their nest in a tree fork rather than hiding it in a hedge.

FACT FILE
Habitat Woodland, more open areas.
Nest Cup-shaped, from vegetation.
Eggs 5–6, blue-white, darker markings.
Food Seeds, also invertebrates.
Distribution Much of the British Isles and mainland Europe, including Denmark but confined to the south of Scandinavia. Also in northern Africa.

IDENTIFICATION
• Red face with black lores. Black area across top of crown broadens to a collar on neck. White extends around throat; brown necklace separates this from paler underparts.
• Brown back and flanks, underparts white. Wings and tail are black with white markings. Hens duller. Young less colourful and barred.
• Size 13cm (5¼in).

EUROPEAN GREENFINCH
Chloris chloris

Greenfinches have quite stout bills that enable them to crack open tough seed casings to reach the edible kernels inside. These birds are most likely to be seen in gardens where there are trees and bushes to provide nesting cover. In winter, European greenfinches visit bird tables, readily taking seeds and peanuts as well as foraging in gardens. Groups of these birds are also sighted in more open areas of countryside, such as farmland, searching for weed seeds and grains that may have been dropped during harvesting. However, as farming has become more intensive in recent decades, so these birds have gradually moved to urban areas to seek food.

They begin breeding in April, usually choosing evergreens as nest sites. Pairs will often nest two or three times in succession during summer, and when there are chicks in the nest the birds consume invertebrates in much larger quantities.

FACT FILE
Habitat Woodland edges and more open areas, gardens, farmland.
Nest Bulky, cup-shaped.
Eggs 4–6, whitish to pale blue with darker markings.
Food Seeds, some invertebrates.
Distribution Range extends throughout Europe and much of northern Africa, but absent from more northern parts of Scandinavia.

IDENTIFICATION
• Cock: greenish head, greyer areas on the sides of the face and wings. Yellowish-green breast, yellow on the flight feathers. Relatively large, conical bill for cracking seeds.
• Hen: duller, greyer tone overall, brownish mantle and less yellow on the wings. Young birds also dull, dark streaking on their upperparts and a little yellow on the wings.
• Size 16cm (6¼in).

EUROPEAN SERIN
Serinus serinus

Although mainly confined to relatively southerly latitudes, these tiny colourful finches are occasionally seen in the British Isles and have even bred successfully in southern England. It appears that European serins are slowly extending their northerly distribution, with records revealing that they had spread to central Europe by 1875 and had started to colonize France within another 50 years. These finches forage for seeds in gardens, parks, orchards, and along the sides of roads. They often seek out stands of conifers as nest sites, although they also frequent citrus groves in the south of their range.

Serins construct a tiny, hair-lined nest where up to four eggs are laid. Two to three broods may be raised between May and July. In autumn, northern populations move south to winter, mainly around the Mediterranean.

FACT FILE
Habitat Parks and gardens.
Nest Cup-shaped, in a tree.
Eggs 3–5, pale blue, darker markings.
Food Seeds and some invertebrates.
Distribution Resident in coastal areas of France south through the Iberian Peninsula to northern Africa and around the northern Mediterranean area. A summer visitor elsewhere in mainland Europe.

IDENTIFICATION
• Cock: bright yellow forehead that extends to a stripe above each eye, encircling the cheeks and joining with the yellow breast. Back is yellow and streaked with brown, as are the white flanks.
• Hens: duller in coloration overall, streaked, greenish-grey upperparts, paler underparts and a pale yellow rump. Young differ from adults in being mainly brown and lacking yellow in the plumage.
• Size 12cm (4¾in).

WOODLAND FINCHES

Many seed-eaters live in open country, but some types of finches prefer woodlands – broad-leaved woodlands in the case of bramblings and bullfinches, while crossbills frequent conifer forests. Here, trees offer shelter and food especially in winter. Crossbills have evolved specialized beaks to extract seeds.

COMMON BULLFINCH
Pyrrhula pyrrhula

These birds are unmistakable thanks to their stocky appearance and the bright pink coloration of the males. They are often seen in gardens but may also be encountered in woodland. Bullfinches are regarded as a potential pest by fruit farmers since they eat buds in the early spring. The seeds of trees such as ash and beech form part of their diet in winter, and they can benefit farmers by eating a range of invertebrates, particularly when rearing their young. Breeding starts from mid-April onwards, with a pair constructing their nest using twigs and a softer lining. The hen sits alone, with incubation lasting 14 days, after which both adults feed their growing brood. The chicks fledge at about two-and-a-half weeks old.

FACT FILE
Habitat Woodland areas.
Nest Cup-shaped, from vegetation.
Eggs 4–6, greenish-blue with dark brownish markings.
Food Seeds, invertebrates.
Distribution Europe, except northern Scandinavia and the southern Iberian Peninsula. Extends east through Asia. Also present on the Azores.

IDENTIFICATION
• Cock: black face and top to the head, with deep pink underparts, lighter around the vent. Grey back, black wings and tail with white area on rump. Black bill, legs and feet.
• Hen: similar but brown underparts. Young birds lack the black cap, and brownish coloration on wing coverts.
• Size 16cm (6¼in).

BRAMBLING
Fringilla montifringilla

Bramblings are winter visitors to British gardens. After breeding in northern Europe, the harsh winter weather forces them to migrate south in search of food. Here, they are seen in fields and other areas of open countryside. These finches feed largely on beech nuts, relying on forests to sustain them over winter. In cold weather they will take seeds scattered on the ground. Although normally occurring in small flocks, millions of individuals occasionally congregate in forests. Bramblings have a rather jerky walk, sometimes hopping along the ground when searching for food.

Their diet is more varied during the summer months, when they are nesting. Caterpillars of moths in particular are eagerly devoured at this time and used to rear the young.

Bramblings have a relatively rapid breeding cycle. The hen incubates the eggs on her own, with the young hatching after about a fortnight. The young leave the nest after a similar interval.

FACT FILE
Habitat Woodland.
Nest Cup-shaped, from vegetation.
Eggs 5–7, dark greenish-blue.
Food Seeds and nuts.
Distribution Breeds in far north of Europe, most of Scandinavia into Russia, extending into Asia. Overwinters south throughout Europe, to parts of north-western Africa.

IDENTIFICATION
• Cocks: black head and bill. Orange underparts, white rump and wing bars. Underparts whitish, blackish markings on orange flanks. Duller in winter: pale head markings, yellowish bill.
• Hens: like winter males, but greyer sides to the face. Young birds like hens but brown, with yellowish rump.
• Size 18cm (7¼in).

HAWFINCH
Coccothraustes coccothraustes

With their stocky, powerful bills, hawfinches are able to crack open cherry stones and the hard kernels of similar fruits and feed on the seeds within. They usually feed off the ground, and may sometimes descend to pick up fallen fruits.

These finches are most likely to be observed in small flocks over the winter, with populations breeding in northerly areas moving southward. It is at this time, particularly in harsh weather, that they are most likely to appear in rural gardens, searching for seeds and berries. In spring, they eat buds and also feed on invertebrates, with their stout bills enabling them to prey on even hard-bodied beetles without too much difficulty.

In spring, they form pairs, with the cock bird harrying the female for a period beforehand. She will then start to build the nest, which can be located in the fork of a tree more than 22m (75ft) above the ground. The incubation period lasts approximately 12 days, and the young leave the nest after a similar interval.

COMMON CROSSBILL
Loxia curvirostra

The crossbill's highly distinctive bill can crack the hard casing of conifer seeds, enabling it to extract the inner kernel with its tongue. These finches also eat the pips of various fruits, and prey on invertebrates, particularly when they have young to feed.

Common crossbills rarely descend to the ground except to drink, unless the pine crop is very poor. When faced with a food shortage, they move to areas far outside their normal range, sometimes seeking food in gardens. This phenomenon, known as an irruption, typically occurs once a decade in Europe. Feeding on seeds, crossbills will also sometimes use birdbaths. The breeding season varies through their range, starting later in the northerly parts. Both birds build the nest, which is constructed in a conifer, sometimes more than 18m (60ft) high.

SPARROWS, WRENS AND DUNNOCKS

Although sparrows, wrens and dunnocks commonly reside in gardens, these birds are not always easily noticed because of their small stature. The dull-coloured plumage provides camouflage, blending in with vegetation. The presence of house sparrows is more obvious because they consort in twittering flocks.

HOUSE SPARROW
Passer domesticus

A common sight on garden bird tables and in city parks, house sparrows have adapted well to living alongside people, even to the extent of nesting under roofs of buildings.

Highly social birds, these sparrows form loose flocks, with larger numbers congregating in places where food is available.

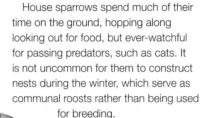

House sparrows spend much of their time on the ground, hopping along looking out for food, but ever-watchful for passing predators, such as cats. It is not uncommon for them to construct nests during the winter, which serve as communal roosts rather than being used for breeding.

The bills of cock birds turn black in the spring, at the start of the nesting period. During this time, several males will often court a single female in what has become known as a 'sparrows' wedding'. In more rural areas, house sparrows sometimes nest in tree holes, and occasionally construct domed nests. They also use nest boxes.

FACT FILE
Habitat Urban and rural gardens.
Nest Tree holes, under roofs of buildings and in birdhouses.
Eggs 3–6, pale with darker markings.
Food Includes invertebrates, seeds.
Distribution Very common, occurring throughout Europe, and eastwards across Asia, northern and south-east Africa.

IDENTIFICATION
• Rufous-brown head with a grey area on top. Black stripe across the eyes, broad black bib over the chest.
• Greyish ear coverts and underparts, whitish area under the tail.
• Hens are a duller shade of brown, with a pale stripe behind each eye and a fawn bar on each wing.
• Size 6in (15cm).

TREE SPARROW
Passer montanus

This woodland bird is a relative of the house sparrow, which it quite closely resembles in size and markings. A distinctive black patch on each white cheek distinguishes these small birds from their cousins. Tree sparrows suffered a disastrous decline in western Europe during the 20th century.

Once widespread, these birds are now absent from many parts of their former range. A sociable species, tree sparrows often form flocks, including mixed flocks with house sparrows outside the breeding season.

Their natural habitat is woodland with scattered clearings, and farmland with clumps of trees. However, these birds are also seen in gardens in urban areas, where they visit bird tables to take seeds and nuts.

They are shyer than house sparrows, but have a similar repertoire of calls, including chirruping and cheeping notes and a ticking sound in flight. In April, they nest colonially in trees, buildings, cliffs or in nest boxes, producing two or even three clutches of eggs which hatch after 11–14 days. The young fledge 12–14 days after hatching. The sexes are alike.

FACT FILE
Habitat Woodland, farmland.
Nest Loose cup shape made of straw or grass.
Eggs 3–6, buff with dark spots.
Food Seeds, grains, buds and invertebrates.
Distribution Breeds in Europe except northern Scandinavia, east England, north Scotland and central Ireland.

IDENTIFICATION
• The top of the head is reddish-brown, with a black bib and bill. White area on the cheeks extend back around the neck, broken by central black patches. Grey chest.
• Light brown and black wings, white wing bar edged by black. Buffish underparts, plain brown tail.
• Size 14cm (5½in).

WREN

Troglodytes troglodytes

Although often difficult to spot due to their size and drab coloration, these tiny birds have a remarkably loud song which usually betrays their presence. Wrens can be found in gardens where there is plenty of cover, such as ivy-clad walls, scurrying under the vegetation in search of spiders and similar prey.

During the winter, when their small size could make them vulnerable to hypothermia, they huddle together in roosts overnight to keep warm. Nevertheless, populations are often badly affected by prolonged spells of severe winter weather.

In the spring, the hen chooses one of several nests that the male has constructed, lining it with feathers to form a soft base for her eggs. Wrens are surprisingly common, although not always conspicuous, with the British population alone made up of an estimated 8 million pairs of birds.

DUNNOCK

Prunella modularis

Once known as the hedge sparrow, the dunnock is actually a member of the accentor family – a group of small, streaked birds. It can be distinguished from the house sparrow, which it resembles in size and in its dull colouring, by its pinkish-orange legs and slender bill. Superficially falling into the category of 'little brown jobs', closer inspection reveals a delicately marked bird.

Dunnocks are frequent garden visitors, but their secretive ways and skulking, mouse-like habits make them difficult to notice. Generally keeping to the cover of hedges and shrubs they sometimes alight on bird tables, but more often peck crumbs and seeds from the ground.

Research has revealed that the unassuming-looking dunnock has a complex sex life. During the breeding season males and females establish separate but overlapping territories, and both sexes often have several mates – sometimes breeding in groups of up to three males and three females, with two males and a female being the most common. Hens build their nests low in dense vegetation and may raise two to three broods in a season.

The rapid, warbling song is similar to a wren's but quieter, with breeding birds keeping in touch with shrill, cheeping calls.

TITS, BUNTINGS AND SONGSTERS

Small and compact birds, tits and buntings, including the yellowhammer, are often talented singers. Cuckoos are considerably larger, but with their distinctive, repetitive call, they are more often heard rather than seen. Cuckoos have unusual breeding habits, relying on other birds to raise their chicks.

CRESTED TIT
Parus cristatus

The crest of this tit is always visible, although the crest feathers can be lowered slightly. This makes it easy to distinguish, even when foraging with other groups of tits, which happens especially during winter. These attractive tits may be seen in gardens near pinewoods in Scotland. They rarely venture high up, preferring to seek food on or near the ground. Invertebrates such as spiders are preferred, although they often resort to eating conifer seeds during winter.

Crested tits frequently create food stores, particularly during autumn, to help them survive the harsh winter months when snow may blanket the ground. Seeds are gathered and secreted in holes in bark and among lichens, while invertebrates are decapitated and stored on a shorter-term basis.

Nesting begins in March, with a pair choosing a hole, usually in rotten wood, which they enlarge before constructing a cup-shaped lining for their eggs. In more southerly areas, two broods of chicks may be reared in succession.

FACT FILE
Habitat Conifer woodland.
Nest In a rotten tree stump.
Eggs 5–8, white with reddish markings.
Food Invertebrates; seeds in winter.
Distribution Spain to Scandinavia (not the far north) and Russia. Present in the British Isles only in northern Scotland. Absent from Italy.

IDENTIFICATION
• Triangular-shaped, blackish-white crest. Sides of the face blackish-white; blackish line running through each eye, curling round hind cheeks. Black collar joins to a bib under bill.
• Upperparts brownish. Underparts paler buff, more rufous on flanks.
• Sexes are alike. Young similar to adults, but have brown irides.
• Size 12cm (4¾in).

SNOW BUNTING
Plectrophenax nivalis

These buntings breed closer to the North Pole than any other passerine (perching bird). They arrive in Britain in autumn to escape the harsh northern winter, when they may visit gardens on coasts. Some pairs also breed in the highlands of northern Scotland. The cock has an attractive display flight, rising to about 10m (30ft) before starting to sing, then slowly fluttering down again. The nest is often sited among rocks, which provide shelter from cold winds. Outside the breeding season, snow buntings are social and can be seen in flocks, searching for food on the ground. They are usually quite wary, flying away to prevent a close approach. These buntings have a varied diet comprised of seeds and berries when invertebrates are scarce in winter.

FACT FILE
Habitat Tundra, grassland.
Nest Scrape on the ground.
Eggs 4–6, white with reddish spots.
Food Seeds, invertebrates.
Distribution Breeds in Iceland, far north Scandinavia and Europe, into Asia. Overwinters father south. Present in North America. Populations from Greenland overwinter in the UK.

IDENTIFICATION
• Breeding males: mainly white, with black on the back, wings, tail and flight feathers. Bill and legs black.
• Hens: dark brown streaking on head, buff ear coverts, brown on wings.
• Non-breeding males resemble hens but with white rump and whiter wings. Young birds greyish and streaked.
• Size 17cm (6¾in).

YELLOWHAMMER
Emberiza citrinella

This long, slender, colourful bunting with a long tail is best known for its song – a rapid, rhythmic series of notes ending with a flourish, often likened to the phrase 'a little bit of bread and no cheese'. The males sing their song in summer near the nest, which is built low along a hedge.

As seed- and grain-eaters, yellowhammers are birds of arable farmland that traditionally fed and nested far from gardens. Like many farmland birds however, their populations have declined in recent years. Formerly found throughout much of rural Britain except the far north and west, they no longer frequent much of their old range, but they are now more often seen in gardens, especially in winter, when they form feeding flocks with other buntings, finches or sparrows.

Yellowhammers pair up in spring and raise two or three broods in a season. The eggs are incubated for 12–14 days with chicks fledging 11–13 days after hatching. The male helps the female to feed the young birds on insects, and takes over feeding altogether when his mate lays a new clutch.

CUCKOO
Common cuckoo *Cuculus canorus*

The distinctive call of the cuckoo, heard when these birds return from their African wintering grounds, is traditionally regarded as one of the first signs of spring. Typically, they are only resident in Britain between April and September, when they are more often heard than seen in gardens.

Adult cuckoos have an unusual ability to feed on hairy caterpillars, which are plentiful in wooded areas in summer. Common cuckoos are parasitic breeders – the hens lay single eggs in the nests of smaller birds such as hedge sparrows (*Prunella modularis*), meadow pipits (*Anthus pratensis*) and wagtails (*Motacilla* species). The unsuspecting hosts hatch a monster, with the cuckoo chick ejecting other eggs or potential rivals from the nest in order to monopolize the food supply.

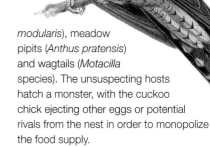

Left: The young cuckoo lifts an egg on to its back to heave it from the nest. If the host's eggs survive long enough to hatch, the cuckoo will eject the chicks.

GARDEN TITS

Given their small size, tits are most likely to be spotted in gardens during winter, when the absence of leaves makes them conspicuous, and they more frequently visit feeders and tables. Tits are very resourceful when seeking food, displaying acrobatic skills as they dart about, even feeding upside down.

COAL TIT
Parus ater

These tits are often seen in gardens feeding on bird tables, sometimes taking foods such as nuts which they then store in a variety of locations, ranging from caches on the ground to suitable holes in trees. The urge to store food in this way becomes strongest in late summer and during autumn, and helps the birds to maintain a food supply through the coldest months of the year. This hoarding strategy appears to be very successful, since coal tit populations rarely crash like many other small birds following a particularly harsh winter.

In fact, these tits have increased their breeding range significantly over recent years, with their distribution now extending to various islands off the British coast, including the Isles of Scilly. During winter, in their natural habitat of coniferous forest, they may form flocks comprised of many thousands of individuals, yet in gardens they are only usually seen in quite small numbers.

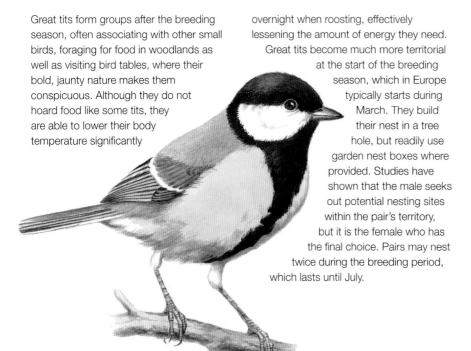

FACT FILE
Habitat Wooded areas.
Nest Cup-shaped, from vegetation.
Eggs 8–11, white with red markings.
Food Mostly invertebrates and seeds.
Distribution All of Europe except for northern Scandinavia. Range extends south to north-western Africa, and spreads across Asia to Japan.

IDENTIFICATION
• Black head, white patches on the sides of the face and on the nape.
• Grey-olive upperparts, white wing bars, brownish-white underparts, some marked regional variations.
• The bill is black. Legs are greyish.
• Sexes very similar; female head markings may be duller. Young birds have pale yellowish cheek patches.
• Size 11cm (4¼in).

GREAT TIT
Parus major

Great tits form groups after the breeding season, often associating with other small birds, foraging for food in woodlands as well as visiting bird tables, where their bold, jaunty nature makes them conspicuous. Although they do not hoard food like some tits, they are able to lower their body temperature significantly overnight when roosting, effectively lessening the amount of energy they need. Great tits become much more territorial at the start of the breeding season, which in Europe typically starts during March. They build their nest in a tree hole, but readily use garden nest boxes where provided. Studies have shown that the male seeks out potential nesting sites within the pair's territory, but it is the female who has the final choice. Pairs may nest twice during the breeding period, which lasts until July.

FACT FILE
Habitat Wooded.
Nest Cup-shaped, made from vegetation; will use nest boxes.
Eggs 5–12, white with red spotting.
Food Invertebrates, seeds.
Distribution All of Europe except northern Scandinavia, across Asia. Ranges south as far as northern Africa.

IDENTIFICATION
• Cock: black head with white cheek patches. Broad band of black down the centre of chest, with yellow on either side. Wings olive-green at the top, becoming bluish on the sides, flight feathers and tail.
• Hens: similar but with a narrower black band. Young paler, yellowish cheeks and lesser black band.
• Size 14cm (5½in).

BLUE TIT
Cyanistes caeruleus

A common visitor to bird tables, blue tits are lively, active birds by nature, and are welcomed by gardeners because they eat aphids. Their small size allows them to hop up the stems of thin plants and, hanging upside down, seek pests under the leaves. Blue tits are well-adapted to garden life and readily adopt nest boxes supplied for them. Their young leave the nest before they are able to fly properly, and are therefore vulnerable to predators such as cats. Those that do survive the critical early weeks can be easily distinguished by the presence of yellow rather than white cheek patches.

LONG-TAILED TIT
Aegithalos caudatus

The tail feathers of these tits can account for nearly half their total length. Those birds occurring in northern Europe have a completely white head and underparts. (The Turkish species *A. c. tephronotus*, in contrast, displays more black feathering.) Long-tailed tits are lively birds, usually seen in small parties, and frequently in the company of other tits. They are often most conspicuous during winter, when small groups of these birds are seen flitting among the leafless branches. In cold weather they roost together, which helps to conserve their body heat – sometimes as many as 50 birds may be clustered together. Groups of these birds can be quite noisy when foraging by day. In harsh winter weather they visit bird tables and feeders to take scraps of fat and peanuts. Their breeding period starts early, in late February, and may extend until June.

Left: *Long-tailed tits build a large nest with a side entrance, made of moss and twigs bound with cobwebs.*

GARDEN THRUSHES AND ORIOLES

The attractive song of some thrushes and orioles forms part of the dawn chorus in woodland areas, being especially conspicuous in spring when they are breeding. Robins, blackbirds and song thrushes may be seen in British gardens at any time of year. Golden orioles may visit eastern Britain in summer.

ROBIN

European robin *Erithacus rubecula*

One of the best-loved garden birds in the UK, the robin's colourful appearance belies its strong aggressive streak, for these birds are highly territorial. That said, in the garden, they can become very tame, regularly hopping down alongside the gardener's fork or spade to snatch invertebrates such as earthworms that come to the surface.

Young, recently fledged robins look very different from mature individuals – they are almost entirely brown, with dense spotting on the head and chest.

Robins sing quite melodiously all year round to defend their territories, also producing a tick-like call which is drawn-out and repeated, particularly when they are alarmed by the presence of a predator such as a cat. Since robins usually feed on the ground, they can be especially vulnerable to these predators.

FACT FILE
Habitat Gardens, parks, woodland.
Nest Under cover, often near the ground, also in nest boxes.
Eggs 5–7, bluish-white, red markings.
Food Invertebrates, fruit and seeds.
Distribution Resident in the British Isles, western Europe and parts of northern Africa. Scandinavian populations winter farther south.

IDENTIFICATION
• Bright orange extends from just above the bill, around the eyes and down over virtually the entire breast. Lower underparts are whitish-grey, becoming browner on the flanks.
• The top of the head and the wings are brown, with a pale wing bar.
• Sexes are alike.
• Size 14cm (5½in).

SONG THRUSH

Turdus philomelos

The song of these thrushes is both powerful and musical. It can be heard particularly in the spring at the start of the breeding season, and is usually uttered from a relatively high branch.

Song thrushes are welcomed by gardeners as they readily hunt and eat snails and other pests on the ground. Having grabbed a snail, the birds choose a special site known as an anvil where they smash it against a rock in order to break the shell and expose the mollusc within.

These thrushes are excellent runners, and this allows them to pursue quarry such as leatherjackets (the larvae of certain species of cranefly, *Tipula* species).

When breeding, song thrushes build a typical cup-shaped nest, which the hen is mainly or even solely responsible for constructing from vegetation.

FACT FILE
Habitat Gardens, parks, woodland.
Nest Cup-shaped.
Eggs 5–6, greenish-blue with reddish-brown markings.
Food Invertebrates, berries.
Distribution Throughout Europe. Eastern populations head to the Mediterranean region for winter. Also northern Africa, to the Sudan.

IDENTIFICATION
• Brown back and wings, with some black evident, and a yellow-buff area across the chest. Dark markings that extend over the chest and abdomen are shaped like arrows.
• Sexes are alike. Young birds have smaller spots, usually less numerous on the underparts.
• Size 22cm (8¾in).

COMMON BLACKBIRD
Turdus merula

One of the most familiar garden birds, blackbirds frequently descend on lawns to search for invertebrates. Earthworms, which feature prominently in their diet, are most likely to be drawn to the surface after rain, and slugs and snails also emerge in wet conditions.

In the 19th century, blackbirds were rarely seen in gardens, but today they have become commonplace. They are vocal and produce a range of fluty notes. Cocks are talented songsters, and both sexes will utter an urgent, harsh alarm call. Although blackbirds do not associate in flocks, pairs can be seen foraging together. As with other thrushes, their tails are surprisingly flexible and can be raised or lowered at will. It is not unusual to see pied blackbirds, with variable amounts of white among the black plumage. The majority of these birds, especially those with the most extensive white, are cocks.

Left: *The hen alone is usually responsible for incubating the eggs, although occasionally the cock bird may share the task.*

EURASIAN GOLDEN ORIOLE
Oriolus oriolus

These summer visitors to gardens in southern and eastern Britain are spectacular birds. However, despite their bright coloration, they are quite inconspicuous, preferring to hide away in the upper reaches of the woodland, although they will sometimes descend to the ground in search of food and water. Their diet varies, consisting mainly of invertebrates from spring onwards, with fruits and berries more significant later in the year.

Migrants arrive at the southern tip of Africa by November, and by March will have set off on the long journey back to Europe. The small north-west African population heads south also, returning by the middle of April. Males establish territories on arrival at their breeding grounds. There is no lasting pair bond.

THRUSHES AND WARBLERS

In some thrushes, the males at any rate are quite brightly coloured, but their shy habits make them fairly inconspicuous. Like thrushes, many warblers are talented singers. Warblers are smaller than thrushes, and their subdued colours make them hard to notice, but they can be recognized by their songs.

COMMON REDSTART
Phoenicurus phoenicurus

This member of the thrush family is most likely to be seen in gardens with mature trees or near woodlands. A summer visitor, it seeks cover when constructing its nest. This is often built inside a tree hole, but sometimes an abandoned building or even an underground tunnel is chosen.

The hen incubates alone for two weeks until the eggs hatch, with both parents subsequently providing food for their growing brood. Fledging takes place around two weeks later. The pair may sometimes nest again, particularly if food is plentiful.

When migrating south, birds from much of Europe take a westerly route through the Iberian Peninsula. The return journey back

north begins in late March. Males generally leave first, enabling them to establish their breeding territories by the time they are joined by the hens.

FACT FILE
Habitat Woodland.
Nest Built in a suitable hole.
Eggs 5–7, bluish with red spotting.
Food Mainly invertebrates, berries.
Distribution Breeding across most of Europe, including Scandinavia, and into Asia. Absent from Ireland. Also parts of north-west Africa. Overwinters south of the Sahara.

IDENTIFICATION
• Cocks: white area above the bill extending back above the eyes. Remainder of the face is black, head and back are grey. Chest is rufous, becoming paler on the underparts.
• Hens: duller, greyish-brown head, buff-white underparts. Young birds have brown heads and rufous tails.
• Size 15cm (6in).

REDWING
Turdus iliacus

The smallest member of the thrush family, the redwing is a winter visitor to Britain from northern Europe. This neat bird with its boldly marked head is named for its russet-coloured underwings and flanks. Redwings arrive from Scandinavia and Iceland in late October or November, often forming mixed flocks with their larger cousins, fieldfares.

These thrushes are not normally garden birds, but harsh or snowy weather will drive them to seek food in gardens in the form of fruit and berries. They feast on windfall apples and on the berries of shrubs such as hawthorn. In a

matter of hours, a flock of redwings can strip a bush of all its berries. In March or April, the birds depart for their breeding grounds in northern Europe. In recent years some pairs have remained to breed in Scotland. Redwing pairs often nest in loose groups, building nests in trees, shrubs or on the ground.

FACT FILE
Habitat Woods, conifer forests, heaths, agricultural land.
Nest Cup-shape of twigs and grass.
Eggs 4–6, pale-blue, red markings.
Food Invertebrates, seeds, berries.
Distribution Breeds in northern and eastern Europe, including Scotland, into Asia. Overwinters in northern and southern Europe, including UK.

IDENTIFICATION
• Small, neat, dark thrush with a well-marked head. The rusty-red patches on the sides of breast and underwings give the bird its name. Upperparts are dark brown; the throat and breast pale, streaked with dark-brown markings. Belly greyish.
• Sexes are alike.
• Size 21cm (8¼in).

DARTFORD WARBLER
Sylvia undata

These small warblers are resident in western Europe, but their most northerly breeding outpost is in southern Britain, where they maintain a tenuous foothold, with numbers becoming severely depleted in harsh winters. They roost in groups, which helps to conserve body heat.

These warblers are most often seen in gardens near heathland. They forage low down in shrubbery, sometimes venturing to the ground, where they can run surprisingly quickly. Berries feature significantly in their diet during winter in northern areas.

Males establish breeding territories in autumn. They sing more loudly and frequently during spring, raising the grey feathers on the sides of their faces as part of the courtship ritual. The nest is built by both adults, usually hidden in a shrub. The hen incubates the eggs mainly on her own, for two weeks, and the chicks fledge after a similar interval.

GRASSHOPPER WARBLER
Locustella naevia

Difficult to observe, these summer visitors may be spotted in gardens close to marshland, heaths and pastures with thorny scrub. They are very adept at clambering through grass and low vegetation. They may be spotted running across open ground, flying low if disturbed and seeking vegetation as cover.

Their song, which is usually heard at dusk, may also betray their presence. They sing in bursts lasting up to a minute in duration, and their calls incorporate ringing notes that have been likened to the sound of a muffled alarm clock.

Grasshopper warblers migrate largely without stopping, and have been observed in West Africa from August onward. They undertake the return journey to their breeding grounds in Europe and Asia between March and May, flying in a more easterly direction, often crossing the Mediterranean from Algeria. The breeding period extends from May until July, with the bulky nest built close to the ground. The chicks hatch after two weeks, and are reared by both adults before leaving the nest as early as 10 days old.

WOODLAND WARBLERS

Spotting these birds in the garden is not always easy because of their small size. In many cases, the neutral coloration also blends in well with the foliage, and the more brightly coloured goldcrest is particularly tiny. Warblers generally favour overgrown areas that contain a good supply of invertebrates.

WILLOW WARBLER
Phylloscopus trochilus

The subdued coloration of these small birds is so effective that, despite being one of Europe's most common species, willow warblers are very inconspicuous. Difficult to observe in their wooded habitat, it is their song, which heralds their arrival in woodlands in early spring, that usually betrays their presence. In the British Isles, the willow species is the most numerous of all warblers, with a population estimated at around three million pairs.

These warblers are most often spotted in rural gardens that are near woodlands and reside in Europe between April and September. They closely resemble chiffchaffs but can be distinguished by their songs. Their nest is hidden among the vegetation and features a low entry point. In late summer, willow warblers can often be seen in loose association with various tits, before they head off to their African wintering grounds.

FACT FILE
Habitat Wooded areas.
Nest Dome-shaped, constructed on the ground.
Eggs 6–7, pale pink with reddish spotting.
Food Insects and other small invertebrates.
Distribution Occurs in the summer from the British Isles right across most of Europe. The species overwinters in Africa.

IDENTIFICATION
• Greyish-green upperparts, with a pale yellowish streak running across each eye. Pale yellow throat and chest, with whitish underparts.
• The yellow plumage is much whiter in birds from more northern areas.
• Size 12cm (4¾in).

GARDEN WARBLER
Sylvia borin

These warblers visit rural gardens with trees in summer, but their dull colours and small size mean they are fairly inconspicuous, particularly when darting among foliage. However, their attractive song and call notes may help identify them in the undergrowth.

Garden warblers arrive in Britain to breed from middle of April onwards, and construct a fairly large nest using a variety of plant matter, usually including stems of grass, and lining it with softer material. The hen sits alone through the incubation period, which lasts about 12 days, but subsequently both parents will seek food for their rapidly-growing brood. The young quickly leave the nest, sometimes when just nine days old, and may be forced to scrabble among the vegetation to escape would-be predators until they are able to fly from danger. In more southern parts of their breeding range, pairs of garden warblers may produce two successive broods of chicks. They return to Africa in September.

FACT FILE
Habitat Gardens with trees, parks.
Nest Made of vegetation.
Eggs 4–5, buff with brown spots.
Food Mainly invertebrates.
Distribution Summer range extends from Scandinavia southwards across virtually all of Europe. Migrates south for the winter, ranging over much of Africa except the Horn and the south-west.

IDENTIFICATION
• Olive-brown head and upperparts, with a greyish area present at each side of the neck. The underparts are greyish-white, buffer along the flanks. Bill and legs are dark greyish.
• Sexes are alike. The young birds are similar to adults.
• Size 14cm (5½in).

FACT FILE
Habitat Wooded areas.
Nest Dome-shaped, from vegetation.
Eggs 4–7, white, brownish spotting.
Food Invertebrates.
Distribution Most of Europe during the summer but absent from parts of northern Scandinavia and Scotland. Resident in parts of southern Britain and Ireland and farther south, near the Mediterranean. Overwinters in northern Africa and south of the Sahara. Also found in Asia.

IDENTIFICATION
• Yellowish stripe above each eye, with a black stripe passing through the centre. Underparts whitish, with variable yellow on sides of the face and flanks. Rest of the upperparts are dark brownish-green. Pointed bill is dark. Legs and feet are black.
• Sexes are alike.
• Size 12cm (4¾in).

CHIFFCHAFF
Phylloscopus collybita

The chiffchaff is a lively warbler, generally common through its range and often seen in gardens, particularly those with trees nearby. Its arrival is a sign of spring. There are regional differences in appearance, with individuals found in western and central areas having brighter yellow coloration than birds occurring farther north and east. Its unusual name reflects its common two-note song pattern.

Pairs are likely to start nesting from April onwards, with the female building the nest on her own. This is positioned relatively close to the ground in a suitable bush or shrub that provides good cover, such as rhododendron, or sometimes in among brambles, offering protection against predators. The chiffchaffs slip in and out of the nest using a side entrance. The hen undertakes the incubation on her own, and this lasts for about 13 days, with the young chicks subsequently fledging after a similar interval. Chiffchaffs may rear two broods during the summer.

GOLDCREST
Regulus regulus

FACT FILE
Habitat Wooded areas, especially conifer woodlands.
Nest Suspended basket, of moss.
Eggs 7–8, buffy-white with brown markings.
Food Mainly invertebrates.
Distribution Much of Europe into Asia, except for northern Scotland and northern Scandinavia, where pairs spend summer. Often overwinters in the Mediterranean.

IDENTIFICATION
• Dumpy appearance, with cock birds having an orange streak (yellow in hens) running down the centre of head, bordered by black stripes on each side. Prominent area of white encircling eyes, much of the rest of the head pale grey.
• White wing bars. Back is greyish-green, underparts paler. Bill is black, legs and feet greyish. Young birds have greyish heads and pale bills.
• Size 8.5cm (3¼in).

These warblers are the smallest birds in Europe and are surprisingly bold, drawing attention to themselves with their high-pitched calls and the way they jerkily flit from branch to branch. They can be easily distinguished from the slightly larger firecrest (*R. ignicapillus*) by the absence of a white streak above the eyes.

Goldcrests may visit gardens especially with conifer trees in both urban and rural settings, but their small size makes them quite hard to detect. They associate in groups both of their own kind and also with other small birds such as tits, seeking food in the branches rather than at ground level.

Pairs split off to breed in the early spring, with both sexes collecting moss and other material to construct their nest. This may be hung off a conifer branch, up to 12m (40ft) off the ground, although it may also be concealed among ivy or similar vegetation. Cobwebs act as thread to anchor the nest together, and the interior is lined with feathers. The young will have fledged by three weeks old, and the adults may nest again soon afterwards and rear a second brood.

CORVIDS

Studies suggest that corvids rank among the most intelligent of birds. Many display an instinctive desire to hoard food, such as acorns, to help sustain them through the winter. Their plumage is often mainly black, sometimes with grey and white areas. Corvids are generally noisy and quite aggressive by nature.

MAGPIE
Common magpie *Pica pica*

Bold and garrulous, magpies are a common sight in gardens, and are regular visitors to bird tables. They are often blamed for the decline of songbirds because of their habit of raiding the nests of other birds to steal eggs and nestlings. They are usually seen in small groups, although pairs will nest on their own.

If a predator such as a cat ventures close to the nest, there will be a considerable commotion, resulting in the nesting magpies being joined by others in the neighbourhood to harry the unfortunate feline. Magpies sometimes take an equally direct approach when seeking food, chasing other birds, gulls in particular, to make them drop their food. These corvids are quite agile when walking, holding their long tails up as they move.

FACT FILE
Habitat Trees with surrounding open areas.
Nest Dome-shaped stick pile.
Eggs 2–8, bluish-green with darker markings.
Food Omnivorous.
Distribution Much of Europe and south to North Africa. Represented in parts of Asia and North America.

IDENTIFICATION
• Black head, upper breast, back, rump and tail, with a broad white patch around abdomen. Broad white wing stripe and dark blue areas below on folded wings. Green gloss on the black plumage in some lights.
• Sexes alike, but the cock may have a longer tail.
• Size 51cm (20¼in).

JAY
Eurasian jay *Garrulus glandarius*

Jays are shy by nature and rarely allow a close approach. They store acorns and other seeds in autumn, and such caches help to sustain them through the winter when the ground may be frozen or covered in snow, restricting their opportunities to find food. This is the time when they are most likely to visit gardens in search of nourishment.

During summer, jays may raid the nests of other birds, taking both eggs and chicks. Throughout their wide range, there is some local variation in their appearance, both in the depth of colour and the amount of black on the top of the head. However, their harsh call, which resembles a hoarse scream, coupled with a flash of colour, helps to identify them.

FACT FILE
Habitat Woodland.
Nest Platform of twigs.
Eggs 3–7, bluish green with dense speckling.
Food Omnivorous.
Distribution Range throughout most of Europe (except Scotland and the extreme north of Scandinavia). Also present in North Africa and Asia.

IDENTIFICATION
• Pinkish-brown with a greyer shade on the wings. Streaking on the head. Broad, black moustachial stripe with whitish throat. White rump and undertail area. Tail is dark.
• White stripe on wings with black and blue markings on sides of wings.
• Sexes are alike.
• Size 35cm (14in).

FACT FILE
Habitat Close to farmland.
Nest Made of sticks, built in trees.
Eggs 2–7, bluish-green with dark markings.
Food Omnivorous, mainly various invertebrates, but also grain, acorns and earthworms.
Distribution Range extends throughout Europe and into Asia. Some populations move south in the winter to the north Mediterranean.

IDENTIFICATION
• Entirely black plumage, with a pointed bill that has bare, pinkish skin at its base.
• The nostrils of adult rooks are unfeathered, distinguishing them from carrion crows. Rooks also have a flatter forehead and a peak to the crown.
• Sexes are alike.
• Size 49cm (19½in).

ROOK
Corvus frugilegus

Rooks are most likely to be seen in gardens near farmland. They nest in colonies, partly because they inhabit areas of open countryside where there are few trees. These are highly social corvids, in which a strong bond also exists between breeding pairs. The rookery serves as the group's centre, which can make them vulnerable to human persecution, but although they eat corn, they are valued for consuming invertebrates as well. The rook's bill is adapted to digging in the ground to extract invertebrates, especially cranefly larvae.

Outside the breeding season, it is not uncommon for rooks to associate with jackdaws, crows or ravens as an alternative to the rookery, which may be used as a roosting site at this time.

FACT FILE
Habitat Relatively open country.
Nest Bulky, made of sticks.
Eggs 3–7, bluish with darker spots.
Food Carrion.
Distribution This species occurs in mainly south-western Europe and North Africa, northwards to Scandinavia. Its range extends eastwards throughout most of northern Asia. It is also present in the British Isles, Greenland, Iceland and North America.

IDENTIFICATION
• These impressive birds are very large in size with a powerful, curved bill. They have entirely black plumage.
• They have a wedge-shaped tail in flight, when the flight feathers stand out, creating a fingered appearance at the tips.
• The males are often larger than the females.
• Size 67cm (26½in).

RAVEN
Common raven *Corvus corax*

Ravens are most likely to appear in gardens in upland areas. They may be recognized by their croaking calls and also their size. The largest members of the crow family occurring in the Northern Hemisphere, the impression of bulk conveyed by these birds is reinforced by their shaggy throat feathers, which do not lie sleekly. There is a recognized decline in size across their range, with ravens in the far north being larger than those occurring farther south.

Pairs of ravens occupy relatively large territories, and even outside the breeding season they tend not to associate in large flocks. When searching for food, ravens are able to fly easily over long distances, flapping their wings slowly.

JACKDAWS, STARLINGS AND THRUSHES

Gregarious birds, jackdaws and starlings are often seen in groups. Both may be seen in British gardens at any time of year. Fieldfares and nightingales are seasonal visitors. Fieldfares visit British gardens in winter. Nightingales arrive in late spring. They are rarely seen but are known for their melodious songs.

JACKDAW
Eurasian jackdaw *Corvus monedula*

These corvids are very adaptable birds, just as likely to be seen foraging on rubbish dumps as visiting garden bird tables. When ants swarm on warm summer days, they are sufficiently agile to catch these flying insects on the wing. In agricultural areas, jackdaws learn to pull ticks off the backs of grazing animals such as sheep, as well as stealing their wool, which they use to line their nests.

Pairs rarely nest in the open, preferring instead the relative security of an enclosed area, often utilizing buildings or even chimneys or church steeples. The hen incubates the eggs alone, with the young hatching after about 19 days. The chicks leave the nest after a further five weeks.

Relatively social birds, jackdaws often associate in large groups in winter, sometimes being seen in the company of rooks (*Corvus frugilegus*) in agricultural areas.

FACT FILE
Habitat Prefers relatively open country.
Nest Made from sticks, sited in a hole.
Eggs 3–8, pale bluish-green with darker markings.
Food Omnivorous.
Distribution Almost all Europe, but absent from parts of Scandinavia. Range extends into Asia. Also occurs in parts of north-western Africa.

IDENTIFICATION
• Glossy blackish overall, darker on crown, around eyes and down on to throat. Back of head and neck lighter, almost silvery, depending on the race. Black bill, legs and feet. Pale bluish irides.
• Young birds have blackish irides and darker, less glossy feathering.
• Size 39cm (15½in).

COMMON STARLING
European starling *Sturnus vulgaris*

Small groups of starlings regularly visit bird tables, and may drive away other visitors. They are equally adept at seeking food on the ground, picking up seeds and probing for invertebrates. These familiar garden birds are resident in a vast range of areas.

However, some populations, especially in the more northerly part of their range, migrate. This prompts the sudden arrival of hundreds of birds in urban areas, especially where there are groups of trees suitable for roosting. They often prove noisy in these surroundings, even singing after dusk if the area is well lit.

In flight, large flocks are adept at avoiding pursuing predators, such as hawks, by weaving back and forth in tight formation. When they are breeding, a pair will often adopt the nest of a woodpecker, or use a nest box.

FACT FILE
Habitat By houses and buildings.
Nest In a tree hole or birdhouse.
Eggs 2–9, white to pale blue or green.
Food Invertebrates, berries and bird table fare.
Distribution Throughout Europe and North Africa, with Scandinavian and eastern European populations migrating south for winter. Also east into Asia. Has been introduced to North America and Australia.

IDENTIFICATION
• Glossy. Purplish-black head, greenish hue on body, overlaid with spots. Dark brown wings and tail.
• Hens: similar, but spots larger and base of tail is pinkish. Young duller, brownish and lack iridescence.
• Size 22cm (8¾in).

FACT FILE
Habitat Breeds in deciduous woodlands and gardens, overwinters in more open areas.
Nest Cup-shaped.
Eggs 4–6, pale-blue with red speckles.
Food Invertebrates, fruit and berries.
Distribution Central and northern parts of Europe, overwintering in the British Isles and south to the Mediterranean. A few pairs are now known to nest in northern and eastern Britain.

IDENTIFICATION
• Large, strikingly marked thrush, with grey head, white eye stripe and small black mask. Bright yellow bill.
• Brown band joins the wings across back. Grey rump. Buff-yellow band across breast speckled with dark markings, including on the flanks. Underparts are otherwise white. The flight pattern is undulating.
• Sexes are alike.
• Size 27cm (10½in).

FIELDFARE
Turdus pilaris

This large member of the thrush family is a winter visitor to British gardens. It arrives from northern Europe and Scandinavia in late autumn, often in large flocks, which may also contain its smaller cousin, the redwing.

Fieldfares generally feed on earthworms, snails and insects, but in harsh winter weather these birds enter gardens in search of fruit and berries. They can be attracted to your garden by fruit left on the ground. Normally quite shy by nature, greedy individuals will aggressively defend fruit or berry-bearing shrubs and trees against other birds. A flock of fieldfares can strip a cotoneaster, hawthorn or holly bush of berries in just a few hours before moving on in search of fresh food.

After returning to their breeding grounds, these birds nest in isolated pairs or loose colonies of up to 50 birds. Breeding birds will vigorously defend their nest in a shrub or tree against cats, people or avian predators such as magpies. They swoop low to dive-bomb intruders while uttering loud cries and even splattering the enemy with droppings until they force a retreat. The call is a harsh, scolding 'chack-chack', most often heard while the birds are in flight.

FACT FILE
Habitat Woodlands, gardens.
Nest Cup-shaped.
Eggs 4–5, greyish-green to reddish-buff.
Food Mainly invertebrates.
Distribution Occurs from southern England and mainland Europe on a similar latitude south to north-western Africa. Overwinters farther south in Africa.

IDENTIFICATION
• Brown plumage extends from above the bill down over the back of the head and wings, becoming reddish-brown on the rump and tail.
• A sandy-buff area extends across the breast, while the lower underparts are whitish. The large eyes are dark and highlighted by a light eye ring.
• Sexes are alike.
• Size 16cm (6¼in).

COMMON NIGHTINGALE
Luscinia megarhynchos

Common nightingales are known for their beautiful singing, and in Europe their arrival is seen as heralding the spring. However, these birds are often difficult to spot, since they utter their musical calls towards dusk and even after dark on moonlit nights.

Their relatively large eyes indicate that these members of the thrush family are crepuscular, becoming active around dusk. Their drab, subdued coloration enables them to blend easily into the dense shrubbery or woodland vegetation that they favour. They are only present in Europe from April to September, when they breed, before heading back to Africa for the winter months.

GARDEN PREDATORS

Kestrels, peregrine falcons and sparrowhawks are agile aerial predators. These opportunistic birds of prey rely on strength and speed to overcome their prey, which frequently includes garden birds. Buzzards are bulkier, with hooked bills and powerful talons. They target small mammals as well as birds.

KESTRELS
Common kestrel *Falco tinnunculus*

These common birds of prey can frequently be seen hovering at the side of busy roads, largely undisturbed by the traffic close by. Roadsides provide them with good hunting opportunities, and their keen eyesight enables them to spot even quite small quarry such as grasshoppers on the ground. They also hunt songbirds in parks and gardens, including in towns. In the winter, they may resort to hunting earthworms that have been drawn to the surface by heavy rainfall.

FACT FILE
Habitat Open countryside.
Nest Platform of sticks in a tree or agricultural buildings.
Eggs 3–7, pale pink, brown markings.
Food Invertebrates, small mammals and birds.
Distribution Throughout western Europe to South-east Asia and North Africa. Also breeds in Scandinavia.

IDENTIFICATION
• Bluish-grey head, black stripe under eyes, whitish throat. Dense black spotting on pale brownish chest, extending to abdomen. Wings chestnut-brown, black markings. Rump and tail feathers grey, black tips.
• Hens similar but browner heads and barring across the tail feathers.
• Size 37cm (14½in).

PEREGRINE FALCON
Falco peregrinus

Peregrine falcons are powerful aerial predators, swooping down incredibly quickly on unsuspecting birds from above. Indeed, it is thought that they can dive at speeds of up to 350kmh (217mph).

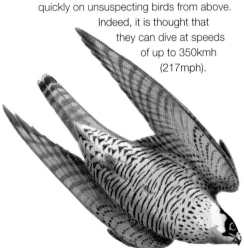

The impact made by their feet when they strike is so great that their quarry is frequently killed instantaneously. Pigeons are generally favoured as prey, although these falcons also hunt waterfowl and songbirds.

Peregrine falcons are highly adaptable hunters and can very occasionally be sighted in cities, where apartment blocks replace the crags from which they would normally fly on hunting excursions. They are one of the most widely distributed birds of prey, occurring on all continents.

FACT FILE
Habitat Near cliffs, open ground.
Nest Cliff ledges.
Eggs 3–4, whitish, red-brown markings.
Food Birds.
Distribution Most of western Europe and Africa, except Sahara and central rainforest. Occur on all continents.

IDENTIFICATION
• Dark grey upperparts. Broad blackish stripe extends below each eye, surrounding white area extends around throat. Barring on chest lighter than on abdomen. Darker markings on grey feathers of back and wings. Tail is barred, with paler grey feathering at base. Yellow feet.
• Hens much larger than male birds.
• Size 38–51cm (15–20¼in).

SPARROWHAWK
Eurasian sparrowhawk *Accipiter nisus*

These hawks favour preying on ground-feeding birds, and males generally take smaller quarry than females, reflecting the difference in their respective sizes. Even females rarely take birds much larger than pigeons, although they will prey on thrushes.

Pairs nest later in the year than many garden birds, so there are plenty of nestlings to prey on and feed to their own chicks. Sparrowhawks have short wings and are very agile in flight, able to manoeuvre easily in wooded areas. They approach quietly with the aim of catching their target unawares, seizing their prey using their powerful clawed feet.

Right: *Young male sparrowhawks fledge several days before their heavier sisters.*

COMMON BUZZARD
Eurasian buzzard *Buteo buteo*

With its rather broad and stocky appearance, the common buzzard's silhouette in flight helps to confirm its identity. Buzzards are capable of soaring for long periods, before suddenly swooping down to seize a rabbit or songbird. They also take the nestlings of garden and woodland birds.

Buzzards can sometimes be observed hunting invertebrates, walking purposefully on the ground in search of their quarry. They may occasionally be spotted on roads too, feeding on road kill, even placing themselves in danger from the passing traffic.

However, buzzards remain one of the most common raptors in Europe, thanks largely to their adaptable feeding habits.

FLYCATCHERS AND INSECT-EATERS

Invertebrates provide nuthatches, creepers and flycatchers with much of their diet, while some also eat other foods – for example, nuts in the case of nuthatches. These insect-hunters use various techniques to capture prey, some combing the bark of trees, while others hunt in the air or on the ground.

EURASIAN NUTHATCH
Sitta europaea

With relatively large, strong feet and very powerful claws, Eurasian nuthatches are adept at scampering up and down tree trunks. They hunt for invertebrates, which they extract from the bark with their narrow bills, but their powerful beaks also enable them to feed on nuts. The nuthatches first wedge the nut into a suitable crevice in the bark, then hammer at the shell, breaking it open so they can extract the kernel. They will also store nuts, which they will eat when other food is in short supply.

These birds are hole-nesters, including in birdhouses. The bill is also used to plaster over the entrance of their nest in spring, until the opening is just large enough to allow the adult birds to squeeze in and out. This helps to protect the young from predators.

Eurasian nuthatches are most likely to be encountered in areas with broad-leaved trees, as these provide food such as acorns and hazelnuts.

FACT FILE
Habitat Mature trees.
Nest In a secluded spot or nest box.
Eggs 6–9, white with heavy reddish-brown speckling.
Food Invertebrates, nuts and seeds.
Distribution Most of Europe, except Ireland, northern England, Scotland and northern Scandinavia. Northern Africa opposite the Strait of Gibraltar.

IDENTIFICATION
• Bluish-grey upperparts.
• Black stripes running from the base of the bill down the sides of the head, encompassing the eyes.
• Underparts vary from white to rusty buff, depending on the race.
• Dark reddish-brown vent area, more brightly coloured in cocks.
• Size 14cm (5½in).

EURASIAN TREECREEPER
Brown creeper *Certhia familiaris*

With relatively large, strong feet and very powerful claws, Eurasian nuthatches are adept at scampering up and down tree trunks. They hunt for invertebrates, which they extract from the bark with their narrow bills, but their powerful beaks also enable them to feed on nuts. The nuthatches first wedge the nut into a suitable crevice in the bark, then hammer at the shell, breaking it open so they can extract the kernel. They will also store nuts, which they will eat when other food is in short supply.

These birds are hole-nesters, including in birdhouses. The bill is also used to plaster over the entrance of their nest in spring, until the opening is just large enough to allow the adult birds to squeeze in and out. This helps to protect the young from predators.

Eurasian nuthatches are most likely to be encountered in areas with broad-leaved trees, as these provide food such as acorns and hazelnuts.

Right: A small crevice in a tree trunk may be used as a nesting site.

FACT FILE
Habitat Dense woodland.
Nest Small hollow.
Eggs 5–7, white with reddish-brown markings.
Food Assorted invertebrates.
Distribution Much of northern Europe, except for the far north of Scandinavia. Sporadic distribution through France and northern Spain. Not present in northern Africa, but range extends eastwards into Asia.

IDENTIFICATION
• Mottled brownish upperparts, variable white stripe above eyes.
• Underparts whitish.
• Narrow, curved bill.
• Sexes are alike. The young are similar to adults.
• Size 14cm (5½in).

PIED FLYCATCHER
Ficedula hypoleuca

FACT FILE

Habitat Where insects are common.

Nest Hole in a tree or nest box.

Eggs 5–9, pale blue.

Food Invertebrates.

Distribution Summer visitor to Europe. Breeding range extends throughout virtually all of Europe except the far north of Scandinavia. Overwinters in Africa north of a line from coastal Nigeria to Djibouti.

IDENTIFICATION

• Cock's summer plumage: white patches above the bill and on the wings. White underparts. The remaining plumage is black.

• Hens: have whitish underparts and white areas on the wings, while their upperparts are brownish.

• Cocks in non-breeding plumage: resemble adult hens, but retain the blackish wings and uppertail coverts.

• Size 13cm (5¼in).

Pied flycatchers are summer visitors to British gardens with mature trees. These flycatchers hawk insects in flight, and will also catch slower-moving prey such as caterpillars by plucking them off vegetation. They can be seen in oak woodlands and nearby gardens in summer. In Europe, these birds may range north to the taiga, where mosquitoes hatching in pools of water during the brief Arctic summer provide an almost constant supply of food. They nest in tree holes and will also use nest boxes. Pied flycatchers are closely related to collared flycatchers (*F. albicollis*), and the two species may sometimes hybridize.

SPOTTED FLYCATCHER
Muscicapa striata

FACT FILE

Habitat Open woodland, woodland edges, parks, large gardens.

Nest Cup-shaped, made of twigs, moss and grass.

Eggs 4–5, buff to greenish with red-brown markings.

Food Flying insects.

Distribution Breeds throughout most of Europe; Britain May–September. Breeding grounds extend east into Asia, south to North Africa. Overwinters south of the Sahara.

IDENTIFICATION

• Greyish-brown upperparts, with darker streaking on the largish head extending to whitish underparts. The area above the bill is also white.

• Relatively long wings. Long, square-tipped tail that can be spread to aid hovering. Blackish bill, legs and feet.

• Sexes are alike. Young birds have dull yellowish markings from the head over the wings, rump and tail.

• Size 15cm (6in).

As its name suggests, this species feeds itself and its young on insects – not only flies, but also aphids, butterflies, and even bees and wasps, whose stings must be first removed. It catches insects in mid-air, swooping from a perch in a tree to chase its prey with an erratic flight. Hovering briefly on long, slender wings to seize victims, it returns to the perch. It moves to a different perch when most of the insects in one area have been taken, only to return later to try its luck again.

This species is one of the last migrants to arrive from Africa, appearing in late May, when it builds its nest of grass, twigs and moss bound with cobwebs in a tree crevice, old nest, open-fronted nest box or on a creeper-covered wall. Its breeding is timed to coincide with the hottest time of year when there will be most insects to feed the young.

In more recent years the spotted flycatcher has suffered a notable decline, probably due to drought in its African wintering grounds.

With its cryptic coloration, this bird is easiest recognized by its relatively large head, upright position on the perch, and insect-catching behaviour. Its quiet song, a series of thin squeaks, is rarely noticed.

SWIFTS, SWALLOWS AND MARTINS

These birds spend most of their lives in flight. They undertake long journeys, migrating south to Africa in autumn, and returning to breed the following spring. Pairs frequently return to the same nest site they occupied previously – a remarkable feat of navigation after a journey covering thousands of kilometres.

SWIFT
Common swift *Apus apus*

Common summer visitors, swifts nest on buildings and sometimes in specialized nest boxes. They are most noticeable when uttering their distinctive, screaming calls, flying low overhead in search of winged insects. At other times they may appear as little more than distant specks in the sky, wheeling around at heights of 1,000m (3,300ft) or more. Their flight pattern is quite distinctive, consisting of a series of rapid wingbeats followed by gliding into the wind. Their tiny feet do not allow them to perch, although they can cling to vertical surfaces.

Except when breeding, swifts spend their entire lives in the air, and are apparently able to sleep and mate in flight too. If hunting conditions are unfavourable, such as in a cool summer, nestling swifts respond by growing more slowly.

FACT FILE
Habitat In the air.
Nest Cup-shaped, built under cover.
Eggs 2–3, white.
Food Flying invertebrates, such as midges and moths.
Distribution Found across virtually the whole of Europe, extending to northern Africa and Asia. Overwinters in southern Africa.

IDENTIFICATION
• This species is dark sooty brown overall, with relatively long, pointed wings. They have a pale whitish throat.
• Tail is slightly forked, but not as much as a swallow's.
• Brown legs and a short, black, thin beak.
• Sexes are alike.
• Size 16.5cm (6½in).

SWALLOW
Barn swallow *Hirundo rustica*

The swallows' return to their European breeding grounds is one of the most welcome signs of spring. They are seen mainly in the countryside and rural gardens. Although pairs return to the same nest site every year, they do not migrate together. Cock birds arrive back before their partners and jealously guard the site from would-be rivals. Cocks fight with surprising ferocity if one of the birds does not back down. Although swallows may use nesting sites such as caves, they more commonly nest inside buildings such as barns, choosing a site close to the eaves. It can take up to a thousand trips to collect enough damp mud, carried back in the bill, to complete a new nest.

FACT FILE
Habitat Open country, close to water.
Nest Made of mud, built off the ground.
Eggs 4–5, white with reddish-and-grey spotting.
Food Flying invertebrates.
Distribution Throughout virtually the entire Northern Hemisphere. European populations overwinter in Africa south of the Sahara.

IDENTIFICATION
• Chestnut forehead and throat, dark blue head and back, and a narrow dark blue band across the chest. The wings are blackish and the underparts are white. Long tail streamers.
• Sexes are alike.
• Size 19cm (7½in).

HOUSE MARTIN
Delichon urbica

House martins are a familiar sight in gardens both in the town and the countryside in summer. The breeding habits of this species have changed significantly due to an increase in the number of buildings in rural areas. They traditionally nested on cliff-faces, but over the past century began to prefer the walls of houses and farm structures as sites, as well as beneath bridges and even on street lamps, where a ready supply of nocturnal insects are attracted to the light.

The nest is usually spherical and normally made of mud. The base is built first, followed by the sides. On average, the whole process can take up to two weeks to complete.

House martins are highly social by nature, nesting in huge colonies made up of thousands of pairs where conditions are suitable. Even outside the breeding period, they sometimes associate in large flocks comprising of hundreds of individuals.

SAND MARTIN
African sand martin, bank swallow
Riparia riparia

Sand martins are migrants, and the first members of their group to arrive in Britain in spring. They are most often to be observed in gardens in the vicinity of lakes and other stretches of water, where they forage for food, frequently swooping down over the surface to catch flying insects. They are most likely to be nesting in colonies nearby, in tunnels excavated in suitable sandy banks or into soft rock. These burrows can extend up to 1m (3ft) into the bank, with the nesting chamber at the end being lined with grass, seaweed and similar material. The eggs are laid on a soft bed of feathers.

Once the young martins leave the nest, they stay in groups with other chicks, waiting for their parents to return and feed them. The adults typically bring around 60 invertebrates back from each hunting expedition. Parents recognize their own offspring by their distinctive calls.

If danger threatens, the repetitive alarm calls of the adult sand martins cause the young to rush back into their nesting tunnels for protection.

This species can be identified by its weak-seeming, fluttery flight pattern and by its low, rasping or chattering call.

WOODPECKERS

Few groups of birds are more closely associated with woodlands than woodpeckers. They are well-equipped to thrive there, using their powerful bills as tools to obtain food and also create nesting chambers. However, not all are exclusively arboreal, since some species forage for food on the ground.

GREAT SPOTTED WOODPECKER

Dendrocopus major

Great spotted woodpeckers can be found in both coniferous and deciduous woodland, and in gardens where the trees are mature enough for the birds to excavate nesting chambers. Their powerful bills enable them to extract grubs hidden under bark and to wrest the seeds from pine cones – the birds use tree holes as vices to hold the cones fast. They also visit gardens to peck from feeders and to forage at bird tables, especially in winter.

FACT FILE
Habitat Woodland.
Nest Tree hollow.
Eggs 5–7, white.
Food Invertebrates, eggs and seeds.
Distribution Most of Europe except for Ireland, northern Scandinavia and much of south-eastern Europe. Also in North Africa. Ranges into Asia.

IDENTIFICATION
• Black top to head. Black areas also from sides of the bill around neck, linking with red area at back of head.
• Wings and upperside of tail mostly black, white area on wings and white barring on flight feathers. Underside of tail mostly white. Red around vent.
• Hens: similar to males but lack the red on the hindcrown.
• Size 25cm (10in).

LESSER SPOTTED WOODPECKER

Dendrocopus minor

The smallest of the three woodpeckers seen in Britain, the lesser spotted is not much larger than a robin. Its small size and shy, secretive habits mean that its presence often goes unnoticed. A bird of woodlands and large gardens with mature trees, it lives higher in trees than other woodpeckers. There, it hides among the foliage of the crown and circles the bark in the manner of a treecreeper, searching for insect food.

Two-thirds the size of the great spotted, it shares its cousin's pied plumage, with even more extensive barring on the wings and back. However, the barring is somewhat blurred. Unlike other woodpeckers it is very seldom seen on lawns, bird feeders or in the open generally. It produces a weaker drumming sound than the great spotted, and its high-pitched,

peevish-sounding call is also weaker. The flight pattern is undulating.

Lesser spotted woodpeckers breed between March and June, having excavated a nest hole high in a tree, where the female lays a single clutch of eggs.

FACT FILE
Habitat Woodland.
Nest Tree hole
Eggs 4–6, white.
Food Invertebrates: insects, grubs.
Distribution Most of Europe except for Iceland, Ireland, northern Britain and much of Spain and Portugal. Also present south into Algeria and Tunisia, and eastwards into Asia.

IDENTIFICATION
• Largish head mostly white with black stripes on sides of face, and buff around bill.
• Males have a red area on crown; hens have black cap. Black wings have white barring, tail is black. Underparts predominantly white with black streaking, reddish area around vent.
• Size 16cm (6¼in).

EURASIAN GREEN WOODPECKER
Picus viridis

Unlike many of its kind, green woodpeckers hunt for food mainly on the ground, using their powerful bills and long tongues to break open ants' nests. They are equally equipped to prey on earthworms, which are drawn to the surface of garden lawns after rain, and may catch small creatures such as lizards. In the autumn, fruit forms a more significant part of their diet, but they avoid seeds, and so are not drawn to bird feeders.

Pairing begins during the winter, with excavation of the nesting chamber taking two weeks to a month to complete. Unlike many woodpeckers they do not drum loudly with their bills to advertise their presence, but pairs can be quite vocal. Incubation is shared, with the hen sitting during the day. Hatching takes just over a fortnight, with the young fledging when a month old.

EURASIAN WRYNECK
Jynx torquilla

Once found throughout Britain, the wryneck has declined dramatically, and now breeds only in Scotland. A woodland bird, it is a hole-nester which will take to using nest boxes. It appears in gardens in other parts of Britain only when blown off course on its way to or from its African wintering grounds. Wrynecks return to their breeding grounds by April, when pairs are very territorial. They seek a suitable hollow, which may be in a tree, on the ground or in a bank. When displaying, pairs face each other and shake their heads, opening their bills to reveal pink gapes.

The two-week incubation is shared, and both adults care for their young, who fledge after three weeks. They are independent in a further two weeks. Two broods may be reared. If disturbed on the nest, a sitting adult will stretch out its head and neck, before suddenly withdrawing it, hissing like a snake. Wrynecks use their long, sticky tongues to rapidly pick up ants and other invertebrates, such as spiders.

WAGTAILS AND PIPITS

Small and relatively slender birds with long tails, most wagtails and pipits are mainly insect-hunters, while pied wagtails also take molluscs and some seeds. Pied wagtails and tree pipits are birds of open countryside. Grey wagtails and particularly water pipits are notable for living and breeding close to water.

GREY WAGTAIL
Motacilla cinerea

Grey wagtails are most likely to be observed in gardens near fast-flowing streams and rivers, where they dart fearlessly across rocks in search of invertebrates. They live in pairs and construct their cup-shaped nest in a well-concealed locality, usually close to water and sometimes in among the roots of a tree or an ivy-clad wall.

These birds have benefited from some changes in their environment, taking advantage of millstreams and adjacent buildings to expand their area of distribution, but they can still be forced to leave their territory in search of food in severe winters, especially if the water freezes.

FACT FILE
Habitat Near flowing water.
Nest In rock crevices and similar.
Eggs 4–6, buff, greyish markings.
Food Invertebrates, and occasionally small fish and amphibians.
Distribution Most of western Europe, except Scandinavia. Also in North Africa and Asia.

IDENTIFICATION
• Grey head and wings, narrow white band with black beneath running across eyes. White border to black bib on throat. Underparts yellow, brightest on chest and tail base.
• Sexes similar but hens have a grey or greyish-white bib and much whiter underparts. Darker feathering disappears from the throat in winter.
• Size 20cm (8in).

PIED WAGTAIL
Motacilla alba

These lively birds are commonly seen in both rural and urban gardens, having adapted well to changes in their environment. Once birds of coastal areas and marshlands, they are now seen in farmland, and even hunting on and beside roads. Pied wagtails are not especially shy birds, and the movements of their tail feathers, which give them their common name, strike an unmistakable jaunty pose.

The race that breeds in the British Isles is different from that observed elsewhere in Europe as cocks have black plumage on their backs during the summer. This area turns to grey for the rest of the year. The mainland European form is often described as the white wagtail as these birds have a greyish back for the whole year.

FACT FILE
Habitat Open areas.
Nest Concealed, sometimes in walls.
Eggs 5–6, whitish with grey markings.
Food Invertebrates.
Distribution Europe and western North Africa; winter distribution there more widespread. Scandinavia, Iceland and Asia in summer.

IDENTIFICATION
• Variable through range. Prominent white area on head with black crown and nape. Black area extends from throat down on to chest. The remainder of underparts are white.
• Grey or black back depending on where the wagtail is from.
• Hens: more ashy-grey backs, smudged border with feathers above.
• Size 19cm (7½in).

TREE PIPIT
Anthus trivialis

Habitat Woodland.
Nest Made of grass.
Eggs 4–6, greyish, variable markings.
Food Mainly invertebrates.
Distribution Widely through Europe up into Scandinavia and into Asia. Overwinters across Africa south of the Sahara, continuing down the eastern side, isolated populations in Namibia and South Africa.

IDENTIFICATION
• Brownish upperparts with dark streaking. White edging to wing feathers. Buff stripe above eyes, darker brown stripes through and below. Throat whitish. Underparts pale yellowish with brownish streaking. Bill dark, especially at tip. Legs and feet pinkish.
• Sexes are alike. Young birds are more buff overall.
• Size 15cm (6in).

Tree pipits sing with increasing frequency at the start of the breeding period. These summer visitors are most likely to be seen in rural gardens. Their nest is built close to the ground in open countryside, hidden from predators. This need for camouflage may explain the variable coloration of the eggs. Long-distance migrants, they overwinter in Africa, reaching the south towards the end of October.

Tree pipits feed on the ground, moving jauntily and pausing to flick their tails up and down, flying to the safety of a nearby branch at any hint of danger. As well as invertebrates, tree pipits also eat seeds.

These solitary, quiet birds are not easily observed away from their breeding grounds. They begin returning to Europe in April.

WATER PIPIT
Anthus spinoletta

FACT FILE
Habitat Overwinters by marshes and still-water areas. Nests by streams in mountainous areas.
Nest Made of vegetation.
Eggs 3–5, greenish with darker markings.
Food Largely insectivorous.
Distribution Southern England and much of western Europe, extending to the northern African coast and into South-east Asia.

IDENTIFICATION
• In breeding plumage, white stripe above the eye, a white throat with a distinctly pinkish tone to the breast, and a white abdomen. Slight streaking evident on the flanks. The head is greyish and the back and wings are brownish.
• During winter, breast becomes whitish with obvious streaking. Wings lighter brown overall. Regional variations apply. Sexes are alike.
• Size 17cm (6¾in).

These aquatic pipits are lively birds, and are sometimes encountered in small flocks. They undertake regular seasonal movements, nesting at higher altitudes in the spring, where they often frequent fast-flowing streams. Pairs nest nearby, choosing a well-concealed location. Subsequently they retreat to lower altitudes for the winter months, sometimes moving into areas of cultivation, such as watercress beds in southern Britain. At this time they are most likely to be seen in gardens near coasts and wetlands, where they search the lawn for invertebrates, but quickly retreat to cover should there be any hint of danger.

Their song is attractive, and rather similar to that of the closely related rock pipit (*A. petrosus*), with studies of their song pattern revealing regional variations between different populations. Water pipits, like others of their kind, often utter their song in flight, and this is most likely to be heard at the start of the nesting period.

PHEASANTS, PIGEONS AND DOVES

Introduced and bred for sport, pheasants are game birds. Pigeons and doves have adapted well to living alongside people, although their presence is sometimes unwelcome. Large flocks of feral pigeons now inhabit urban areas. Their adaptability is shown by their ability to breed through much of the year.

COMMON PHEASANT
Ring-necked pheasant *Phasianus colchicus*

Common pheasants occur naturally in Asia. Introduced to Europe by the Romans, they have been widely bred and released for shooting – it is one of the world's most hunted birds – and are now commonly seen in British gardens, including in towns, especially in autumn and winter.

Common pheasants usually live in small groups comprised of a cock bird with several hens. They forage on the ground, flying noisily and somewhat clumsily when disturbed, and may choose to roost off the ground.

Right: *Mottled plumage provides the pheasant hen with good camouflage.*

FACT FILE
Habitat Light woodland.
Nest Scrape on the ground.
Eggs 7–15, olive-brown.
Food Plant matter, invertebrates.
Distribution Most of western Europe, except much of Spain and Portugal. In a band east across central Asia to Japan. Also USA, Australia and New Zealand.

IDENTIFICATION
• Cock: red skin on sides of face, surrounded by metallic dark green plumage. Variable white area at base of neck. Remainder brown, underparts chestnut with dark blotches.
• Hens lighter brown, with darker mottling on back and wings.
• Size cock 89cm (35½in); hen 62cm (24¾in).

COLLARED DOVE
Streptopelia decaocto

The collared dove only appeared in north-western Europe in the 1940s. Since then their spread has been dramatic, to the extent that they are now a common sight in British gardens. These birds were recorded in Hungary in the 1930s, and then moved rapidly over the next decade west across Austria and Germany to France, and also north to the Netherlands and Denmark. The species was first sighted in eastern England during 1952, and a pair bred there three years later. The earliest Irish record was reported in 1959, and by the mid-1960s the collared dove had colonized almost all of the UK.

No other bird species has spread so far and so rapidly in recent times, to the extent that the collared dove's range now extends right across Europe and Asia.

Above: *The collared dove is a frequent visitor to towns and cities, where it will happily construct its nest on the rooftops.*

FACT FILE
Habitat Parks and gardens.
Nest Platform of twigs.
Eggs 2, white.
Food Mostly seeds and plant matter.
Distribution Much of Europe excluding far north of Scandinavia and the Alps, ranging into Asia. More localized on the Iberian Peninsula and in northern Africa particularly.

IDENTIFICATION
• Pale greyish-fawn with narrow black half-collar around back of neck.
• Dark flight feathers, with white along the leading edges of the wings. White tips to tail feathers, visible when spread. Depth of individual coloration can vary.
• Sexes are alike.
• Size 34cm (13½in).

FERAL PIGEON (ROCK DOVE)
Columba livia

True rock doves have a localized range, favouring cliffs and ruined buildings as breeding sites. In the past, these doves were kept and bred by monastic communities, where the young doves (known as squabs) were highly valued as a source of meat.

Inevitably, some birds escaped from their dovecotes and reverted to the wild, and their offspring gave rise to today's ubiquitous feral pigeons, which are a common sight in gardens and streets in almost every town and

Left: *The rock dove nests on loose twigs.*

city, scavenging whatever they can from our leftovers. Colour mutations have also occurred, and as well as the so-called 'blue' form there are now red and even mainly white individuals.

WOOD PIGEON
Columba palumbus

Wood pigeons are one of the most common large birds seen in British gardens. They are often observed pecking on the lawn or drinking from birdbaths. In towns they frequent parks with stands of trees,

descending into nearby gardens and allotments to raid growing crops. These pigeons can be significant agricultural pests in arable farming areas. However, they also occasionally eat crop pests such as snails.

Pairs sometimes nest on buildings, although they usually prefer a suitable tree fork. Their calls are surprisingly loud and are often heard soon after dawn. Outside the breeding season these birds will often congregate in large numbers. If danger threatens, they can appear quite clumsy when taking off thanks to their relatively large size.

OWLS AND NIGHT-TIME HUNTERS

More likely to be heard rather than seen, owls and the nightjar become more active after dark. Nightjars feed on night-flying insects, while the diet of most owls includes rodents. It is possible to determine the diet of owls by examining their pellets, which are the indigestible remains of their prey.

TAWNY OWL
Strix aluco

The distinctive double call notes of these owls reveal their presence, even though their dark coloration makes them difficult to spot. Tawny owls prefer ancient woodland and nearby gardens, where trees are large enough to provide hollow nesting cavities. They will, however, often adapt to using nest boxes, which has helped to increase their numbers.

Nocturnal by nature, these owls may nevertheless occasionally also hunt during the daytime, especially when they have chicks in the nest. They usually sit quietly on a perch, waiting to swoop down on their quarry.

Young tawny owls are unable to fly when they first leave the nest, and during this vulnerable time the adults can become very aggressive in protecting their offspring from any threats.

FACT FILE
Habitat Favours ancient woodland.
Nest Tree hole.
Eggs 2–9, white.
Food Small mammals, birds and invertebrates.
Distribution Across Europe (not Ireland) to Scandinavia and eastwards into Asia. Also occurs in North Africa.

IDENTIFICATION
• Tawny-brown, white markings across wings and darker striations over wings and body. Slight barring on tail. White stripes above almost plain brown facial disc. Some have a greyer tone to their plumage, others more rufous. Bill is yellowish-brown.
• Sexes similar, females larger and heavier, higher-pitched song.
• Size 43cm (17¼in).

LITTLE OWL
Athene noctua

Little owls can be seen resting during the daytime, on telegraph poles and similar perches in the open. Introduced to Britain in the 1800s, they have since spread right across southern England, where they venture into gardens near farmland. They hover in flight, but are rather ungainly when walking on the ground.

One factor that has assisted their spread is their adaptability in choosing a nest site – disused factories and even rabbit warrens may be used.

The hen sits alone during incubation, which lasts 24 days. Both adults feed the young, who fledge after five weeks, and are independent of their parents in a further two months.

FACT FILE
Habitat Prefers relatively open country.
Nest Tree hole or a cliff hole.
Eggs 3–5, white.
Food Invertebrates, small vertebrates.
Distribution Southern Britain, most of Europe at a similar latitude (not as far as Scandinavia) into Asia. Northern Africa, to parts of Middle East.

IDENTIFICATION
• White spotting on head, white above eyes, whitish moustache. Heavy brown streaking on white chest. Larger whiter spots on wings, barring on flight feathers and banding across tail. Whitish legs and feet. Bill yellowish, irides yellow.
• Young lack white spotting on forehead. Sexes alike, hens larger.
• Size 25cm (10in).

BARN OWL
Tyto alba

Barn owls seek out dark places in which to roost, using buildings. They may be seen in gardens near open country or swooping over farmland, and will sometimes nest in large oblong boxes placed high in outhouses. Males in particular will often utter harsh screeches when in flight, which serve as territorial markers, while females make a distinctive snoring sound for food at the nest site.

They pair for life, which can be more than 20 years. Barn owls have adapted to hunting along roadside verges, but here they are in danger of being hit by vehicles.

NIGHTJAR
European nightjar *Caprimulgus europaeus*

Nightjars are regular summertime visitors to heathlands and nearby gardens in Britain, but their small size and cryptic coloration mean that they are seldom noticed. Perhaps even more significantly, these birds are nocturnal by nature, which makes them extremely difficult to observe. However, they have very distinctive calls, likened both to the croaking of a frog and to the noise of a machine, which are uttered for long periods and can carry over a distance of 1km (⅝ mile).

During the daytime, nightjars spend much of their time resting on the ground, where their mottled plumage provides them with excellent camouflage, especially in woodland areas. Additionally, they narrow their eyes to slits, which makes them even less conspicuous.

Nightjars are sufficiently agile in flight to catch moths and other nocturnal invertebrates, flying silently and trawling with their large gapes open. If food is plentiful, breeding pairs of nightjars may rear two broods in succession, before beginning the long journey south again to reach their African wintering grounds.

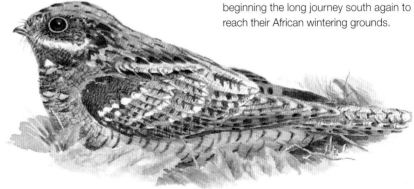

RARE VISITORS AND INTRODUCTIONS

Hoopoes and spoonbills are rare but welcome visitors to Britain during the summer months. The latter recently nested for the first time in 300 years. Red-legged partridges were introduced for sport, while ring-necked parakeets arrived as cage birds, but populations of both now exist in the wild.

HOOPOE

Eurasian hoopoe *Upupa epops*

Hoopoes are occasional visitors to gardens near farmland in southern England, especially in spring and summer. The distinctive appearance of these birds helps to identify them with ease. When in flight, the broad shape of the wings is clearly visible and the tall crest is held flat over the back of the head. Hoopoes often raise their crest on landing. They use their long bills to probe for worms in the ground, or grab insects scurrying through the grass. They can also often be observed dust-bathing, which keeps their plumage in good condition. Hoopoes are not especially shy of people, and pairs will sometimes nest in buildings. Their common name is derived from the sound of their 'hoo, hoo' call.

Left: *The black-and-white barring is shown to best effect in flight.*

FACT FILE
Habitat Open country.
Nest Secluded hole.
Eggs 5–8, whitish to yellowish-olive.
Food Mainly invertebrates, especially worms, also lizards.
Distribution Most of Europe, sometimes appearing in Britain. Overwinters in Africa south of the equator. Also occurs in parts of Africa, and extends east to the Arabian Peninsula and across Asia.

IDENTIFICATION
• Mainly pale buff, but more orange on crown and black edging to the feathers. Alternate bands of black-and-white coloration on the wings. Long, narrow, downward-curving bill.
• Sexes are alike.
• Size 29cm (11½in).

RING-NECKED PARAKEET

Rose-ringed parakeet *Psittacula krameri*

The ring-necked parakeet is the most widely distributed member of the parrot family in the world. Found naturally across Asia and Africa, flocks of these birds first appeared in Great Britain in the 1960s, having bred from escaped captive birds. These distinctive birds are now regularly seen in gardens and parks in cities all across Britain, from the south-east of England where they were initially most common to many other parts of the country – well outside their natural range.

This adaptable species in its natural habitat is usually observed in farmland and woodland. Historically, the spread of agriculture in Africa and Asia led to an increased food supply which helped these birds to expand their distribution to urban gardens and parks, too.

Ring-necked parakeets fly quite high, often in small groups, and their distinctive, screeching calls carry over long distances. These are unmistakable parakeets, especially when silhouetted in flight, with their long, tapering tails streaming behind their bodies.

FACT FILE
Habitat Light woodland.
Nest Tree cavity high off the ground, sometimes on a rocky ledge.
Eggs 3–6, white.
Food Cereals, fruit, seeds.
Distribution Across Africa in a band south of the Sahara. Eastwards through the Arabian Peninsula and across Asia to China. Widely in UK.

IDENTIFICATION
• The African race (*P. k. krameri*) has black on the bill and is more yellowish-green than the Asiatic form (*Psittacula k. manillensis*) (illustrated), which is now widespread across the UK.
• Hens and young birds of both sexes lack the distinctive black and pink neck collar seen in cocks.
• Size 40cm (16in).

EURASIAN SPOONBILL
Platalea leucorodia

A rare sight but has been spotted. The enlarged surface area of these birds' bills enables them to feed more easily as they move their heads from side to side in the water. Young spoonbills, however, have a much narrower, light-coloured bill with no enlargement at the tip. They can also be identified in flight by the black tips to their outer flight feathers. It may be up to four years before they start nesting. Spoonbills can swim if they need to, but usually prefer to inhabit calm, shallow stretches of water. When resting, they may perch on one leg and tuck their bills over their backs, but while in flight they will extend their necks. They can live for nearly 30 years.

RED-LEGGED PARTRIDGE
Alectoris rufa

The red-legged partridge was brought to England as long ago as the late 1600s for shooting, and its adaptable nature ensured that its range steadily expanded. It is now widely seen in arable farmland and nearby gardens. However, during the 20th century the chukar partridge, which hybridizes with the red-legged variety, was also introduced to Britain.

Today, it can be difficult to determine whether partridges are pure or cross-bred red-legged individuals, thanks to their similarity in appearance to chukars.

Red-legged partidges form individual pairs when breeding. The cock bird chooses and then prepares the nest site.

SEABIRDS AND DUCKS

Gulls are linked in many people's minds with the seaside, but some species have adjusted to living alongside people, and generally profiting from the association. A number of gulls have now spread inland. Ducks are usually freshwater birds whose appearance and distribution can differ through the year.

COMMON GULL
Mew gull *Larus canus*

Common gulls often range inland over considerable distances, searching for earthworms and other invertebrates to feed on. In sandy coastal areas they will seek out shellfish as well. There is a distinct seasonal variation in the range of these gulls. At the end of the summer they leave their Scandinavian and Russian breeding grounds and head farther south in Europe, to France and various other locations in the Mediterranean. Here, they overwinter before migrating north again in the spring.

In spite of its rather meek appearance, this species will bully smaller gulls and garden birds to steal food from them. When venturing inland, common gulls show a preference for agricultural areas and grassland, but they will also enter domestic gardens in search of food.

FACT FILE
Habitat Coasts and inland areas close to water.
Nest Raised nest of twigs, debris.
Eggs 2–3, pale blue to brownish-olive in colour, with dark markings.
Food Shellfish, fish, invertebrates.
Distribution Iceland and Europe. Breeding grounds in Scandinavia and Russia, Asia to western North America.

IDENTIFICATION
• White head and underparts with yellow bill and yellowish-green legs. Wings greyish with white markings at tips. Flight feathers black with white spots. White tail. Dark eyes. Greyish streaking on head in winter plumage.
• Sexes are alike. Young birds have brown mottled plumage until age two.
• Size 46cm (18¼in)

BLACK-HEADED GULL
Larus ridibundus

These gulls are a common sight not only in coastal areas but also in parks and gardens with or near lakes and large ponds, including in cities. They move inland during winter, where they can often be seen following ploughing tractors searching for worms and grubs in the soil.

Above: The black feathering on the head is a transient characteristic, appearing only in the summer (far right).

Black-headed gulls nest close to water in what can be quite large colonies. Like many gulls, they are noisy birds, even calling at night. On warm, summer evenings they can sometimes be seen hawking flying ants and similar insects in flight, demonstrating their airborne agility.

FACT FILE
Habitat Woodland, farmland.
Nest Loose cup shape, straw or grass.
Eggs 3–6, buff with dark spots.
Food Seeds, grains, buds, invertebrates.
Distribution Breeds in Europe except northern Scandinavia, east England, north Scotland and central Ireland.

IDENTIFICATION
• Throughout summer, this gull has a distinctive black head with a white collar beneath and white underparts. Wings are grey and flight feathers mainly black.
• In winter, head is mainly white except for black ear coverts and a black smudge above each eye. The bill is red at its base and dark at the tip.
• Size 39cm (15½in).

HERRING GULL
Larus argentatus

These large gulls are often seen on fishing jetties and around harbours, searching for scraps. They have also moved inland and can be seen in areas such as rubbish dumps, where they scavenge for food, often in quite large groups.

Herring gulls are noisy by nature, especially when breeding. They frequently nest on rooftops in coastal towns and cities, a trend that began in Britain as recently as the 1940s.

Pairs can be very aggressive at breeding time, swooping menacingly on people or animals who venture too close to the nest site (and even including their chicks once they have fledged).

Above: *The herring gull's pink legs are a distinctive feature.*

FACT FILE
Habitat Coasts and inland.
Nest Small pile of vegetation.
Eggs 2–3, pale blue to brown with darker markings.
Food Fish and carrion.
Distribution Northern Atlantic including north of Iceland and south to northern Africa and the Mediterranean. Also in the North Sea and Baltic areas to northern Scandinavia and Arctic Russia.

IDENTIFICATION
• White head and underparts, grey on back and wings. Prominent large, white spots on black flight feathers. Pink feet. Reddish spot towards tip of lower bill. Some dark streaking on the head and neck in winter.
• Sexes are alike. Young birds are mainly brown, with dark bills and prominent barring on their wings.
• Size 60cm (24in).

MALLARD
Anas platyrhynchos

These ducks are a common sight by lakes, rivers and canals in towns and cities. They are also seen in gardens with or near ponds and streams.

They may congregate in quite large flocks, especially outside the breeding season, but are most evident in the spring, when groups of unpaired males chase potential mates.

The nest is often constructed close to water and is frequently hidden under vegetation, including in urban gardens. They feed on water, upending themselves or dabbling at the surface, and on land.

FACT FILE
Habitat Open areas of water.
Nest Usually a scrape lined with down feathers.
Eggs 7–16, buff to greyish-green.
Food Mostly plant matter, but some invertebrates.
Distribution Occurs throughout the northern hemisphere and resident through western Europe. Also occurs in north Africa.

IDENTIFICATION
• Drake: metallic green head, white ring around neck. Chest brownish, underparts grey, and a blackish area surrounds vent. Bluish speculum in wing, most evident in flight, bordered by black-and-white stripes.
• Hen: brownish-buff overall with darker patterning, same wing markings as drake. Hen's bill is orange, whereas male bill in eclipse plumage (outside breeding season) is yellow, with a rufous tinge to breast.
• Size 60cm (24in).

AQUATIC BIRDS

Coots, moorhens and rails belong to the group known as crakes. These water-loving birds can often be observed out in the open, but when frightened will usually scuttle away to the safety of reeds or dense vegetation by the water's edge. Cormorants are marine birds that may be seen inland.

CORMORANT

Great cormorant *Phalacrocorax carbo*

This species has a surprisingly wide range, being represented on all inhabited continents except South America. The isolated South African form *P. c. lucidus* ('white-breasted cormorant'), however, is often regarded as a distinct species, differing in appearance, with a more extensive white throat area, and dark, greenish-black wing plumage.

Cormorants can be seen in habitats ranging from the open sea to inland freshwater lakes, where they are despised by fishermen, as they prey on their quarry, diving and chasing the fish underwater. Although they nest colonially in a wide variety of sites it is not uncommon to see odd individuals perched on groynes and similar places. While human persecution and oil spillages represent dangers, these cormorants can have a life expectancy approaching 20 years.

FACT FILE
Habitat Mainly coastal, inland.
Nest Made of seaweed and flotsam.
Eggs 3–6, pale with darker markings.
Food Largely fish.
Distribution Scandinavia and British Isles south via Iberian peninsula and the Mediterranean to north-western Africa and South Africa. Also North America, southern Asia, Australia.

IDENTIFICATION
• Predominantly black once adult, with white throat area. White patch at top of each leg in birds in breeding condition. Some regional variations. Bluish skin around eyes. Bill is horn-coloured at its base, dark tip.
• Sexes are alike. Young birds are brownish with paler underparts.
• Size 94cm (37in).

WATER RAIL

Rallus aquaticus

Water rails frequent ponds, reed beds and bog gardens, but their skulking habits make them hard to notice. Being very adaptable, these rails have an extensive distribution, and are even recorded as foraging in tidal areas surrounded by seaweed in the Isles of Scilly off south-west Britain. In parts of their range they migrate to warmer climates for the winter.

They are very territorial when breeding and, as in other related species, their chicks hatch in a precocial state. Calls include squealing and pig-like grunts.

FACT FILE
Habitat Reed beds and sedge.
Nest Cup-shaped, from vegetation.
Eggs 5–16, whitish with reddish-brown spotting.
Food Animal matter, some vegetation.
Distribution Extensive, from Iceland throughout most of Europe, south to northern Africa and east across Asia to Siberia, China and Japan.

IDENTIFICATION
• Long, reddish bill with bluish-grey breast and sides to head. Narrow brownish line over top of head down back and wings, which have black markings. Black-and-white barring on flanks and underparts. Short tail with pale buff underparts.
• Sexes are alike.
• Size 26cm (10¼in).

COOT
Eurasian coot *Fulica atra*

Coots may set up home by large ponds and lakes in parks and gardens. Open stretches of water are important to them, enabling them to dive in search of food. During the winter, these birds may sometimes assemble in flocks on lakes that are unlikely to freeze over.

Coots may find their food on land or in the water, although they will dive only briefly in relatively shallow water. Pairs are very territorial during the breeding season, attacking the chicks of other coots that venture too close and even their own chicks, which they grab by the neck. The young usually respond by feigning death, and this results in them being left alone.

MOORHEN
Common moorhen *Gallinula chloropus*

Even a relatively small garden pond can attract moorhens, and they may nest in gardens with dense vegetation near the pond. Although usually found in areas of fresh water, they are occasionally seen in brackish areas. Their long toes enable them to walk over aquatic vegetation.

These birds feed on the water or on land and their diet varies according to the season, although seeds of various types make up the bulk of their food. If danger threatens, moorhens will either dive or swim underwater. They are adept divers, remaining submerged by grasping on to underwater vegetation with their bills.

In public parks, moorhens can become quite tame, darting in to obtain food provided for ducks.

POND AND GARDEN PREDATORS

Aerial agility is a feature associated with birds of prey, particularly those that hunt other birds. Kites and harriers are nimble predators whose diet includes small birds and also carrion. Herons and kingfishers generally hunt by water. Both are opportunistic feeders, going after fish and other aquatic creatures.

GREY HERON
Ardea cinerea

Grey herons sometimes hunt in gardens with ponds and on other waterways soon after dawn. These opportunistic hunters are shy and can be difficult to spot, despite their size. They are usually seen in flight, with their long necks tucked back on to their shoulders and their legs held out behind their bodies. They fly with relatively slow, quite noisy wing beats.

Grey herons are very patient predators. They stand completely motionless, looking for any sign of movement in the water around them, then lunge quickly with their powerful bills to grab any fish or frog that comes within reach.

During winter, when their freshwater habitats are frozen, grey herons will often move to river estuaries in search of food. These birds frequently nest in colonies, and some breeding sites may be used for centuries by successive generations.

FACT FILE
Habitat Water with reeds.
Nest Large platform of sticks built off the ground.
Eggs 3–5, chalky-blue.
Food Fish, amphibians and any other aquatic vertebrates.
Distribution Most of Europe into Asia, except far north. Also in Africa, except the Sahara and the Horn.

IDENTIFICATION
• Powerful yellow bill, white head, black above eyes extending to long plumes off back of head. Long neck and chest whitish with black stripe running down the centre. Grey wings and black shoulders. Underparts lighter grey. Long yellow legs.
• Sexes are alike.
• Size 100cm (40in).

KINGFISHER
Common kingfisher *Alcedo atthis*

A flash of colour may be all you see of a kingfisher visiting your garden pond. These birds are surprisingly difficult to spot, as they perch motionlessly while scanning the water for fish. Once its prey has been identified, the predator enters the water, where a protective membrane covers its eyes. Its wings provide propulsion, and having seized the fish in its bill it darts out of the water and back onto its perch with its catch. The whole sequence happens incredibly fast, taking just a few seconds. The kingfisher then stuns the fish by hitting it against the perch, then swallows it head first. It later regurgitates the bones and indigestible parts.

Above: *Kingfishers dive at speed into the water, aiming to catch their intended quarry, such as fish and amphibians, unawares.*

FACT FILE
Habitat Slow-flowing water.
Nest Tunnel excavated in a sandy bank by the water.
Eggs 6–10, white.
Food Small fish, aquatic insects, molluscs, crustaceans.
Distribution Most of Europe, except much of Scandinavia. Northern Africa, through the Arabian Peninsula and South-east Asia to Solomon Islands.

IDENTIFICATION
• Bluish-green extends over head and wings. Back is pale blue, blue flash on cheeks. White throat, white areas below orange cheek patches. Underparts orange. Black bill.
• Hens: the bill is reddish at the base of the lower bill.
• Size 18cm (7¼in).

RED KITE
Milvus milvus

The red kite in a rare visitor to gardens, where it may take songbirds up to the size of crows. Although very agile hunters, these kites also seek carrion such as dead sheep. This behaviour has resulted in their persecution in some areas because of misplaced fears that they actually kill the lambs.

When seeking prey, red kites circle repeatedly overhead, relying on their keen eyesight to spot movement on the ground. They then drop and sweep down low, homing in on their target.

Up until the 1700s, flocks of red kites were common scavengers on the streets of London, where they were sufficiently tame to swoop down and steal food from children. It was their willingness to scavenge, however, that led to a reduction in their numbers, since they were killed using carcasses laced with poison.

FACT FILE
Habitat Light woodland.
Nest Large nest of sticks, built in a tree and usually well concealed.
Eggs 1–4, white, red-brown markings.
Food Small birds, mammals, carrion.
Distribution Across Britain, the Iberian Peninsula and the adjacent area of North Africa. Extends north-eastwards across Europe as far as the Baltic and southern Sweden, and also found in Russia.

IDENTIFICATION
• Predominantly reddish-brown, with a greyish head streaked with darker markings. Darker mottling over wings, some variable streaking on underparts as well. Feet are yellowish with black talons. White areas under the wings and forked tail can be clearly seen in flight.
• Sexes are alike.
• Size 66cm (26¼in).

WHITE STORK
Ciconia ciconia

White storks are very rare visitors to southern Britain, most often seen in warm spring weather. In Europe, where they are considered to bring good fortune, these birds often return each year to the same site, adding annually to their nest, which can become bulky. The return of the storks in April from their African wintering grounds helped to foster the myth of the link between storks and newborn babies.

Migrating birds are a spectacular sight, flying with necks extended and legs trailing behind. However, in many parts of Europe they are now declining due to changes in farmlands and also wetlands.

FACT FILE
Habitat Wetland areas.
Nest Large, bulky platform of sticks sited off the ground, including on rooftops and towers.
Eggs 3–5, chalky-white.
Food Amphibians, fish, small mammals, invertebrates.
Distribution Summer visitor to much of mainland Europe, but only very occasionally seen in southern Britain. The species overwinters in western and eastern parts of North Africa, depending on the flight path. Also occurs in Asia.

IDENTIFICATION
• The white stork is a tall, mainly white bird with prominent black areas on the back and wings.
• It has distinctive long red bill and red legs.
• Sexes are alike. Young birds are smaller than adults, with a dark tip to the bill.
• Size 110cm (43in).

DIRECTORY OF BACKYARD BIRDS (NORTH AMERICA)

There is a lot of enjoyment to be gained from watching birds, many of which can be attracted to your garden by offering a range of foodstuffs, along with suitable nest facilities after the winter period. Here are profiles of some of the most common and notable North American species that you may encounter, both regular backyard residents and more occasional visitors. Although there is not space to include all the varieties, you will find plenty of examples to guide your bird-spotting. Descriptions are given of their distribution, size and appearance, behavior, nesting habits and food preferences.

Left: *Woodpeckers favor well-established trees; this pileated woodpecker (*Dryocopus pileatus*) is found in deciduous woodland of the eastern US and Canada.*

Above: *Hummingbirds are drawn to flowers. This broad-billed (*Cynanthus latirostris*) can be spotted in south-western gardens.*

Above: *Virginian cardinals (*Cardinalis cardinalis*) are among the most colorful birds that visit backyards.*

Above: *Jays like areas where there is some woodland nearby; this blue jay (*Cyanocitta cristata*) is found in eastern US and Canada.*

FINCHES

Members of this group have benefited from changes to the environment. Along with a greater availability of food, urban areas provide a multitude of nesting sites as people seek to attract these birds into their backyards. Pairs may establish breeding territories, but these birds form flocks for much of the year.

HOUSE FINCH
Carpodacus mexicanus

Two separate populations of these finches occur in North America: one native to the west and the other in the east. The eastern population is descended from birds released on Long Island, near New York City, during the 1940s. There, they bred successfully, but it was not until the 1960s that they began to spread more widely and become established. They appear to have benefited significantly from bird feeders, although they also forage for berries and other items in backyards.

Males have an attractive song that is not unlike that of a canary. Nesting pairs are very adaptable and often breed in loose colonies, commonly utilizing nesting baskets secured under the eaves of houses. They frequently raise two or more broods of chicks in rapid succession.

During the fall, house finches often associate together in large flocks, and in more rural areas may be seen feeding in the fields. In spring, flocks can cause damage in orchards by pecking the buds and flowers.

FACT FILE
Habitat Open areas, cities, backyards.
Nest Cup shape.
Eggs 4–5, pale blue, black spots.
Food Seeds and invertebrates.
Distribution Southwestern Canada through western parts of the USA to Texas and into Mexico. Separate population in eastern USA south of the Great Lakes. Also on Hawaii.

IDENTIFICATION
• Cock: brown cap on head and brown ear coverts. Remainder of head and breast red, may be more orange. Streaked white underparts, browner on flanks. Back streaked, dark wing feathers edged with white.
• Hens: much duller, streaked over their entire head and underparts.
• Size 6in (15cm).

PURPLE FINCH
Carpodacus purpureus

Purple finches are bold and conspicuous in backyard settings, often visiting feeders, with oil-rich seeds, such as sunflower, being favored foods. These birds are territorial by nature, especially during the breeding season. Males sing loudly from branches and also undertake display flights to attract a partner. The nest is built on the branch of a conifer, often at a considerable height from the ground. Although some individuals remain on their breeding grounds throughout the year, others move south, where they may be sighted in small flocks.

The availability of pine seeds influences their distribution during winter in particular, since in years when the crop fails these finches move to new areas in search of other food. Although their breeding range is continuous, the population splits into distinct western and eastern groups for the duration of the winter.

FACT FILE
Habitat Backyards, parks, woodland.
Nest Cup shape.
Eggs 5–6, pale bluish, dark markings.
Food Seeds and invertebrates.
Distribution Canada south of Hudson Bay, most common in east. Extends to southern California. Winters in the west and much of eastern USA along the Gulf coast, into northern Mexico.

IDENTIFICATION
• Cocks: rose red over much of the body, especially on the head and rump. The back is red with brown streaking, lower underparts are whitish in the center.
• Hens: brownish, light stripes around eyes. White area under throat. Pale underparts streaked with brown.
• Size 6in (15cm).

PINE GROSBEAK
Pinicola enucleator

As their name suggests, pine grosbeaks are closely linked with coniferous forests, although they move into deciduous woodlands and also backyards in fall.

Living in flocks, these finches prefer to feed off the ground, resorting to nibbling buds when seeds and fruit are scarce and snow covers the ground. In some areas, such as the western United States, they are regular bird-feeder visitors. Their winter range is influenced by availability of food, with flocks sometimes moving south of their normal range when berries, such as mountain ash, fail.

Pine grosbeaks are not active by nature. They are also tame, so are fairly easy to observe. The nest is built in a tree, often close to the ground, with the young fledging after three weeks.

EVENING GROSBEAK
Coccothraustes vespertinus

These large, thick-set finches have a powerful bill. When they were first described in the 1820s, it was believed that they emerged from cover only at dusk. This is incorrect, but they became known as evening grosbeaks. Their range has expanded since then.

Up until the 19th century, these finches were restricted to northern Canada, but suddenly, perhaps because of persistent food shortages, evening grosbeaks started traveling and ultimately breeding in northeastern parts of the United States. They continued to spread, partly thanks to bird table offerings, reaching Maryland by the 1960s, and Florida and the Gulf coast a decade later.

Pairs build their nest at the end of a branch, up to 70ft (21m) off the ground, choosing a site where it will be hidden. The hen sits alone, with the chicks hatching after about two weeks. They fledge after a similar interval.

TOWHEES AND MIGRATING SPARROWS

Brown predominates in the coloration of these adaptable birds, but there can actually be a huge variety in appearance through what is often a wide range. Despite their fairly small size, a number of towhees and sparrows undertake extensive migrations to and from their breeding grounds in spring and fall.

CALIFORNIA TOWHEE
Pipilo crissalis

The taxonomy of the towhees can be confusing. In the past, the Californian towhee and the closely related canyon towhee, which occurs farther west, were grouped together under the name brown towhee, although it is now clear that they are, in fact, distinct species. Even so, eight distinctive races of California towhee are recognized through the bird's relatively small range.

Pairs, which bond for life in many cases, are most likely to be observed in backyards during the breeding season, because this is when the cock bird sings loudly from a prominent perch. Even after egg laying, he continues this behavior, laying claim to their territory; any intruders will be driven away aggressively. Their nest, made of various plant materials, is hidden low in vegetation and the hen incubates alone. Once the chicks have hatched, these towhees become largely insectivorous, frequently foraging on the ground, using their feet to scratch around in the hope of discovering invertebrates hiding under leaves or other vegetation.

FACT FILE
Habitat Chaparral, parks, backyards.
Nest Cup shape.
Eggs 3–4, bluish green, dark markings.
Food Seeds and invertebrates.
Distribution Range extends along coastal western North America, from Oregon to Baja California, and eastward as far as the Cascades and Sierra Nevada Mountains.

IDENTIFICATION
• Predominantly brown, with crown a warmer shade. Buff throat marked with dark spots that are largest across upper chest. Undertail coverts are cinnamon brown.
• Sexes are alike. Young birds are duller with more extensive speckling on their underparts.
• Size 9¼in (23cm).

CHIPPING SPARROW
Spizella passerina

These sparrows are not easy to observe in backyards, partly because their coloration provides camouflage, but also because they hide among vegetation. Even when singing, the cock chooses a fairly secluded location. The sound is a distinctive, monotonous 'chip'-like call, which explains the species' common name.

These sparrows forage mainly on the ground, although they may visit bird feeders to take seeds, especially during winter when snow blankets the ground. Each fall, chipping sparrows desert most of their North American range, migrating to southern states and farther south in late September. They return to their breeding grounds in the far north the following May. The well-hidden nest is constructed from vegetation, with incubation and fledging each lasting about 12 days. This rapid breeding cycle means that in favorable conditions, they may rear two broods, especially in the south, in quick succession.

FACT FILE
Habitat Parks, wooded backyards.
Nest Cup shape.
Eggs 3–5, light blue, darker markings.
Food Seeds and invertebrates.
Distribution Most of North America south of Hudson Bay, except for central-southern USA. Winters along southern Mexican border and through Central America to northern Nicaragua.

IDENTIFICATION
• Breeding adults have a chestnut crown, white stripes beneath, black stripe running through eyes. Grayish neck and underparts, whitish throat.
• Wings are black and brown with whitish markings. Dark notched tail. Head coloration is brownish, darker speckling outside nesting season.
• Size 5½in (14cm).

LARK SPARROW
Chondestes grammacus

Lark sparrows have a very musical song, incorporating trills and buzzes. In common with larks, they are terrestrial birds, foraging on the ground not just for seeds but also insects, especially grasshoppers, during summer, which are used to rear their chicks. They breed on the ground or in a low bush, frequently in scrubland, where the nest can be hidden from predators, and sometimes in loose colonies.

Northern populations fly south in late July and August, returning again the following spring. During the winter period, they can often be seen in flocks, including in fields and by roadsides. They sometimes visit rural bird feeders in search of seeds.

The range of the lark sparrow has declined over recent years.

This may be due to changes in habitat. Their distribution formerly extended up the East Coast to Maryland and New York, while today they are relatively scarce east of the Mississippi.

SAVANNAH SPARROW
Passerculus sandwichensis

These widely distributed birds are as adept at running as they are flying. It is not unusual for them to escape danger by dropping down into vegetation and scurrying away.

Savannah sparrows can be found in a wide range of habitats, from the tundra of the far north to the grassy sand dunes of Mexico. They breed on the ground, with spiders usually featuring in the diet of the young. In fall, large numbers migrate southward, appearing in parks and backyards in both cities and rural areas.

Various distinctive races of these sparrows are recognized; some have very limited distributions. The so-called Ipswich sparrow *(P. s. princeps),* breeds on tiny Sable Island, Nova Scotia. It winters more widely along the East Coast, including around Ipswich, Massachusetts. Another localized and distinctive form, *P. s. rostratus* from the western side of the United States, has a much broader bill and a different song pattern from other savannah sparrows.

DOVES AND PIGEONS

The characteristic dumpy appearance of doves and pigeons, along with their relatively subdued coloration, makes them easy to identify. There is actually no strict zoological distinction between these two groups, although the term 'pigeon' is usually applied to larger species.

WHITE-WINGED DOVE

Mesquite dove *Zenaida asiatica*

Flocks of white-winged doves often congregate in crop-growing areas around harvest time, foraging on the ground for cultivated grains. They are very adaptable by nature and can also be found in habitats ranging from semidesert to mangrove swamps. They are attracted to backyards by sunflower and other seeds on bird tables.

During the breeding season in the USA, pairs of white-winged doves from eastern areas breed in large colonies, while those occurring farther west tend to nest individually. Subsequently, many head south for winter, with birds from Texas flying as far as Costa Rica.

Although they are often hunted for game, these doves are still common in most areas, and the species is expanding its distribution in parts of the Caribbean.

FACT FILE
Habitat Farmland, parks, backyards.
Nest Loose platform of twigs.
Eggs 2, creamy buff.
Food Various seeds and grains.
Distribution Across southern USA and Mexico, except the southeast, southward to Costa Rica and Panama. Also in the Caribbean.

IDENTIFICATION
• So-called because of white area on leading edge of wings when folded. Wings and tail feathers otherwise mainly brownish, with an adjacent grayer band. Head, neck and upper chest have a pinker tinge. Prominent area of bare blue skin around eyes.
• Hens: duller, with less iridescence on the neck.
• Size 12in (30cm).

MOURNING DOVE

Carolina dove *Zenaida macroura*

These doves are so-called because of the plaintive, mournful sound of their calls. Their scientific name *macroura* means 'long-tailed.' They have benefited from the provision of bird tables, particularly in the northern part of their range, and often visit rural and urban backyards for food, such as seeds and millet.

Their powerful wings and sleek shape help these doves to fly long distances on migration, and northerly populations overwinter in Central America. In southern USA, such as Florida, mourning doves are resident throughout the year. They prefer to look for food on the ground if not feeding on a bird table, and groups often wander across fields in search of seeds and other edible items. Mourning doves are now recorded overwintering farther north than they did in the past, partly as a result of more feeding opportunities from backyard bird tables.

FACT FILE
Habitat Lightly wooded areas.
Nest Loose pile of twigs.
Eggs 2, white.
Food Seeds and some invertebrates.
Distribution Across much of North America, from southern Canada across the USA and Central America to Costa Rica and Panama. Affected by the season. Also on Greater Antilles.

IDENTIFICATION
• Some variation in appearance through range.
• Cocks: pinkish buff coloration on face, extending to underparts, with dark streak just above neck. Upper surfaces of wings and tail brown, with large dark spots evident on wings.
• Hens: duller and browner overall.
• Size 13½in (34cm).

FACT FILE

Habitat Open areas, including fields, parks, and backyards.
Nest Fragile platform of twigs and other vegetation.
Eggs 2, white.
Food Seeds, fruits, berries.
Distribution Southwestern USA south as far as Costa Rica. Range is extending north and south.

IDENTIFICATION

• Brownish upperparts, with a pinker tinge to the underside. Black scalloping on both wings and body. Finer scalloping on the head, which is grayer.
• Tail is relatively long and tapering. Rufous underwing coverts seen in flight, with a rufous bar evident when wings are closed.
• Hens: similar, but underparts less strongly suffused with pink.
• Size 8¾in (22cm).

INCA DOVE
Columbina inca; previously *Scardafella inca*

Inca doves are typically encountered in relatively open countryside, but can also be seen in urban backyards throughout the year. The population is largely sedentary through its range, although sometimes these doves may be seen north of their breeding range in the USA, which extends across Oklahoma, Arkansas, and Nebraska. They were first recorded there around 1870.

Too small to be hunted as game, these doves are relatively tame and will nest in urban backyards. Like many doves, pairs will breed two or three times in rapid succession when conditions are favorable, but their limited nest-building skills means that some nests will collapse, resulting in the loss of both eggs and chicks. A well-concealed site in vegetation is usually chosen, with both birds sharing incubation duties; the cock normally sits by day, while the hen takes over in late afternoon. The young grow rapidly and may leave the nest when only 12 days old, although they will not be able to fly strongly at this age.

FACT FILE

Habitat Narrow ledges of city buildings.
Nest Loose pile of twigs.
Eggs 2, white.
Food Prefers seeds, but adaptable.
Distribution Much of North America except the far north, through Central America and across most of South America, except for central Amazonia and extreme southern tip; also occurs in the Caribbean.

IDENTIFICATION

• Dark, bluish gray head with slight green iridescence on neck. Light gray wings with two black bars on each wing.
• Reddish purple coloration on sides of upper chest. The remainder of plumage is gray, with a black band at the tip of the tail. Various color morphs exist, typically displaying orangish red or white areas of plumage.
• Sexes are alike.
• Size 14in (35cm).

FERAL PIGEON (ROCK DOVE)
Columba livia

These birds are not native to the Americas, but were introduced from Europe, where they evolved from rock doves. This helps to explain why they often nest on narrow ledges high above sidewalks, just as their ancestors still do on windswept cliffs.

Feral pigeons are common city birds, scavenging from leftovers and having virtually no fear of people. Large flocks can cause serious damage to buildings, with their droppings and also by pecking away at the mortar, which provides calcium.

SONGBIRDS

One of the most welcome signs of spring in temperate regions is the dawn chorus, indicating the onset of the breeding period and the return of migrant songbirds. At this hour of day, the songs of birds can be clearly heard in backyards and parks, and early morning is an excellent time to watch birds, too.

VIRGINIAN CARDINAL
Northern cardinal *Cardinalis cardinalis*

One of the most colorful backyard birds, the range of these cardinals continues to increase both in northern and western areas, especially since the first breeding record from Canada, dating to 1901. This expansion probably results from bird-table offerings. The stout, conical bill of these birds is adapted to crushing seeds, although Virginian cardinals will also hunt invertebrates, particularly when they have chicks in the nest.

FACT FILE
Habitat Edges of woodland, parks, backyards.
Nest Cup shape, made of vegetation.
Eggs 3-4, whitish or grayish white, with darker spots and blotches.
Food Seeds and invertebrates.
Distribution Southern Ontario, Canada, south through USA to Gulf of Mexico, and southward to Belize.

IDENTIFICATION
• Cock: mainly red, with a pointed crest. Black mask surrounds bill extending to eyes and onto throat. Wings, back, and tail duller shade.
• Hen: mainly brown, with reddish suffusion over wings and tail.
• Adult bills bright red, young birds' bills blackish.
• Size 9¼in (23cm).

SCARLET TANAGER
Piranga olivacea

These tanagers undertake long flights each year to and from their breeding grounds. Individuals sometimes venture farther afield, and are observed in more northerly and westerly areas than usual, even reaching Alaska on rare occasions.

A pair of scarlet tanagers rears only one brood during the summer before returning south. These birds catch invertebrates in the undergrowth and also in flight. More unusually, scarlet tanagers rub live ants onto their plumage. This behavior, known as anting, results in formic acid being released by the ants among the feathers, which in turn drives out parasites, such as lice, from the plumage. The bright coloration of these birds is linked in part to their diet.

FACT FILE
Habitat Light forest and woodland.
Nest Cup shape, stems and roots.
Eggs 2–5, whitish to greenish blue with dark markings.
Food Mainly invertebrates.
Distribution Migrates to southeastern Canada and eastern USA. Overwinters in Central and South America, east of Andes to Peru and Bolivia.

IDENTIFICATION
• Mainly yellowish olive, underparts more yellowish than upperparts.
• Cock: distinguishable from hen by black instead of brownish wings and tail. In breeding plumage, cock has vivid scarlet plumage. Young cock birds in their first year have more orange rather than scarlet plumage.
• Size 6¾in (17cm).

FACT FILE
Habitat Brush, often near water.
Nest Cup shape.
Eggs 3–4, pale blue.
Food Seeds and invertebrates.
Distribution Widely across USA, from California through to New Jersey, south to Costa Rica. Northern populations overwinter in Central America, from Mexico to Panama.

IDENTIFICATION
• Adult cock: dull shade of blue, with large, grayish bill. Darker wings, with two wing bars close to shoulder.
• Young cock: displays more widespread blue feathering.
• Hens: predominantly brownish, lighter on underparts, also display two buff-colored wing bars. Some bluish feathering on the rump.
• Size 7½in (19cm).

BLUE GROSBEAK
Guiraca caerulea

Despite the cock bird's distinctive plumage, the blue grosbeak is not as conspicuous as its coloration would suggest. Indeed, in poor light its feathering can appear so dark that, at a distance, it is sometimes confused with the male brown-headed cowbird *(Molothrus ater)*. It is also easily confused with the male indigo bunting *(Passerina cyanea),* which also has blue plumage and a stout, conical beak.

The grosbeak's melodious song is most commonly heard early in the day, although the birds may start singing again at dusk. The song consists largely of short notes interspersed with longer trills.

Cock birds usually return from their winter haunts a few days ahead of hens, frequently spending this time searching for food in groups on the ground before splitting up to nest. Pairs are likely to rear two broods of chicks over summer before migrating south again.

In fall, these birds gather in flocks to comb fields for seeds and insects, and they may also appear at bird tables at this time.

FACT FILE
Habitat Wooded or lightly wooded areas, backyards with mature trees.
Nest Cup shape.
Eggs 2–7, pale blue.
Food Seeds, other plant matter, and invertebrates.
Distribution This species' range extends from Canada southward through much of USA and to northern Mexico.

IDENTIFICATION
• Cock: bright yellow plumage, with a black forehead and black wings and tail, and white bars on the wings. Duller in winter plumage, being a more olive shade with a less distinct black cap.
• Hens: can be identified by their olive-yellow upperparts and more yellowish underparts, becoming brownish during winter, especially on the upperparts. The white wing barring is still apparent, enabling hens to be distinguished easily from juvenile birds.
• Size 5½in (14cm).

AMERICAN GOLDFINCH
Carduelis tristis

These attractive songbirds are common throughout their range. Familiar backyard visitors, they take sunflower hearts, peanut hearts, and thistle supplied on bird tables. Goldfinches in northern areas move south to warmer areas for the winter. They are often seen in larger flocks at this time, frequently in the company of related birds, such as redpolls *(Acanthis* species) and pine siskins.

Their diet varies through the year, being influenced by the availability of food. Shoots and buds of trees, such as spruce and willow, are eaten when other foods are in short supply. Seeds are a principal food, consumed through much of the year, and goldfinches delay their breeding until midsummer when weed seeds are available. Invertebrates also provide protein for rearing chicks in the nest.

TITS, TITMICE AND CHICKADEES

These small birds are most likely to be seen in backyards during winter, when the absence of leaves makes them more conspicuous. They often visit bird tables and feeders during cold weather. They are very resourceful, displaying acrobatic skills as they dart about and hang upside down to feed.

TUFTED TITMOUSE
Baeolophus bicolor

This is the largest member of the tit family in North America. It is conspicuous, thanks to its noisy nature. The vocal range of male tufted titmice is especially varied, with individuals able to sing more than 15 different song patterns. Hens also sing, but not to the same extent, and mainly in spring and early summer.

The range of these titmice has increased northward, largely because bird-table offerings provide them food year round.

Left: *The nest cup is lined with soft material. These small birds can be fierce in defending their nests.*

In the south, they have been recorded as hybridizing with black-crested titmice *(B. atricristatus)* in central parts of Texas. The resulting offspring have grayish crests and a pale orange band above the bill. Despite their small size, these titmice are determined visitors to bird tables, driving off much larger species.

FACT FILE
Habitat Light, deciduous woodland.
Nest Small tree holes, nest boxes.
Eggs 3–8, creamy white, brown spots.
Food Invertebrates in summer; seeds during winter.
Distribution Range extends across eastern North America, from southern Ontario south to the Gulf of Mexico, not present in southern Florida. Range appears to be expanding in some areas of Canada.

IDENTIFICATION
• Characteristic black band immediately above the bill, gray crest and crown. Cheeks and underparts whitish, pale reddish orange flanks.
• Sexes are alike. Young birds are duller overall.
• Size 6in (15cm).

CAROLINA CHICKADEE
Parus carolinensis

A regular visitor to bird tables in eastern states, Carolina chickadees can become

very tame when supplied with food, such as sunflower seeds, suet, and peanut butter. This species is very closely related to the black-capped chickadee *(Poecile atricapillus),* which occurs farther north, and it is not unknown for the birds to hybridize where they overlap. Studies of their song patterns have revealed that the Carolina chickadee has a four-note call, whereas the black-capped type has a two-note whistle.

Although pairs have their own territories during summer, Carolina chickadees form larger groups in the winter months. During cold weather, they spend much longer periods roosting in tree hollows to conserve their body heat, sometimes remaining there for up to 15 hours per day. This is also the time of year when chickadees are most likely to be seen visiting bird tables in search of food.

FACT FILE
Habitat Light, broad-leaved woodland.
Nest In small holes in trees, also uses nest boxes.
Eggs 3–9, white with reddish brown spots.
Food Invertebrates and seeds.
Distribution Range extends from northeastern USA southward to Texas and northern Florida. Occasionally in Ontario, Canada.

IDENTIFICATION
• Black area extends to back of head, black under bill broadening across the throat. White on the sides of the face. Underparts are whitish with a slightly orange cast. Wings and tail are primarily grayish olive.
• Sexes are alike.
• Size 4¾in (12cm).

FACT FILE
Habitat Scrubland, open woodlands, suburbs, backyards.
Nest Pendulous mass.
Eggs 5–13, white.
Food Mainly invertebrates. Berries.
Distribution Range extends from British Columbia in Canada south and eastward through the USA to parts of Mexico and Guatemala in Central America.

IDENTIFICATION
• Three groupings exist. Those from northern areas have brownish ear coverts, a brown cap and gray upperparts, and whitish underparts. Hens have grayer throats and gray coloration extends onto the cap in the lead-colored variety.
• In the Central American black-eared form, cock birds have black areas on the sides of the face.
• Size 4¼in (11cm).

FACT FILE
Habitat Areas of oak woodland, also pinyon-juniper woodlands.
Nest Old woodpecker holes, also birdhouses.
Eggs 3–9, white.
Food Invertebrates, buds, and berries.
Distribution This species' range covers much of western parts of the USA, extending down to Baja California and other parts of northwestern Mexico.

IDENTIFICATION
• Differences in depth of coloration and bill size occur through its range. Grayish brown overall, with a small crest at the back of the head. Underparts are a purer shade of gray than the back.
• Sexes are alike.
• Formerly classified with the juniper titmouse (*B. ridgwayi*) as one species.
• Size 4¾in (12cm).

AMERICAN BUSHTIT
Psaltriparus minimus

Bushtits are the smallest species of North American tit. These lively birds forage in groups of up to 40 individuals, their movements helping to disturb insects and spiders that might otherwise remain hidden. Bushtits will comb plants in this way, which makes them welcome by gardeners, because they can devour unwanted infestations of pests rapidly.

They are very agile birds, able to hang upside down from a branch or feeder when seeking food, and also have a bold nature, so it is often possible to observe them at relatively close quarters. There is a consistent difference in eye coloration between the sexes: the irises of cocks are invariably brown, whereas those of hens may vary from white through to yellow. Remarkably, this change may become apparent within a few days of the young birds fledging, although both sexes have dark eyes at first.

Nesting pairs are surprisingly tolerant of others of their own kind, to the extent that they may allow them to roost in their nest. Flocks subsequently reform once the breeding season has ended.

PLAIN TITMOUSE
Oak titmouse *Baeolophus inornatus;*
previously *Parus inornatus*

Until recently, the plain or oak titmouse was considered one species with the juniper timouse. Since 1996, the two have been classed separately because of differences in their songs and preferred habitat.

The dull coloration of this titmouse helps it to blend in with its wooded habitat. Pairs maintain distinct territories throughout the year, and form lifelong bonds. If one bird dies, the surviving individual may mate with a new partner. Plain titmice breed only once during the year, with the young being driven away by their parents when they are about seven weeks old, and forced to seek their own territories.

When feeding, these titmice will often comb branches in search of insects. During winter, acorns feature prominently in their diet—they can open these easily with their stout bill. They are also more frequent visitors to bird feeders in winter, taking food, such as sunflower seeds, cracked corn, suet, and baked

goods. They will pick up edible items from the ground and convey them to a more secluded location to be eaten.

At night, plain titmice will seek out suitable roosting holes, with pairs of birds using separate locations, although they sometimes prefer a well-hidden perch. They will also roost in nest boxes.

BACKYARD WRENS

These small, rather stumpy birds are often found in residential areas, especially the aptly named house wren, which has one of the widest distributions of all American birds. Other wrens have more localized distributions, benefiting from bird-feeder offerings to sustain themselves during cold winter months.

HOUSE WREN
Troglodytes aedon

The house wren is a nondescript bird, but its lively, jerky movements make it instantly recognizable. These wrens often visit backyards, usually being seen among dense vegetation because they are instinctively reluctant to leave cover for long. Although wrens are small in size, they can be determined and belligerent, especially in defense of a chosen nest site, such as a woodpecker hole in a tree, and are able to force the hole maker to go elsewhere. They will also take occupancy of a birdhouse, particularly when sited in a corner of a backyard where they feel secure. The pair collect a jumble of moss and small twigs to line the interior, adding feathers to make a soft pad for their eggs. House wrens are prolific breeders, frequently producing two broods of chicks during the course of a season.

FACT FILE
Habitat Dense vegetation in parks and backyards.
Nest Pile of twigs and sticks.
Eggs 5–9, white with brown spotting.
Food Invertebrates.
Distribution Present across much of North America except the far north, extending down through Mexico and right across South America.

IDENTIFICATION
• Brown upperparts, black barring evident on wings and tail. Underparts lighter brown, with whitish throat area. Indistinct pale eyebrow stripes. Narrow, relatively short bill.
• Sexes are alike. Young birds have a rufous rump and are a darker shade of buff on the underparts.
• Size 4¾in (12cm).

CAROLINA WREN
Thryothorus ludovicianus

Carolina wrens are relatively easy birds to identify, due partly to their extensive white facial markings. They move with the same jerky movements as other wrens, frequenting dense areas of vegetation through which they can move inconspicuously.

Carolina wrens are also noisy birds, with a song that is surprisingly loud for a bird of their size. It is uttered throughout the year, rather than just at the start of the breeding season, and sounds in part like the word 'wheateater,' repeated over and over.

Unfortunately, young Carolina wrens often have an instinctive tendency to push northward from their southern homelands. Although in mild years they will find sufficient food to withstand the winter cold, widescale mortality occurs in these northern areas when the ground is blanketed with snow for long periods, almost wiping out the species. In due course, however, their numbers build up again, until the cycle is repeated at some future stage.

FACT FILE
Habitat Shrubbery.
Nest Cup of vegetation.
Eggs 4–8, whitish with brown spotting.
Food Invertebrates, some seeds.
Distribution The range of this species extends throughout eastern USA, notably occuring in North Carolina and South Carolina.

IDENTIFICATION
• Chestnut brown upperparts, with black barring on wings and tail, and white bands running across the wings.
• Distinctive white eye stripes, edged with black above and chestnut below. Black and white speckling on sides of face. Throat white, underparts buff.
• Sexes are alike.
• Size 5½in (14cm).

FACT FILE
Habitat Rocky areas, canyons, cliffs, and old stone buildings.
Nest Open cup of vegetation.
Eggs 4–7, white, lightly speckled with reddish brown.
Food Invertebrates.
Distribution Range extends from western parts of the USA south as far as southern Mexico.

IDENTIFICATION
• Black-and-white speckled top to the head, with a white throat and breast. Black barring on the wings and tail, with speckling on the back and underparts.
• Characteristic rufous underparts, with the red extending across the back, wings, and tail. Long, relatively straight, blackish bill.
• Sexes are alike. Young birds lack the white speckling of the adults.
• Size 6in (15cm).

CANYON WREN
Catherpes mexicanus

As with other wrens it is the powerful, musical song of this species that attracts attention. However, it can be difficult to see the songster, partly because of its small size and relatively dull coloration, and especially if it is partly concealed among a loose outcrop of rocks.

Slightly larger than the house wren, this species has a conspicuous white throat. Unlike the house wren, it is shy and secretive by nature. Canyon wrens generally inhabit rocky terrain but will sometimes adopt old stone buildings as refuges. Their long, narrow bills let them seize invertebrates from small crevices without difficulty, their tails often bobbing up and down as they seek their quarry.

Canyon wrens prefer areas around steep slopes or cliffs, whereas rock wrens *(Salpinctes obsoletus)* tend to inhabit flatter areas of countryside. For breeding, these wrens choose a site in a stone wall or a similarly inaccessible place, such as a chimney. The nest is fashioned from a jumble of vegetation on a suitable ledge.

FACT FILE
Habitat Rocky and arid areas.
Nest Made of vegetation.
Eggs 4–10, white with reddish brown speckling.
Food Insects, other invertebrates.
Distribution Occurs in western North America. Breeding range extends to British Columbia. The species wanders widely outside the breeding period. Separate populations are found in parts of Mexico, Guatemala, Honduras, Nicaragua, and northwest Costa Rica.

IDENTIFICATION
• This species has dark, grayish brown upperparts with black streaky markings. It has a chestnut brown rump. Underparts are whitish gray with fine dark streaking on the breast. Narrow, pointed grayish bill.
• Sexes are alike. Young birds are duller. Extent of black barring differs between races.
• Size 5½in (14cm).

ROCK WREN
Salpinctes obsoletus

As its name suggests, this wren is mainly found in rocky terrain, although it may appear at picnic sites and in backyards in this habitat. Rock wrens are lively and easy to observe because they are naturally tame and conspicuous, moving from boulder to boulder in search of invertebrates. If danger threatens, they slip away.

Their relatively loud song is especially evident during the breeding period. These wrens seek out small crevices in rocks as nest sites, creating a snug lining. They often build the nest on a bed of small stones that they collect themselves, for reasons that are unclear, but may have to do with nest sanitation. They gather a wide variety of material to incorporate into the nest site, ranging from rabbit bones to small pieces of rusty metal

Six subspecies of this wren have been identified, although one of these, the San Benedicto rock wren *(S. o. exsul)*, from an island on Mexico's west coast, was wiped out by a volcanic explosion there in 1952.

HUMMINGBIRDS AND WARBLERS

Hummingbirds are one of the unique sights of the Americas and are fascinating to watch as they hover in front of a nectar-rich flower while feeding. Some warblers, too, have developed a highly specialized style of feeding, while others are more opportunistic, which has helped them spread widely.

RUBY-THROATED HUMMINGBIRD

Archilochus colubris

The small size of these hummingbirds is no barrier to their flying long distances back and forth to their wintering grounds. Cock birds usually arrive back in their breeding areas about a week before the hens are seen in May. Temperate areas hold insufficient plant nectar to sustain them through the winter. These hummingbirds are relatively unspecialized in their feeding habits, feeding from over 30 types of plants. They are attracted to tubular red flowers and also to feeders filled with sweet liquid. Hens build their nest alone, binding it with the silk threads of spiderwebs.

FACT FILE
Habitat Lightly wooded areas with flowering plants, suburban backyards.
Nest Cup built in trees bound with spiders' silk.
Eggs 2, white.
Food Nectar, pollen, sap, invertebrates.
Distribution Breeds in eastern USA, moving south to Florida, Texas, as far as Panama for winter. Sometimes seen in the Caribbean.

IDENTIFICATION
• Metallic, green-bronze upperparts. Large, glossy red area of plumage under the throat. The remainder of the underparts are whitish.
• Hens: similar in appearance, but have dusky white area on throat instead of glossy red patch of cocks.
• Size 3½in (9cm).

ANNA'S HUMMINGBIRD

Calypte anna

These hummingbirds are a familiar sight in backyards west of the Sierras, where they sip nectar from flowers and also from artificial feeders. They are sometimes seen feeding at holes in tree bark drilled by sapsuckers (*Sphyrapicus* species), which results in nutrient-rich sap oozing.

At the outset of the breeding season, males become very territorial. Soon after, hens begin to seek out suitable nest sites, which can include human-made structures. They gather small lengths of plant fibers and bind them together with silk from spiderwebs. Lichens are used to fill in gaps between the stems, and the cup is then lined with feathers. The chicks leave the nest for the first time when they are only 18 days old.

FACT FILE
Habitat Generally woodland areas with flowers, backyards.
Nest Cup bound in spiders' silk.
Eggs 2, white.
Food Nectar, pollen, sap, invertebrates.
Distribution Western USA, from California and offshore islands southeast to Arizona; may move to southern Oregon during winter. Sometimes recorded in Alaska.

IDENTIFICATION
• Mostly rose-colored head, with a bronzy green area behind eyes and a small white spot. Upperparts metallic, bronzy green, underparts green and whitish.
• Hens: lack rose-colored plumage on head, have a brownish throat.
• Size 4in (10cm).

YELLOW WARBLER
Dendroica petechia

Yellow warblers are one of the most widespread warblers in the Americas. They regularly visit bird tables to take sunflower seeds, peanut hearts, suet, and raisins. They are popular with people seeking a natural form of pest control, because they comb the ground for invertebrates. When breeding, their nests are sometimes parasitized by cowbirds.

As winter approaches, these warblers head south to southern Mexico, Peru and Brazil. The small resident population of yellow warblers *(D. p. gundlachi)* in Florida are of Caribbean origin, which explain the green plumage on their crown. Farther south, the so-called mangrove warblers of Mexican coasts are a variety of yellow warbler.

There is also wide diversity in the plumage of young birds, which can vary from pale yellow with greener upperparts to a browner shade, or gray with white underparts in the case of young Florida birds.

FACT FILE

Habitat Orchards, backyards, open woodland.
Nest Cup of plant material in tree fork.
Eggs 4–5, bluish white with darker speckling.
Food Mainly invertebrates.
Distribution Range extends from northern Alaska east and south across much of northern North America. Ranges down into Central America and through the Caribbean, with a tiny localized population in Florida.

IDENTIFICATION

• Coloration varies, especially in young birds. Yellowish, with red streaking on the underparts, and greener upperparts.
• Adults from northern areas are greener than those found farther south, while birds from Mexico often have chestnut brown on the head.
• Size 4¾in (12cm).

BLACK-AND-WHITE WARBLER
Mniotilta varia

With its bold patterning and a call likened to a noisy wheelbarrow, this warbler is relatively conspicuous. These birds arrive back in their breeding grounds during April, although they may head north before then, appearing in backyards and parks.

They are also known as black-and-white creepers, due to their habit of foraging on tree trunks, probing for insects in the bark.

They are agile, being able to move both up and down the trunk. In their breeding territories, they prefer deciduous woodland, where cover is available, because they breed on the ground. The pair construct a well-disguised nest, usually close to a tree.

They start to head south again from July onward. Like other wood warblers, these birds often forage in mixed flocks, especially in winter.

FACT FILE

Habitat Woodland, backyards, parks.
Nest Cup shape.
Eggs 4–5, white with purple spots.
Food Invertebrates.
Distribution Range extends from Canada (southern Mackenzie through central Manitoba to Newfoundland) to much of southern USA east of the Rockies. Overwinters along the Gulf coast and down through Central America into northern South America.

IDENTIFICATION

• Breeding cocks: black feathering on cheeks and throat, with lower throat becoming white in winter. White stripe above the eyes, black-and-white streaking on flanks. Lower underparts white.
• Hens: whitish cheeks, with buff suffusion on flanks, more apparent in young.
• Size 4¾in (12cm).

GRACKLES AND ORIOLES

The colors of grackles are subdued, but they can display a striking iridescent sheen when sunlight catches their plumage. Orioles are small, colorful birds, often graced with an attractive song. A glimpse of yellowish orange and black plumage and a pointed bill is indicative of an oriole sighting.

COMMON GRACKLE
Quiscalus quiscula

These familar birds thrive alongside humans, and particularly relish cracked corn on bird tables. Opportunistic feeders, they will raid trash cans for scraps. They have a powerful pointed bill and long tail.

The song of the common grackle is highly distinctive, making it easy to recognize individual birds. While singing, they perform a so-called 'rough out' display, in which they fluff up their plumage. This may be accompanied by dancing on the perch and flashing their yellow eyes. Males sometimes react more to other males than to females.

In flight, the tail feathers are splayed to create a wedge shape. As fall approaches the grackles leave northern and western haunts; they only reside all year in southern areas. These can be long-lived birds, surviving to 22 years.

FACT FILE
Habitat Open country, marshland to suburban areas and parks.
Nest Large cup-shape structure.
Eggs 3–7, pale green to pale rust.
Food Seeds, invertebrates, fish, birds.
Distribution Central and eastern North America, British Colombia to southeastern USA. Occasionally in Pacific states and Alaska spring.

IDENTIFICATION
• Bronze form of northern and western areas has bronze feathering and blue head; purplish suffusion characterizes purple grackle from Appalachian region. Florida race has olive green body and purplish head.
• Hens: smaller and less iridescence, especially on their underparts.
• Size 12¾in (32cm).

GREAT-TAILED GRACKLE
Quiscalus mexicanus

The great-tailed grackle is rapidly extending its North American range in a northwesterly direction, nesting for example in Montana for the first time in 1996. This trend is probably due to these birds' bold, adaptable nature, especially since they thrive in areas with relatively few trees.

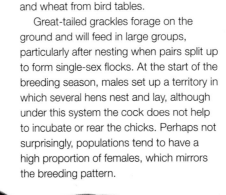

They are common in backyards in the southwest, and will take many different foods including seeds, sunflowers, suet, and wheat from bird tables.

Great-tailed grackles forage on the ground and will feed in large groups, particularly after nesting when pairs split up to form single-sex flocks. At the start of the breeding season, males set up a territory in which several hens nest and lay, although under this system the cock does not help to incubate or rear the chicks. Perhaps not surprisingly, populations tend to have a high proportion of females, which mirrors the breeding pattern.

FACT FILE
Habitat Open areas, including farmland and suburbs.
Nest Cup shape, twigs lined with grass.
Eggs 3–4, blue, brown-black markings.
Food Varied, including seeds, invertebrates, small vertebrates.
Distribution Oregon south and east through Mexico (except Baja California) into South America, eastward to Venezuela as far as northern Peru.

IDENTIFICATION
• Cocks: glossy black, with a purplish suffusion on the head, back, and underparts. Keel-shaped tail feathers and yellow eyes.
• Hens: smaller and mainly brown.
• The young birds resemble the hens, but with striped underparts.
• Size 15–18¼in (38–46cm).

FACT FILE
Habitat Open woodland close to water, moving into grassland and marshes, also backyards with mature trees.
Nest Hanging cup of grass.
Eggs 3–7, bluish white with darker blotches.
Food Fruit, insects, nectar.
Distribution South-central Canada, down across central and eastern USA to Florida and Mexico. Occasionally in westerly US states. May overwinter in South America.

IDENTIFICATION
• Mature cock: black head, back, and chest, with the remainder of the body being a distinctive shade of chestnut.
• Hens: olive upperparts, yellowish beneath. Young males are similar to females but with a black bib.
• Size 7¼in (18cm).

ORCHARD ORIOLE
Icterus spurius

Each year these small orioles fly long distances to and from their northern breeding grounds, often not being sighted in the far north of their range until the end of May. Some head north through Florida, while the majority fly directly across the Gulf of Mexico. Having reached their breeding grounds they will nest in backyards with large trees, especially oaks.

Oriole pairs tend to be solitary, although they may sometimes associate with eastern kingbirds *(Tyrannus tyrannus)*, which defend their nest sites vigorously. Even so, the number of orchard orioles is declining, partly, it is feared, because of nest parasitism by bronzed and brown-headed cowbirds *(Molothrus)*, where the young cowbirds hatch first from eggs laid in the host nest and then eject the oriole eggs or chicks. In some areas, over one-quarter of orchard oriole nests host the young of these species,

which greatly reduces the rate of survival of their natural offspring.

In their wintering quarters, hundreds of orchard orioles may congregate together, feeding on the nectar of various flowering trees and shrubs.

FACT FILE
Habitat Deciduous woodland.
Nest Pendulous woven structure.
Eggs 4–6, grayish, darker markings.
Food Invertebrates and fruit.
Distribution British Columbia in Canada eastward to Nova Scotia and across virtually all of the USA, except Florida and parts of Gulf coast. Overwinters in Central America down to northern South America.

IDENTIFICATION
• Breeding adult cock: black head, black extending over back and wings. Narrow white bar above flight feathers, which are edged with white. Rest of body orange, vivid on chest but paler on underparts. Rump orange, with black upper tail feathers, and orange below. Narrow, pointed grayish bill, blacker on upper surface.
• Hens: brown head and upperparts.
• Young have olive-brown upperparts, dull underparts with orange coloring.
• Size 8¾in (22cm).

NORTHERN ORIOLE
Icterus galbula

These orioles and particularly their young vary in appearance, which makes them hard to identify. To add to the confusion, this species used to be called the Baltimore oriole, and was considered distinct from the Bullock's oriole found in the west. New studies suggest they are the same species, now known as the northern oriole.

The orange eyebrows and cheeks of the cock distinguish the western form from the eastern. The forestation of the Great Plains enabled these birds to meet and hybridize, to create what is in some respects a new species.

These orioles may be seen in backyards with mature trees. Large flocks migrate south in September, and return in April.

BACKYARD HUNTERS

Studies suggest that corvids rank among the most intelligent of birds, a trait that they put to good use when hunting for food. Kestrels and owls are agile aerial predators and opportunistic hunters that rely on strength and speed to overcome their prey, which often includes smaller birds.

BLACK-BILLED MAGPIE

Pica hudsonia

Distinguishable from its European relative by its calls rather than its appearance, the black-billed magpie is a common sight through much of its range. These members of the crow family are agile, holding their tail feathers up as they hop along the ground. They are often blamed for the decline of songbirds because of their habit of raiding nests, taking both eggs and young chicks. They will also chase other birds, particularly gulls, to force them to drop their food. Bold and garrulous by nature, a pair of black-billed magpies create a commotion if their nest is threatened by a predator, such as a cat. Their calls draw other magpies, who then join in harrying the feline. Their nest is a large structure, with a protective dome of twigs.

FACT FILE
Habitat Trees with surrounding open areas, grasslands, by streams.
Nest Dome-shape stick pile.
Eggs 2–8, blue-green, darker markings.
Food Omnivorous.
Distribution Western North America, from Alaska eastward to Ontario down to northeastern parts of California and northern New Mexico.

IDENTIFICATION
• Black head, upper breast, back, rump and tail, with a broad white patch around the abdomen. When folded, wings have broad white stripe and dark blue areas below. Black plumage may have green gloss.
• Sexes are alike, but the cock frequently has a longer tail.
• Size 19¼in (48cm).

AMERICAN CROW

Common crow *Corvus brachyrhynchos*

Few birds have more highly developed communication skills than these crows. It is almost impossible to approach them without being noticed, because even when feeding they have sentinels keeping a lookout for danger. They are heavily persecuted in farming areas, due to the damage they can inflict on crops; however, the benefit they bring to farmers and gardeners in foraging for harmful invertebrates is often overlooked.

American crows are highly adaptable birds, just as likely to be encountered in suburban backyards as in open countryside. Noisy by nature, they tend to be much less vocal in the vicinity of their nests, which are sited in tall trees, often in public parks.

The height at which they build—60ft (20m) or more off the ground—keeps the nests safe from most predators.

FACT FILE
Habitat Ranges widely, including into suburban areas.
Nest Platform of sticks.
Eggs 3–7, greenish, brown blotches.
Food Omnivorous.
Distribution Present in much of North America, from British Columbia to Newfoundland and south to Baja California, Colorado, and central Texas.

IDENTIFICATION
• Jet black plumage, with dark eyes and a large black bill.
• Sexes are alike.
• Calls help to distinguish this species from other crows, while the fan-shape appearance of the tail in flight distinguishes them from ravens
• Size 17½in (45cm).

AMERICAN KESTREL
Falco sparverius

The smallest North American falcon, the American kestrel can easily be overlooked unless it is hovering conspicuously by a roadside. Keen eyesight allows it to see a mouse from up to 90ft (30m) away. It dives down quickly to seize the unsuspecting

quarry in its sharp talons. After making a kill, the kestrel flies up to a convenient perch with its meal, or back to the nest if it has young.

In urban backyards, house sparrows and other small birds fall prey to these falcons. In summer, insects such as grasshoppers can play a vital part in nourishing a growing brood. The vast range of these kestrels shows them to be adaptable feeders.

EASTERN SCREECH OWL
Otus asio

Lightly wooded areas, including backyards, are favored by these birds of prey. In true owl fashion, eastern screech owls hunt at night, and despite their size are able to take relatively large quarry, including adult rats. They are opportunists, catching anything from earthworms to snakes and even moths, which can be seized in flight. In urban areas, they are even known to plunge into backyard ponds at night, seizing unwary fish who venture near the surface.

The shape of their wings means that virtually no sound betrays their presence until after they have launched their deadly strike. As with other owls, the study of the pellets regurgitated after meals has allowed ornithologists to confirm their feeding habits.

In the breeding season, these owls lay up to eight eggs in a tree hole or nest box. They will harry intruders, including humans, if they feel the nest is threatened. The red and gray morphs of these owls are equally

common, sometimes even cropping up in the same nest. Habitat appears to play no part in determining coloration.

NATIVE INSECT-EATERS AND INVADERS

The present-day distribution of some birds is the direct result of past human interference. The effects of this can be seen in North America, where some introduced European species have become established across virtually the entire continent. Mimics such as the catbird may even pick up the songs of these invaders.

BROWN THRASHER
Toxostoma rufum

Thrashers are a native American group of birds. They are common yet inconspicuous, being shy by nature, tending to hide away in woodland or backyards with dense vegetation. They venture down to the ground to flick over leaf litter and snatch up any invertebrates disturbed.

At the outset of the breeding season it is difficult to overlook the courtship of the brown thrasher, because the cock takes up a prominent position from which to sing to his would-be mate. He perches with his head up and bill open, but any hint of danger will stop his song. The hen responds by offering a piece of vegetation, which probably marks the start of nest building.

Pairs work together to construct a bulky nest of plant matter, including grass and twigs. Incubation and fledging each take about 13 days, which allows two broods of chicks to be reared during a single breeding season.

FACT FILE
Habitat Woodland, hedges, shrubbery.
Nest Cup shape.
Eggs 2–5, whitish to pale blue with brown speckles.
Food Invertebrates and berries.
Distribution Widely in eastern parts of North America, as far as Florida and the Gulf coast. It has even been recorded in Newfoundland.

IDENTIFICATION
• Reddish brown upperparts, streaking across wings. Long chestnut tail feathers. Underparts marked with black streaks in vertical lines running on to flanks; plumage whitish near throat, fawn on lower parts of abdomen.
• Long, down-curved black bill.
• Sexes are alike.
• Size 11½in (29cm).

GRAY CATBIRD
Dumetella carolinensis

The song of these relatives of the mockingbird incorporates a sound like a cat's meowing, which is the reason for their common name. This plaintive song is commonly heard in suburban backyards. Catbirds also possess a harsher alarm call in their vocal repertoire. They can often be heard singing after dark, especially on moonlit nights.

Catbirds are shy by nature, and their coloration also helps them to blend into the background. Their chestnut underparts are most conspicuous during the cock's courting display, when he chases the hen in the early stages of courtship.

When on the move, the catbird flicks its long tail repeatedly. Insects are a vital part of the diet of these birds, especially when they are rearing chicks, when invertebrates provide valuable protein. Catbirds may catch their insect prey above water, and these birds may be observed hunting in backyards close to ponds and streams.

FACT FILE
Habitat Scrubland, hedges, backyards.
Nest Loose cup of vegetation.
Eggs 4–6, glossy blue-green.
Food Fruit and insects.
Distribution Range extends from southern Canada south and eastward across the USA, as far down as Florida. Southerly winter range extends as far down as Panama and Cuba.

IDENTIFICATION
• Smaller than the American robin, this species is slate gray in color, with a distinctive black cap. It also has chestnut underparts, which may not be clearly visible.
• Sexes are alike.
• Size 9¼in (23cm).

HOUSE SPARROW
Passer domesticus

A common visitor to bird feeders and city parks, house sparrows have adapted to living close to people. They were originally brought to New York from Europe in 1850, and by 1910 had spread west to California. There are now noticeable differences within the North American population: northern individuals are larger, while those from southwestern arid areas are paler.

House sparrows form loose flocks, with larger numbers gathering where food is plentiful. They spend much time on the ground, hopping along while watching for predators, such as cats. It is not uncommon for them to build nests during winter to serve as communal roosts.

The bills of cock birds turn black in the spring, at the start of the nesting period.

During this time, several males will often court a single female in what has become known as a 'sparrows' wedding'. In more rural areas, house sparrows sometimes nest in tree holes, and occasionally construct domed nests. They also sometimes use nest boxes.

COMMON STARLING
European starling *Sturnus vulgaris*

The common European starling is a New World invader, introduced in 1890 when a small flock of 60 starlings brought from England was set free in New York's Central Park. A further 40 were released there the following year, making the millions of starlings now present in the whole of North America direct descendants of this initial group of 100 birds. This release came about as part of an unfulfilled plan to introduce all the birds described in the works of British playwright William Shakespeare to North America.

Small groups of starlings are often to be seen feeding in backyards, although occasionally much larger groups comprised of hundreds of birds may visit an area.

In flight, European starlings are adept at avoiding predators, such as hawks, by weaving back and forth in close formation, to confuse a would-be attacker. Their belligerent nature means that these starlings sometimes commandeer backyard bird tables and even nest holes from native species.

MIGRANTS

Many New World species undertake marked seasonal movements in the course of a year. Though the focus is often on birds from inhospitable northern latitudes flying south for the winter, others in the southern hemisphere also move north toward the equator before the southern winter.

SAND MARTIN

Bank swallow or African sand martin *Riparia riparia*

In the summer months, bank swallows sometimes appear in backyards with large ponds. They are usually observed relatively close to lakes and other stretches of water, often swooping down to catch invertebrates near the surface. They are likely to be nesting in colonies nearby, in tunnels that they excavate on suitable sandy banks. These can extend back for up to 3ft (1m), with the nesting chamber lined with grass, seaweed, or similar material. The eggs are laid on top of a soft bed of feathers.

When the young birds leave the nest, they stay in groups with other chicks until their parents return to feed them, typically bringing about 60 invertebrates back on each visit. Parents recognize their offspring by their distinctive calls. If danger threatens, the repetitive alarm calls of the adults cause the young to rush back to the protection of the nest.

FACT FILE
Habitat Open country, close to water.
Nest Holes in sandbanks.
Eggs 3–4, white.
Food Flying invertebrates.
Distribution Throughout North America, except in the more arid regions of southwestern USA. Winters in South America.

IDENTIFICATION
• Mainly brown, with white plumage on the throat, separated from the white underparts by a brown band across the breast. Long flight feathers. Small black bill.
• Sexes are alike. Immature bank swallows have shorter flight feathers and are browner than the adults.
• Size 4¼in (11cm).

NORTHERN ROUGH-WINGED SWALLOW

Stelgidopteryx serripennis

These swallows take their name from the tiny hooks on the feather vane of the outermost primary feather on each wing, near the shaft. These can only be seen with magnification; their purpose is unknown. Although they range over a wide area, northern rough-winged swallows are likely to be seen in backyards close to lakes and other wetlands, where they catch insects, such as midges, on the wing. They also hunt prey, such as caterpillars and spiders, near the ground.

Often seen in groups, they sometimes roost communally in holes to conserve warmth in cold weather. Pairs of these swallows start to nest in May and adopt a variety of existing cavities as nest sites, rarely excavating their own burrows. The nest chamber is lined with available materials, from seaweed to pine needles.

FACT FILE
Habitat Open country.
Nest Existing burrows in riverbanks.
Eggs 4–8, white.
Food Invertebrates.
Distribution Breeds from southern Alaska and Canada south through British Columbia, the southern prairies of Canada, and across most of the USA to southern California and the Gulf Coast. Migrates to Central America, as far as Panama.

IDENTIFICATION
• Mainly brown, darker on head and wings, with long, broad flight feathers. Tail brown, underparts whitish. Thin, narrow bill.
• Sexes are alike. Young birds have a cinnamon tone to the upperparts.
• Size 4¾in (12cm).

FACT FILE
Habitat Urban and agricultural areas.
Nest Twigs held together with saliva.
Eggs 2–7, white.
Food Flying insects.
Distribution This species' range extends through eastern North America. It migrates through Central America on its way to and from its South American winter quarters in Peru and northern Chile.

IDENTIFICATION
• Dark brown overall, with a paler area around the throat. It has a stocky body with short tail feathers and long wings.
• This species is usually seen in flight from beneath, often at a great height as they soar high.
• Sexes are similar.
• 4¾in (12cm)

CHIMNEY SWIFT
Chaetura pelagica

Chimney swifts have long wings and actively fly rather than glide, flapping their wings fast to stay airborne. When seen up close, their square-shape tails have spines at their tips.

Dependent on flying insects for food, they are forced to head south for the winter, returning north to their breeding grounds in March and April. Just prior to migration, thousands may congregate at favored roosts. Their habits have changed following the spread of cities. Instead of the hollow trees that they would formerly have used for roosting, they have switched to using chimneys, barns, and similar sites, even breeding in these surroundings.

FACT FILE
Habitat Open areas near buildings.
Nest Gourd-shape structure of mud.
Eggs 3–6, white with brown speckles.
Food Invertebrates.
Distribution North America and Mexico, except northern Alaska and the far northeast. Migrates via Central America to southern Brazil, Paraguay, parts of Argentina, and even Chile.

IDENTIFICATION
• Pale forehead, with blue top to the head, which is encircled with chestnut. Blackish area at the base of the throat.
• Upper chest and rump orangish brown, underparts otherwise whitish, with dark edging to undertail coverts.
• Back and wings are dark, streaked with white.
• Young have blackish heads.
• Size 5½in (14cm).

CLIFF SWALLOW
Petrochelidon pyrrhonota

The cliff swallow has adjusted its habits to benefit from the spread of urbanization in its North American breeding grounds. In the past, these swallows built their nests on cliff faces, as their name suggests, but now pairs will breed in barns, bridges, and similar structures. They will also use dry, hollowed gourds placed in suitable sites in backyards as artificial nests.

These swallows may also nest in large colonies. The mud that forms the nest is scooped up in the swallow's bill, and, unlike in related species, is the only building material. The interior is lined with vegetation.

Pairs typically take five days to build the nest. In fall, the swallows head south for winter, although a few fly no farther than Panama. Their return is greeted as a sign of spring.

TREE-DWELLERS

Few groups of birds are more closely associated with woodlands than woodpeckers. They are well-equipped to thrive in these surroundings, using their powerful bills to obtain food and also carve nest holes. Nuthatches are similarly well-adapted, with strong toes and claws and a compact shape.

BLACK-HEADED THREE-TOED WOODPECKER
Picoides arcticus

Ranging over a huge area, these woodpeckers are most likely to be seen where there are numerous dead pine trees, especially if the surrounding area is flooded. They often occur in groups, breeding together in close proximity where conditions are favorable. In some years, flocks may move further south than usual, occasionally crossing into the states of Nebraska, New Jersey, and Ohio in the USA. This type of movement, known as an irruption, is usually the result of a shortage of food.

These birds are burnt-forest specialists that feed on the wood-boring beetles that in turn feed on the burnt wood. The woodpeckers peck the beetles or sometimes glean them off branches.

The short inner hind toe, equivalent to the thumb, is missing, helping these birds to climb vertically.

FACT FILE
Habitat Coniferous forest.
Eggs Tree hollow.
Eggs 2–6, white.
Food Invertebrates, vegetable matter.
Distribution Canada and northern USA, from Alaska east to Newfoundland in the north and south to New York State and California.

IDENTIFICATION
• Yellowish plumage on head and crown, two white stripes on each side of face separated by irregular, broad, black band. Wings and back blackish, with some whitish feathering. Flanks of some subspecies blacker than others.
• Hens: smaller with no yellow on the crown. Young birds browner, but more white plumage on wings.
• Size 9½in (24cm).

RED-HEADED WOODPECKER
Melanerpes erythrocephalus

Red-headed woodpeckers sometimes appear in backyards near farmland or close to orchards with dying trees, containing plentiful dead wood. They eat a wide range of plant and animal foods, with their diet being influenced by the season. They are unusual in that they hunt not only by clambering over the bark of trees, but also by hawking insects in flight. They will even swoop down onto the ground and hop along there seeking prey. These woodpeckers will raid the nests of other birds, seizing both eggs and chicks, and they also catch mice.

In northern parts of their range, they often migrate southward during the cold months of the year, seeking plentiful supplies of acorns and beech nuts when other foods are scarce. They also lay down stores of food, concealing nuts, acorns, and large insects in cavities or hiding them under the bark, and returning to eat them later. European starlings occasionally evict these birds from their nest holes, chiseled out of rotten wood in a tree.

FACT FILE
Habitat Open woodland, farmland, country roads, golf courses.
Nest Hole in a tree or fence post.
Eggs 4–10, white.
Food Plant matter, invertebrates, rodents, eggs and nestlings.
Distribution Canada and the USA, from Manitoba and southern Ontario south to Florida and the Gulf Coast.

IDENTIFICATION
• Scarlet plumage covering the head, bordered by a narrow band of black feathering. White underparts, bluish black coloration on back and tail.
• Prominent white patch on wings, which are otherwise bluish black.
• Sexes are alike. Young birds much browner overall, including the head.
• Size 9½in (24cm).

DOWNY WOODPECKER
Picoides pubescens

Downy woodpeckers are relatively common and can be found in a variety of habitats. These small woodpeckers are relatively tame, and it is possible to attract them to backyard feeding stations by offering suet, particularly in the wintertime when other foods are likely to be scarce. They feed largely on wood-boring insects, but are usually forced to seek out plant matter, such as nuts, through the winter.

The breeding period varies across their extensive range, being later in the north, where egg laying is unlikely to occur before May. Unusually for a woodpecker, the nest site is chosen by the female, and is almost invariably sited in a dead tree. At this time, their distinctive drumming sounds can be heard echoing through the forest, as they tap on branches within their territory to keep in touch. Nesting duties are evenly shared, with pairs subsequently splitting up over the winter period to seek food and roost in tree hollows on their own.

RED-BREASTED NUTHATCH
Sitta canadensis

Lively and active by nature, red-breasted nuthatches are well-adapted to an arboreal lifestyle. Their small size and compact shape enable them to climb up and down tree trunks with ease, their strong toes and claws providing sufficient anchorage for them to descend headfirst. They are adept at pulling insects out from under the bark, and move along narrow branches to pluck invertebrates off leaves. The seeds of conifers help to sustain them through winter, when invertebrates are scarce. At this time, they will also take seeds, suet, and wheat from bird tables.

These birds have an unusual method of deterring predators from the nest hole by smearing it with pine oil. This helps to obscure their scent, but their plumage becomes heavily stained as they pass in and out of the nest.

INVERTEBRATE-EATERS

Insects provide these birds with much of their diet, and all also eat other foods, for example, seeds, fruit, and in the case of the omniverous black-billed cuckoo, eggs, chicks, and lizards. They use various techniques to feed. For instance, the ruby-crowned kinglet hovers before darting down on to its prey.

BLACK-BILLED CUCKOO
Coccyzus erythrophthalmus

Black-billed cuckoos are typically found below 3,300ft (1,100m). They are not easy to spot, being mainly solitary birds that prefer to hide in dense vegetation. Their calls are not very distinctive, resembling those of doves.

Pairs sometimes nest quite close to the ground in a bush that gives good cover, or higher up in a tree fork.

The diet of black-billed cuckoos varies with location, since they are opportunistic feeders. They may steal both eggs and chicks from the nests of smaller birds, as well as eating fruit and catching prey ranging from insects to lizards. In North America, these cuckoos are highly valued in farming areas due to the number of pests, especially tent caterpillars, they eat, which lessens damage to crops.

FACT FILE
Habitat Various types of woodland.
Nest Platform of sticks.
Eggs 2–4, pale bluish green.
Food Omnivorous feeding habits.
Distribution From Alberta and Montana to the eastern coast of North America, south as far as South Carolina, Arkansas and Texas. Migrates to western South America as far south as northern Peru, but also recorded from Paraguay.

IDENTIFICATION
• Bronze-brown on upperparts, underparts white. Long, narrow tail feathers black with white tips. Orbital skin encircling eyes is red. Black bill.
• Size 11¼in (28cm).

AMERICAN PIPIT
Anthus rubescens

American pipits leave their northern breeding grounds in early September, and head south for the winter. At this time, they may appear on farms and golf courses, sometimes in large flocks.

Active birds by nature, they tend to walk rather than hop across the ground, bobbing their tails up and down regularly. Their range does not extend to the northeastern United States, probably because until recently this area was heavily forested. The males establish their territories once they reach their breeding grounds in the Arctic tundra. The nest site is carefully chosen to reduce the risk of the eggs becoming chilled. It may be partly buried, or sheltered by a rock, often apparently orientated to catch the rays of the sun. It is not uncommon for hens to reuse a nest built previously. The hen sits alone. The eggs hatch after about 14 days. The chicks fledge after a similar period, and are reared on invertebrates.

FACT FILE
Habitat Tundra, grassland, fields.
Nest Cup shape.
Eggs 4–5, gray, dark spots and streaks.
Food Seeds and invertebrates.
Distribution Arctic North America and western USA, parts of northern New Hampshire, California, and New Mexico. Winters throughout southern USA, and up to British Columbia in the west and New England in the east.

IDENTIFICATION
• Gray upperparts, indistinct whitish stripe passing through each eye, becoming brownish gray over back.
• Wings blackish. Streaking on reddish buff underparts, varying according to race. Rump brown, tail black above. Darker, brownish upperparts outside breeding period, more streaked overall.
• Sexes are alike.
• Size 6¾in (17cm).

RUBY-CROWNED KINGLET
Regulus calendula

These small warblers breed in the taiga forest in the far north of North America. They often search for food by hovering around the branches, darting down to seize caterpillars, and are able to balance right at the tips of branches thanks to their small size. It is not always easy to recognize the distinctive ruby red crown of the cock bird, because this feathering may be obscured.

Ruby-crowned kinglets are active birds, always on the move, and frequently flick their wings, as if they are startled and about to take off. The nest is located close to the end of a branch of a spruce tree or similar conifer, where the young will be fairly safe from predators.

After the breeding season, they travel southward, arriving at their wintering grounds in September. In northern states, they are very rare in winter, but are familiar residents in the south, visiting backyards for peanut picks, fruit, and baked goods.

DARK-EYED JUNCO
Junco hyemalis

These sparrows display variable coloration through their wide range, but the fact that they breed together freely and produce fertile offspring means that they rank as one species, not four.

Rather tame, they are widely seen in woodlands, and also backyards, particularly in winter when they take seeds, millet, and peanuts from feeders.

Dark-eyed juncos are mainly terrestrial in their habits, living in loose flocks that may forage widely. They are prolific when nesting, with incubation lasting just 12 days and the young fledging after a similar period. The nest is well-disguised and sited close to the ground, so that if the young are disturbed

they can escape a predator by running away on their surprisingly large feet.

Hens produce up to three rounds of chicks over the summer. The young feed largely on invertebrates.

FACT FILE
Habitat Forests and woodland.
Nest Woven from plant matter.
Eggs 5–10, creamy, fine speckling.
Food Insects and other invertebrates.
Distribution From Alaska, across Canada south of Hudson Bay to Newfoundland, south to the Great Lakes and New England. Overwinters from southern USA south through Central America as far as Guatemala.

IDENTIFICATION
• Olive-brown upperparts, paler, whitish area encircling eyes. Throat area pale gray, becoming yellowish on underparts.
• Wings dark, white band at top and across wings of cock bird. Ruby red patch of feathering on top of crown.
• Hens: lack the red patch; more dusky stripes across wings. Young have more brownish upperparts.
• Size 4¼in (11cm).

FACT FILE
Habitat Woodland, backyards.
Nest Cup of vegetation.
Eggs 3–6, pale green to blue, with brown spots.
Food Seeds, berries, invertebrates.
Distribution Breeds from Alaska to Newfoundland, south to Mexico and Georgia in the east. Winters along the Gulf coast and into Mexico.

IDENTIFICATION
• Variable appearance. Eastern North American birds mainly slaty gray, with brownish gray hens. In the west, the Oregon junco (*J. h. thurberi*) has a black head and orange-red flanks and back, with paler brown hens. Other variants include the pink-sided *J. h. mearnsi* of the central Rockies, and the white-winged *J. h. aikeni*, gray with white wing bars and white underparts. All have dark eyes.
• Sexes are alike. Young birds have streaked patterning.
• Size 6¼in (16cm).

VARIATIONS ON A THEME

It is not always easy to identify birds with certainty, especially in the case of immatures coming into their adult plumage, which can involve several moults. There can also be regional variations, particularly birds that are widely distributed, and distinctive color forms can crop up among normally-colored individuals.

MEXICAN JAY
Gray-breasted jay *Aphelocoma wollweberi*

Seven different races of the Mexican jay have been identified, though it is not always easy to distinguish them in the field, especially since juvenile coloration is a key factor. The length of time taken for the bills of young birds to change color varies greatly, sometimes taking up to two years. Differences in vocalizations and lifestyle have also been identified.

The race *A. w. couchii*, found in southern Texas and south across the border, has a harsher call and has adopted a more territorial lifestyle than the Arizona race (*A. w. arizonae*), which lives in flocks of up to 20 birds. These flocks are usually made up of an adult pair and their young from previous years that are not yet breeding, and so are able to help the parents rear the new brood.

FACT FILE
Habitat Arid woodland.
Nest Cup-shaped platform of sticks.
Eggs 4–7, blue to greenish blue.
Food Omnivorous.
Distribution From Texas, Arizona, and New Mexico in southwestern USA, down much of Mexico.

IDENTIFICATION
• Bluish gray overall, differing in depth of color through range. Bluish-gray plumage on head and neck, extending over wings, tail also bluish.
• Grayish-white underparts, becoming white around vent and on undertail coverts. Northern birds paler than southerly ones.
• Sexes are alike. Young birds duller, with yellowish area at base of the bill.
• Size 13in (34cm).

AMERICAN ROBIN
Turdus migratorius

The return of the American robin to its northern haunts is a long-awaited sign of spring. Adult cock birds usually arrive first, followed by the hens. Last to arrive are the young of the previous year, making their first flight back to the area where they were hatched. American robins are alert hunters, hopping across lawns and pausing at intervals, their head tilted slightly to one side as if listening. It is actually their keen eyesight that allows them to spot earthworms and other invertebrates in the grass. Berries also feature in their diet.

Their nest is well-built, with mud serving as cement to hold the vegetation together, and carefully sited in dense vegetation to avoid the attention of predators. Eastern birds tend to be more brightly coloured than their western counterparts. It is not uncommon for pale leucistic individuals to occur in this species, and even pure white albinos.

FACT FILE
Habitat Woodlands, parks and suburban areas.
Nest Cup of vegetation and mud.
Eggs 3–6, bright blue.
Food Invertebrates and also fruit.
Distribution All of North America apart from the central far north, down as far as Mexico. Overwinters in the south of its range, including some Caribbean islands.

IDENTIFICATION
• Cocks have a blackish head with white around the eyes and streaking under the throat. Back and wings greyish brown, with brick-red underparts and white under the vent.
• Hens have browner heads and orangish underparts.
• Size 10in (25cm).

AMERICAN REDSTART
Setophaga ruticilla

Belonging to the wood warbler rather than the thrush family, American redstarts are naturally very lively and active, almost constantly on the move seeking food, fanning open their tails and lowering their wings. Invertebrates may be hawked in flight or grabbed off bark.

In parts of Latin America, where they overwinter, they are known as 'candelita,' because their jaunty nature and the coloration of cock birds combine to resemble the movements of a candle flame.

One of the most widespread warblers in North America, they may be seen in backyards with wild areas or near second-growth woodlands. Males will sing loudly even before they gain adult plumage, which is not attained until they are over a year old. The song is most evident in spring at the start of the breeding season.

The nest is built at a variable height in a suitable bush or tree, up to 75ft (23m) above the ground. The hen incubates alone, with the eggs hatching after approximately 12 days. The young birds are reared almost entirely on invertebrates, and fledge about three weeks later.

VARIED THRUSH
Ixoreus naevius

Varied thrushes are common in the coniferous woodlands of the Northwest, where they sometimes appear in backyards. This migratory member of the thrush family is fairly hard to observe in its habitat, dark woods and areas near water.

Varied thrushes are not shy birds, however, and have a powerful song with buzzing tones, which is most often uttered in the rain. They sing most at the start of the breeding period in March, from the upper branches of conifer trees.

Varied thrushes normally feed close to the ground, foraging for invertebrates as well as eating berries. They normally nest about 15ft (4.5m) off the ground. The bulky nest often includes moss.

After the breeding period the thrushes leave Alaska, with many overwintering in British Columbia, while others head farther south, where they are sometimes seen in backyards near open woodland.

OWLS

Owls rank among the most distinctive of all birds, thanks partly to their facial shape. Representatives of this group are very widespread in America, ranging from the coniferous forests of the far north, through the Amazon rainforest and right down to Tierra del Fuego at the southern tip of South America.

NORTHERN SAW-WHET OWL

Aegolius acadicus

Despite their distinctive calls, which resemble the sound of a saw being sharpened, northern saw-whet owls are hard to observe due to their small size and nocturnal nature. They are also able to fly very quietly.

This is strictly a woodland species, not found in northern coniferous areas. In southern areas it can be seen in more open, drier deciduous forest. During the day the owls rest on a branch close to a tree trunk, where their color and size make them hard to locate.

They eat a variety of prey, especially rodents but also birds, invertebrates and frogs.

Pairs only come together for breeding, with the male seeking a mate by singing close to his nest hole. The young remain in the nest for a month.

FACT FILE
Habitat Mainly coniferous forest.
Nest Tree hole.
Eggs 3–7, white.
Food Mainly small vertebrates.
Distribution North America from British Columbia to Newfoundland, and Mexico. *A. a. brooksi* occurs on Queen Charlotte Islands and *A. a. acadicus* in the full range.

IDENTIFICATION
• Brown and white area on face above eyes, white spotted area on nape. Brown markings on sides of face.
• Underparts white, rufous-brown markings. Wings and tail brownish, white spotting. Black bill, irides yellow.
• Young have white eyebrows and lores and brown face and underparts.
• Size 7½in (19cm).

NORTHERN HAWK-OWL

Surnia ulula

These owls, occurring in the far north where day length varies significantly through the year, can be encountered at any time. Northern hawk-owls are solitary by nature outside the breeding season. In late spring the male calls to attract a mate.

The pair may choose from a variety of nesting sites, making use of a hole created by a woodpecker, taking over an abandoned stick nest, or simply choosing a site on top of a tree whose crown has snapped off, creating a depression. They make no attempt at nest-building themselves. The eggs are laid at two-day intervals, with the hen sitting alone and the male bringing food for her.

Lemmings usually predominate in their diet, but in years when the lemming population plummets other prey, even small fish, may be caught. Breeding success is directly related to the availability of food.

The young fledge at four weeks old, but it will be a further two weeks before they can fly, and they remain dependent on their parents for food for a further month.

FACT FILE
Habitat Coniferous forest.
Nest Tree holes.
Eggs 5–13, white.
Food Mainly small mammals.
Distribution The owls' range is circumpolar, right across North America in the boreal region from southern Alaska east to Labrador. Also present in Newfoundland.

IDENTIFICATION
• Prominent white eyebrows and white cheeks, with whitish spotting on the dark head and wings. Broad black bars on each side of the neck.
• More brownish on the underparts and tail, with the underparts barred too. Eyes and bill pale yellow.
• Sexes are alike.
• Size 16in (40cm).

Habitat Coniferous forest.
Nest Often a platform of sticks.
Eggs 3–6, white.
Food Small vertebrates, especially voles.
Distribution Circumpolar, from northern Canada and Alaska south to California, Idaho and Wyoming. A separate population extends across the far north of Europe and Asia.

IDENTIFICATION
• Plumage coloration consists mainly of gray streaking and barring on a white background.
• The dark markings on the so-called facial disk that surrounds the eyes form concentric rings.
• Yellowish bill, with a blackish patch beneath. The tail is relatively long.
• Hens: larger in size than males.
• Size 27½in (69cm).

GREAT GRAY OWL
Strix nebulosa

These very large owls are documented as being the world's largest owls by length, though it is not the heaviest. They move quite extensively through their large range, which spans the Eastern and Western Hemispheres, with North American individuals even having been sighted in the vicinity of New York on occasion.

Much of this movement is triggered by the availability of food, especially voles, which these owls hunt almost exclusively during the breeding season. They are mostly silent, but when they do call it is a deep, rhythmic 'whoo' sound, and usually occurs in relation to territory or when interacting with offspring.

Pairs will often take over the abandoned nests of other birds of prey such as buzzards, although they sometimes nest on the ground. The number of eggs in the clutch is directly related to the availability of food, with breeding being closely correlated to fluctuations in vole populations.

FACT FILE
Habitat Lightly wooded areas.
Nest Abandoned nest or on the ground.
Eggs 2–6, white.
Food Small vertebrates.
Distribution Present in Alaska and Canada south over virtually the entire USA and Central America. Also in South America from Colombia and Ecuador through Peru to Bolivia and east to Guyana; and south to Brazil and central Argentina.

IDENTIFICATION
• Variable through the species' wide range. Northerly populations generally have more brown in their plumage and on the facial disc. Populations further south have a more buff tone to the feathering.
• The bill is grayish black. The iris is yellow.
• Underneath the feathers, the legs and feet are black.
• Hens are larger than cocks.
• Size 22¼in (56cm).

GREAT HORNED OWL
Bubo virginianus

These owls are not found in areas of dense forest. They prefer instead to hunt in semi-open terrain, where their keen eyesight enables them to swoop down on small mammals that form the basis of their diet. They are opportunistic hunters, however, and will take a much wider range of prey, from insects and amphibians to other birds, including smaller owls. Males are quite vocal, and sing loudly to attract a mate. Pairs split up at the end of the breeding season, but may reunite later. They breed in a wide range of locations; an unpleasant stench may give away the location of the nest site because the male may stockpile food there for the offspring.

Below: *The name of these owls comes from the appearance of their so-called ear tufts.*

WOODLAND DWELLERS

A variety of game birds are found in the woodlands of North America, extending southward. The most significant is the wild turkey, the original ancestor of all modern domestic strains worldwide. Grouse also occur in this region. All are shy, relying on cover to elude detection, and seeking food at ground level. Some migrate.

AMERICAN WOODCOCK
Scolopax minor

The mottled appearance of this bird provides exceptional camouflage when on the ground in forests, where they blend in with the leaf litter. They tend to rely on camouflage to escape danger, but if flushed will take off with a noisy flapping of their wings, flying not in a straight line but swerving from side to side.

The courtship display of these woodcocks is spectacular, with males taking off and flying almost vertically before circling and plunging down again. The nest is sited in a secluded spot, and even the eggs blend in with the leaves, which are used to line the nest scrape.

American woodcocks have relatively large eyes, which help them see in the gloom of the forest. The position of the eyes high on the head also gives them excellent vision, so it is difficult for predators to creep up on them. The long bill is used to extract worms and to catch insects.

FACT FILE
Habitat Wet woodland.
Nest On the ground.
Eggs 4, buff with brown spots.
Food Invertebrates.
Distribution From Newfoundland and southern Manitoba in Canada down through eastern parts of USA to Texas, Florida and the Gulf coast. Overwinters in these southerly areas.

IDENTIFICATION
• Pale buff sides to face, barred crown, gray above bill and around throat.
• Gray stripe down the edge of wings, broader gray area across wings. Rest of back is mottled. Pale rufous-brown underparts, undersides of flight feathers gray, black band across short tail. Long, tapering bill.
• 11¼in (28cm).

WILSON'S SNIPE
Gallinago delicata

Not easy to observe, Wilson's snipe tends to feed either at sunrise or toward dusk, probing the ground with jerky movements of its stocky bill. It remains out of sight for most of the day. If surprised in the open these birds will sometimes freeze in the hope of avoiding detection, relying on their cryptic plumage to provide camouflage. More commonly they take off in a zigzag fashion, flying quite low and fast before plunging back down into suitable cover. Cocks perch and call loudly on their display grounds in the far north.

When plummeting down as part of their display flight, the movement of air through their tail feathers creates a hooting sound that has been likened to the call of the boreal owl. They migrate south in the fall, flying in flocks under cover of darkness. Subsequently they split up and forage separately, which helps to conceal their presence.

FACT FILE
Habitat Lightly wooded areas, and fields offering plenty of concealment.
Nest Hidden in grass.
Eggs 4, olive-brown with black spots.
Food Mainly invertebrates.
Distribution Breeds across northern Alaska and Canada, southward to New Jersey and California. Wintering grounds up to British Columbia, to western and southeastern USA, and along Gulf coast.

IDENTIFICATION
• Pale buff stripe along crown, pale stripes above and below eyes. Dark mottled plumage on chest and wings.
• Blackish stripes on sides of body, white underparts. Wings have white stripes, tail is rufous. Long, pointed bill.
• Size 11¼in (28cm).

WILD TURKEY
Meleagris gallopavo

FACT FILE
Habitat Wooded areas, including swampland.
Nest Scrape on the ground.
Eggs 8–15, buff with dark brown spots.
Food Berries, seeds, and nuts, also invertebrates.
Distribution Southern USA south into Mexico. It has a very patchy distribution that has given rise to numerous localized subspecies, especially in more western parts of the range.

IDENTIFICATION
• Bare head, which is predominantly bluish. Prominent red beard extending down the throat, which is absent in hens.
• Body is bronzy brown in color, with black barring on the wings and tail.
• Size cock: 49in (120cm); hen: 36¼in (91cm).

These large members of the fowl family are difficult to spot in their natural woodland habitat because the barring on their plumage breaks up their outline very effectively to create good camouflage. Shafts of sunlight filtering through the trees highlight the natural iridescence in the plumage, with shades of green appearing on the feathering from some angles.

The wild turkey is unmistakable, especially when the male erects his tail feathers into a fan-shape as part of his courtship display. The color of his bare skin intensifies during the breeding season, and he often utters a loud gobbling call. Males, called stags, frequently live in the company of several females. It is only these wild turkeys that have rusty brown tips to their tail feathers, those of domestic turkeys being white.

OVENBIRD
Seiurus aurocapilla

FACT FILE
Habitat Largely deciduous woodland.
Nest Scrape on the ground.
Eggs 8–15, buff with brown markings.
Food Seeds, berries and invertebrates.
Distribution Restricted to specific areas of Central America, such as the Yucatan Peninsula in Mexico, Belize and Guatemala.

IDENTIFICATION
• Rufous stripe edged with black extending back from the bill and up the crown. Upperparts are olive brown, throat is white with a dark stripe running down the sides from the lower corner of the bill.
• Dark streaking on underparts, including flanks. Narrow ring of white feathers encircles each eye.
• Bill darker on the upper surface, paler below. Legs and feet are pinkish.
• Sexes are alike.
• Size 5½in (14cm).

These unusual warblers spend most of their time on the ground searching for insect prey, walking rather than hopping like most birds. Ovenbirds prefer mature areas of woodland, where there is relatively little undergrowth. Their presence may be revealed by their song, which sounds like the word 'teacher' repeated constantly. Their precise song pattern varies with region, with several dialects being identified.

The ovenbird gets its name from the appearance of its nest, a domed structure that has been likened to a Dutch oven. The nest is located on the ground and made from a pile of leaves and other vegetation. The entrance hole is to the side, and the interior is lined with grass. Some males have more than one mate, while on occasions several males have been observed feeding a brood of chicks.

QUAILS AND OTHER GROUND BIRDS

It is no coincidence that many of these birds have mottled upperparts, since they face danger from above, in the guise of avian predators swooping overhead. They move largely on foot, which also helps to conceal their presence, and often fly only if they detect danger nearby.

COMMON BOBWHITE

Northern bobwhite *Colinus virginianus*

Taxonomists have recognized at least 22 different races of these quail, and color variation is quite marked in some cases. Differences in size are also apparent, with individuals found in southern parts of their range being smaller than those occurring in northern regions. Common bobwhites live in groups, typically numbering around a dozen birds or so. They will invade agricultural areas to forage for food, especially when crops are ripening. These birds generally prefer to seek cover on the ground, where their cryptic coloration helps to conceal them from predators, but they will fly if threatened. Populations of these quails have also been introduced well outside their normal range, not only in other parts of the USA, including the northwest and on Hawaii, but also further afield in New Zealand.

FACT FILE
Habitat Woodland and farmland.
Nest Scrape on the ground lined with vegetation.
Eggs 10–15, dull white, often with blotches.
Food Seeds and invertebrates.
Distribution Northeastern USA southward through Mexico into western Guatemala.

IDENTIFICATION
• There is considerable variation. Most races have black stripe running from bill through eyes, white stripe above and broader white area on throat. Chestnut underparts, usually speckled with white. Wings brownish.
• Hens: duller, having buff rather than white patches on the head.
• Size 10in (25cm).

CALIFORNIA QUAIL

Callipepla californica

California quail are highly adaptable through their range, and this characteristic has enabled breeding populations of these popular game birds to be established in locations as far apart as Hawaii, Chile and King Island, Australia.

Nesting on the ground makes California quail vulnerable to predators, and although the young are able to move freely as soon as they have hatched, relatively few are likely to survive long enough to breed themselves the following year. Overgrazing by farm animals can adversely affect their numbers, presumably because this reduces the food that is available to the birds. However these quail also forage in cropgrowing areas, and sometimes associate in groups of up to a thousand individuals where food is plentiful.

FACT FILE
Habitat Semi-desert to woodland.
Nest Grass-lined scraping on ground.
Eggs 15, creamy white with brownish patches.
Food Seeds, vegetation, invertebrates.
Distribution Native to western North America, ranging from British Columbia in Canada southward to California and Mexico.

IDENTIFICATION
• Prominent, raised black crest that slopes forward over the bill. Top of the head is chestnut, with a white band beneath and another bordering the black area of the face. Chest is grayish, flanks are speckled.
• Hens: lack black and white areas, grayish faces and smaller crests.
• Size 10½in (27cm).

GREATER PRAIRIE CHICKEN
Tympanuchus cupido

The greater prairie chicken's range has declined significantly in recent years. The nominate race, called the heath hen, once had an extensive range in eastern parts of the USA, but is now presumed extinct. The smaller and darker form, Attwater's prairie chicken (*T. c. attwateri*), is now extinct in southwest Louisiana and struggling to survive in Texas. This is the result of hunting and clearance of prairie habitat.

Breeding males display communally at a lek, inflating their neck sacs and uttering a far-carrying, booming call. The nest is concealed by vegetation. Egglaying occurs from early April, usually 5–17 per clutch.

FACT FILE

Habitat Prairies and associated agricultural areas.
Nest Scrape lined with feathers.
Eggs 5–17, olive with brown blotching.
Food Seeds and invertebrates.
Distribution Occurs mainly to the south and west of the Great Lakes, as far south as Oklahoma, with a separate population found in the coastal area of Texas.

IDENTIFICATION

• Cock: yellowish-orange areas on head. Adjacent golden air sacs are inflated as part of the display, when dark neck feathers are also raised. Body is barred with shades of brown. Paler underparts. Short tail is blackish in cock, barred in the hen.
• Hen: side of head and throat are speckled, with underparts having dark markings on a white background.
• Size 18½in (47cm).

WHITE-TAILED PTARMIGAN
Lagopus leucura

The white-tailed is the only species of ptarmigan ranging south into the USA from Canada. It usually occurs at higher altitudes, although it descends in October to escape the worst winter weather. During summer, white-tailed ptarmigans are found close to the tree-line, where pairs establish breeding territories.

The nest is concealed on the ground, and lined with feathers. Eggs are laid any time from late May until July. Hens incubate alone, with the young able to follow their parent after hatching.

The population divides in winter, with males forming flocks on their own. When food is hard to find because of snow, ptarmigans feed on the buds of willow, birch and alder. Their fully feathered legs and feet afford protection from the cold.

FACT FILE

Habitat Tundra and mountainous areas.
Nest Scrape on the ground.
Eggs 5–9, brown with dark spots.
Food Vegetation.
Distribution Western North America, from Alaska through Canada into USA in Rocky Mountains, as far south as New Mexico. Now re-established in the High Sierras of California.

IDENTIFICATION

• In winter, both sexes are completely white, with males retaining a narrow red comb above eyes. In summer, males have evident red comb with mottling on head and upper breast, extending over back and part of wings, with white underparts.
• Hens slightly smaller, more mottled, with prominent black markings over back, lacking comb. Slight variations depending on race.
• Young have barring all over wings.
• Size 13in (34cm).

HAWAIIAN BIRDS

In appearance and lifestyle, native birds occurring on the Hawaiian Islands are among the most unusual found anywhere, having developed in isolation from mainland species until relatively recently. However, a number have become extinct over recent years, as a result of human interference in their environment.

I'IWI
Drepanis coccinea

As with many of Hawaii's birds, the common name of this honeycreeper is derived from its native name. It is most likely to be spotted around flowering plants. In spite of their vivid coloration i'iwis are not easy to observe; like other red forest birds, they blend with the background. Even if only briefly glimpsed, however, their downward-curving bill sets them apart from other similar Hawaiian birds.

I'iwis' calls range from whistles to gurgles, their most distinctive vocalizations being likened to the sound of a rusty hinge creaking open. They also replicate the calls of other species such as the Hawaii elepaio (*Chasiempis sandwichensis*). I'iwis are mostly found above 2,000ft (600m), being less common on O'ahu and Molokai.

FACT FILE
Habitat Woodland.
Nest Cup-shaped, made of vegetation.
Eggs 1–3, white with brown markings.
Food Nectar and invertebrates.
Distribution Confined to the Hawaiian Islands; extinct on Lanai, and now occurs only on Hawaii itself, Kaua'i, Maui, O'ahu and Molokai.

IDENTIFICATION
• Red coloration over body. Black wings and tail, area of white plumage at top of wings. Red legs and bill.
• Youngsters yellow-green, dark barring over body. Back darker than underparts. Black tail and wings, paler edging on some wing feathers.
• Size 6in (15cm).

'AKOHEKOHE
Crested honeycreeper *Palmeria dolei* (E)

Another honeycreeper that is not always easy to spot. Its rather dark overall coloration and relatively small size help to conceal its presence in the treetops where it feeds. However, the 'akohekohe has a very lively nature and is highly vocal, uttering a series of buzzing and histling sounds, some not unlike a person whistling.

Unfortunately this species has seriously declined in numbers. It has already vanished from Molokai, although it is not uncommon on the eastern side of East Maui, where it inhabits the upland forest areas, frequenting ohia-lehua trees in particular. Here, it can sometimes be seen in flight, although sightings are made difficult by the frequent misty weather that obscures visibility in this area.

From a distance, it is possible that the 'akohekohe may be confused with the smaller apapane (*Himatione sanguinea*).

FACT FILE
Habitat Flowering trees.
Nest Cup-shaped, of vegetation.
Eggs 2, white with brown markings.
Food Nectar and invertebrates.
Distribution Hawaiian Islands; now believed to be extinct on Molokai, but still survives on Maui.

IDENTIFICATION
• Bushy crest up between eyes, buff above each eye, blue beneath on cheeks. Rest of head dark, reddish nape. Bluish markings on throat, blue and brown patterning on underparts.
• Wings similarly colored on top, blue band running across and blue edging to flight feathers. Black fan-shaped tail with white tip, undercoverts grayish.
• Sexes are alike. Young birds duller with much shorter crest.
• Size 7¼in (18cm).

MAUI NUKUPU'U
Hemignathus affinis (E)

The Maui nukupu'u occurs in thick ohia forest, using its strong legs to clamber up the bark of trees. Its slender bill is used to probe for invertebrates among the moss and crevices in the bark, and it may often be seen hanging upside down looking under leaves as well. Once three species existed. The O'ahu nukupu'u (*H. lucidus*) is already extinct and the Kaua'i species (*H. hanapepe*), with its distinctive white undertail coverts, was restricted to the Alakai swamp, however there have been no recent sightings. On Maui most sightings are likely to be on Haleakala's upper slopes.

Much of the confusion surrounding its distribution there arose from its close likeness to the akiapola'au (*H. wilsoni*), which occurs on Hawaiian islands too. A very detailed comparison will reveal that the akiapola'au's straight rather than slightly curved lower mandible sets it apart.

FACT FILE
Habitat Forest.
Nest Apparently unrecorded.
Eggs Believed to be 2, white with brown markings.
Food Mainly invertebrates.
Distribution Now restricted to Maui.

IDENTIFICATION
• Cock: yellow head and underparts, with paler undertail coverts. The plumage on the back of the head is relatively long. Back and wings are dark olive-green. There is a small black area of plumage around the eyes, with the legs black too. The narrow bill is dark, with the upper part being curved and much longer than the short lower part.
• Hens easily distinguished by their dull olive-green plumage.
• Young birds resemble hens.
• Size 5½in (14cm).

BISHOP'S OO
Moho bishopi (E)

This relatively large nectar-feeder has very distinctive, flute-like tones in its song that are unlike those of other native birds. The bishop's oo is exceedingly difficult to spot, however, as it inhabits dense areas of rainforest and prefers the upper level of the forest canopy.

It is regarded now as being extinct, having vanished from both of the islands where it was sighted at the start of the 20th century. However, the bishop's oo did have an unconfirmed sighting on Maui in 1981 so it is possible that it still survives there today, notably on the northeastern slope of Haleakala, but sadly there have been no sightings of the Molokai population since 1904.

Like other honeyeaters, bishop's oos have tiny swellings on their tongue, called papillae, which act as brushes, helping them to collect flower pollen. They favor lobelia (*Campanulaceae*) flowers. Not surprisingly, honeyeaters are important pollinators of forest trees. Nothing is known about its nesting biology and little is known about its life history.

FACT FILE
Habitat Dense forest.
Nest Cup-shaped.
Eggs 2, pinkish with some dark spotting.
Food Mainly nectar.
Distribution Restricted to the Hawaiian Islands, being recorded only from Molokai and Maui.

IDENTIFICATION
• Predominantly blackish, with faint yellow streaking on the body and more prominent yellow areas behind the eyes and at the bend of the wing.
• This bird has yellow undertail coverts and long tail feathers, tapering to a point. The yellow tail feathers were used by early Hawaiians to make long, flowing cloaks and feathered capes and for feathered standards.
• The bill is slightly down-curving, also tapering to a point, and it has black legs.
• Sexes are alike.
• Size 12in (30cm).

PREDATORY AQUATIC BIRDS

Gulls in particular are highly adaptable species that feed on a wide range of food, from invertebrates, fish, and young birds to garbage. The belted kingfisher and little blue heron, too, are versatile birds that are well-adapted to their predatory lifestyle, with powerful, sharp bills.

CALIFORNIA GULL
Larus californicus

California gulls are particularly adaptable, as is reflected in the wide range of habitats they frequent. They will eat an equally diverse range of food, including grain and various types of invertebrates, and will scavenge at garbage dumps for anything edible. These gulls will also take eggs and hunt ducklings and other young birds, and may even cannibalize the carcasses of their own dead.

They seem to have an insight into where food may be readily available, often appearing to plague strawberry farms for fruit when the crop is ripening. Famously, flocks of California gulls rescued the early Mormon settlers around the Great Salt Lake from imminent starvation by devouring a plague of locusts that was threatening to destroy their crops, an event marked by a statue in Salt Lake City. California gulls breed in colonies on islands in large inland lakes.

FACT FILE
Habitat Coastal areas and inland.
Nest Twigs and other vegetation.
Eggs 2–3, buff olive with blotches.
Food Omnivorous.
Distribution Central northwestern North America, in the prairie regions, overwintering on the coast from Oregon south via California to Baja California.

IDENTIFICATION
• White underparts and head, with back of head being mottled in winter. Wings gray, flight feathers appearing black and white with wing closed.
• Bill is yellow with a red tip. Legs and feet also yellow.
• Sexes are alike. Young birds have brown mottling, dark bill and pink legs.
• Size 23¼in (58cm).

RING-BILLED GULL
Larus delawarensis

Winter sees a return to the coastline for these gulls. Most move to the more southerly parts of their range, although some wander north as far as Alaska. Over recent years they have become relatively common in Florida, where they were first recorded in 1930. They have also extended their distribution from California in 1940 up to British Columbia by 1974. Even more remarkably, since the 1970s they have been crossing the Atlantic in large numbers, so that they are no longer considered rare vagrants in the UK.

Ring-billed gulls are adaptable feeders. In the prairies they congregate in flocks to pick up grubs from the soil as the land is ploughed. They catch fish underwater when hunting at sea.

FACT FILE
Habitat Coastal areas and inland.
Nest Made of vegetation.
Eggs 3, buff-colored and blotched.
Food Omnivorous.
Distribution Range extends north to the prairie region of Canada, and east to the Great Lakes. Also extends down the Atlantic seaboard, past Florida and around the Caribbean to Central America.

IDENTIFICATION
• Named for the black ring circling yellow bill close to tip. Typical gull patterning, with white head showing mottling in winter. Wings grayish, white markings on black tips. Legs yellow.
• Sexes are alike. Young show light mottling.
• Size 21¼in (53cm).

FACT FILE
Habitat Ponds, lakes, marshes.
Nest Platform of sticks.
Eggs 3–5, pale blue-green.
Food Invertebrates.
Distribution Southern parts of the USA; breeds in various locations from southern California east to New England. Moves south in winter from New Jersey down to Florida, along the Gulf coast, and down through Central America to southern Peru and southern Brazil.

IDENTIFICATION
• Slateblue, with dark purple feathers on head and neck. In breeding birds, these areas are reddish purple, with plumes on the chest and a head crest. Legs and feet change from dull green to black.
• Sexes are alike.
• Young birds are white, with black tips to flight feathers.
• Size 24¼in (61cm)

LITTLE BLUE HERON
Egretta caerulea

These herons are a common sight through much of their range. They prefer to feed on invertebrates rather than fish, hunting crayfish in the water, and crickets on drier ground. These birds sometimes follow behind ploughs to hunt worms brought to the surface. Breeding starts in April in the north, earlier in Florida and the Caribbean. Pairs often breed in mixed groups with larger herons. Young birds are occasionally seen well beyond their normal range, even as far as Greenland and Paraguay.

FACT FILE
Habitat Ponds, lakes and rivers.
Nest In a burrow.
Eggs 5–8, white.
Food Mainly fish.
Distribution Ranges from the Aleutian Islands into southwest Alaska and down through southern Canada to the Gulf coast and Mexico. May be seen in other parts of Central America, the Caribbean and along the northeastern coasts of South America in winter.

IDENTIFICATION
• Cock: mainly gray on the head, back and wings, except for a white collar, white underparts below a gray breastband, and a white spot by each eye.
• Hens: have a rufous breastband with gray markings. and are rufous on the flanks too. Young have a second tawny breastband.
• Size 14½in (37cm).

BELTED KINGFISHER
Megaceryle alcyon

The loud, rattling call of these kingfishers, uttered in flight, betrays their presence. Their preference for fish means they will move south in the winter, to areas of water that will not freeze over. They are generally found on tranquil stretches of water, where they can observe fish easily, but on occasions they have been spotted feeding up to 0.6 miles (1km) offshore. They may also visit backyard ponds.

Various invertebrates from butterflies to crayfish feature in the diet of belted kingfishers. Their large size means they can also prey on water shrews and the young chicks of other birds. If they are faced with a shortage of food in winter, they will even resort to feeding on berries. The area beneath their regular roosting spot is littered with regurgitated pellets containing the indigestible remains of their prey. As in the case of owls, this evidence enables zoologists to pinpoint the feeding preferences of these and other kingfishers.

COMMON WATER BIRDS

Coots and moorhens belong to the group known as crakes. These water-loving birds can often be seen out in the open, but when frightened they usually scuttle to the safety of dense vegetation by the water. Geese rank among the longest-lived of all waterfowl, with a potential life expectancy of more than two decades.

CANADA GOOSE
Branta canadensis

A number of different races of Canada goose are recognized, which all differ from one another a little in terms of plumage and size. This species has proved to be highly adaptable. Its numbers have grown considerably in Europe, specially in farming areas, where these geese descend in flocks to feed on crops during the winter once other food has become more scarce. When migrating, flocks fly in a clear V-shaped formation.

The smallest race occurs in western Alaska, while geese from the Canadian prairies are almost four times as heavy.

In common with many waterfowl, Canada geese are not able to fly when moulting, but they take

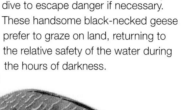

readily to the water at this time and can dive to escape danger if necessary. These handsome black-necked geese prefer to graze on land, returning to the relative safety of the water during the hours of darkness.

FACT FILE
Habitat Usually near water.
Nest Vegetation on the ground.
Eggs 4–7, whitish.
Food Vegetarian.
Distribution Breeds across North America from Alaska to Labrador, south to California and south of Great Lakes. Overwinters near west and east coasts of USA, to the Caribbean.

IDENTIFICATION
• Black head and neck. Area of white in a broad stripe from behind eyes to under throat. Whitish area at base of neck merges into brown on chest. Dark brown wings. White on abdomen. Blackish legs and feet.
• Sexes are alike.
• Size 22–43in (55–110cm).

AMERICAN AVOCET
Recurvirostra americana

These avocets head north to their breeding grounds in April, nesting around shallow lakes and similar expanses of water, sometimes in large numbers. Females

sometimes lay in nests other than their own. Both sexes share the incubation and rearing, with the young fledging at around four weeks of age.

American avocets leave their nesting grounds from August, often heading to coasts. They are less common on the eastern seaboard, but appear to be increasing there after being hunted and almost exterminated in the 1800s.

The species winters in the vicinity of Florida, Texas and the Caribbean, as well as California. It also ranges south to Guatemala.

These birds have a distinctive method of feeding in water, sweeping their head from side to side in search of worms, crustaceans, and other prey. On land, they catch grasshoppers in a more conventional way, grabbing them with their bill, and sometimes eat seeds too.

FACT FILE
Habitat Marshes and ponds.
Nest Grass-lined scrape.
Eggs 4, olive-buff with darker spots.
Food Invertebrates.
Distribution Breeds from southeastern parts of British Columbia to southwestern Ontario, to Baja California and central Texas. Also in eastern USA and central Mexico.

IDENTIFICATION
• Slender and long-legged. Narrow, grayish bill slightly upturned at tip, especially in females, longer in males.
• Black areas on wings separated by broad white band, white underparts. Head and neck are rusty shade when breeding, grayish-white in winter.
• Young birds have a slight cinnamon wash on their neck.
• Size 18¼in (46cm).

MOORHEN
Common moorhen *Gallinula chloropus*

Even a relatively small pond can attract moorhens, and they may nest in backyards with dense vegetation near the pond. Although usually found in areas of fresh water, they are occasionally seen in brackish areas. Their long toes enable them to walk over aquatic vegetation.

These birds feed on the water or on land. Their diet varies according to the season, although seeds of various types make up the bulk of their food.

Moorhens are less wary than most rails or crakes, swimming in open water. If danger threatens, they will either dive or swim underwater. They are adept divers, remaining submerged by grasping onto underwater vegetation with their bills. In public parks, moorhens can become tame, darting in to obtain food provided for ducks.

During the breeding season, pairs of moorhens set up and defend territories and perform complex courtship rituals.

FACT FILE
Habitat Ponds and other areas of water edged by dense vegetation.
Nest Domed structure hidden in reeds.
Eggs 4–7, buffish with dark markings.
Food Omnivorous.
Distribution South from the Great Lakes to much of the eastern USA. Also Florida, the Gulf Coast, and California, and through Central America. Common in much of South America except northeast and south.

IDENTIFICATION
• Slate gray head, back, and underparts. Grayish black wings. Prominent white line runs down sides of body. Area under tail is white and has a black central stripe. Greenish yellow legs have a small red area at the top. Red bill, apart from yellow tip.
• Sexes are alike.
• Size 12in (30cm).

AMERICAN COOT
Fulica americana

American coots may set up home by large ponds and lakes in parks and backyards. They can become tame when supplied with bread. The cock and hen look similar, but can be distinguished by their different calls.

These coots have proved to be highly adaptable, to the extent that their numbers appear to have increased overall recently.

They rapidly colonize new areas of suitable habitat, although populations can be adversely affected by very cold springtime weather, which makes food harder to find. For this reason, American coots commonly migrate south in large numbers in order to avoid the worst of the winter weather.

FACT FILE
Habitat Permanent areas of wetland, including coastal inlets in winter.
Nest Floating heap of dead aquatic vegetation.
Eggs 3–12, buff with dense, fine blackish spotting.
Food Aquatic vegetation.
Distribution This species ranges from Alaska southward across much of North America, and right through Central America and the Caribbean into parts of Colombia in South America.

IDENTIFICATION
• Predominantly slategray, more blackish on the head. White undertail coverts. Bill is whitish, with red near the tip, enlarging into a broad shield with red at the top.
• Sexes are alike, although hens are often significantly smaller.
• Young birds are predominantly brown, with duller bills.
• Size 17¼in (43cm).

DUCKS

Ducks are a diverse group of waterfowl, but can be distinguished by their relatively small size compared with swans and geese. They inhabit stretches of open water, though typically become more secretive when nesting. Drakes usually moult into more colorful plumage before the onset of the breeding season.

MOTTLED DUCK
Anas fulvigula

Closely related to the well-known mallard (Anas platyrhynchos), these dabbling ducks are usually encountered in relatively shallow waters, where they dip their heads down under the surface to obtain water plants and invertebrates.

During the summer they are more likely to be found on stretches of fresh water, but will usually be seen in salt marshes through the winter period. Flocks start to pair off early in the year, beginning in January. They breed on the ground, choosing a secluded site under vegetation for their nest and lining it with feathers.

The incubation period takes approximately four weeks, with the young ducklings having dark brown upperparts at first, and much lighter underparts. They will be sexually mature at one year old.

Mottled ducks can be distinguished from mallards by their darker overall plumage, with females having no white area in their tails.

FACT FILE
Habitat Coastal waters.
Nest Made of grass.
Eggs 4–18, grayish-green.
Food Aquatic vegetation, invertebrates.
Distribution From just north of Florida on Atlantic coast around the Gulf of Mexico down to south Mexico. Now introduced to South Carolina.

IDENTIFICATION
• Drake has yellow bill with a dark tip. Predominantly brownish plumage, paler, unstreaked sides to face and on throat. Mottled underparts, more scalloping to feathers on flanks, over back and on wings. Blue wing speculum. Yellow-orange legs and feet.
• Sexes are similar, although ducks have greener coloration of bills.
• Size 22¼in (56cm).

MALLARD DUCK
Anas platyrhynchos

These ducks are a common sight, even on stretches of water in towns and cities, such as rivers and canals. They may congregate in quite large flocks, especially outside the breeding season, but they are most evident in the spring, when groups of unpaired males chase after potential mates.

The nest is often constructed close to water and is frequently hidden under vegetation, especially in urban areas. These birds feed both on water, up-ending themselves or dabbling at the surface, and on land.

FACT FILE
Habitat Open areas of water.
Nest Scrape lined with down feathers.
Eggs 7–16, buff to grayish green.
Food Plant matter, invertebrates.
Distribution Much of North America, though is more scarce in the far north of Canada. Also in Mexico.

IDENTIFICATION
• Drake: metallic-green head, white neck ring. Brownish chest, gray underparts, blackish area around vent. Bluish speculum in wing, bordered by black and white stripes.
• Duck: brownish buff overall, darker patterning. Same wing markings as drake. Bill is orange, whereas drake's in eclipse plumage is yellow, with a rufous tinge to the breast.
• Size 24in (60cm).

CAROLINA WOOD DUCK
American wood duck *Aix sponsa*

Although these ducks have been seen as far north as Alaska, they move south to warmer climates for the winter months. In some areas their numbers have benefited from the provision of artificial nesting boxes, so that today they rank among the most common waterfowl in the United States. Carolina wood

ducks are likely to be seen dabbling for food in open stretches of water, dipping their heads under the surface, but they also come ashore to nibble at vegetation. Although vagrants sometimes appear in the Caribbean, wood ducks observed in other parts of the world will be descendants of escapees from waterfowl collections.

COMMON MERGANSER
Goosander *Mergus merganser*

Like many waterfowl found in the far north, the common merganser occurs at similar latitudes in Europe and Asia. Diving rather than dabbling ducks, they are called sawbills because of the small sharp projections running down the sides of their bills, which help them to grab fish.

Seen in wooded areas close to water, pairs will nest in a hollow tree or even a nest box, lining it with down to insulate the eggs and prevent them rolling around.

Outside the breeding period, common mergansers form large flocks numbering thousands of birds on lakes and similar stretches of fresh water. They may, however, prefer to fish in nearby rivers, returning to the lake at dusk.

Common mergansers tend to remain in their nesting location until the water starts to freeze over, whereupon they head south. They pair up mainly over winter, returning north to breed the following spring.

TEMPLATES

These templates will enable you to complete some of the more wordworking projects in this book. They should be used in conjunction with the instructions and cutting lists for timber in the steps. Dimensions are listed in both metric and imperial measurements – choose and use just one system.

PALLADIAN BIRD TABLE, page 110

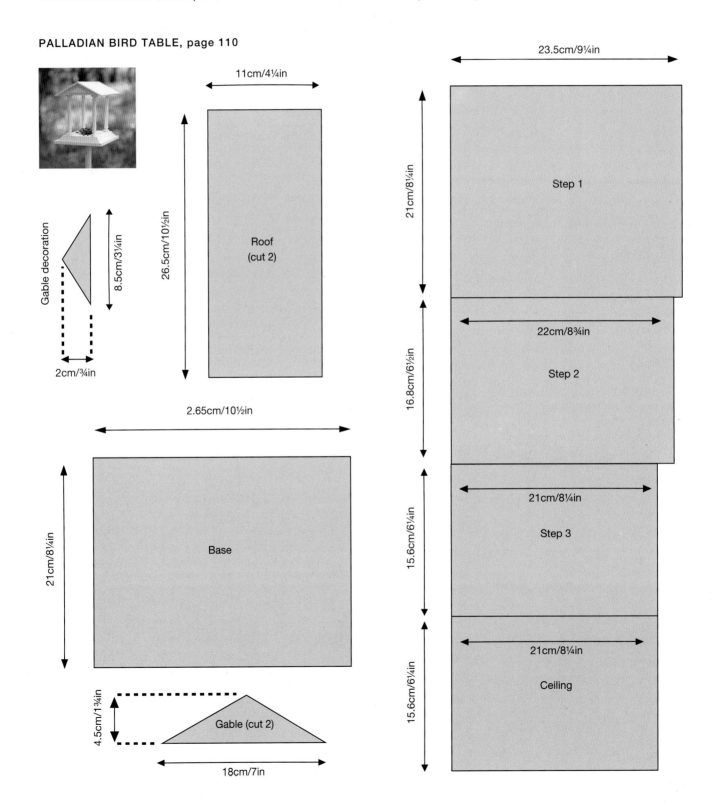

11cm/4¼in

Roof
(cut 2)

26.5cm/10½in

Gable decoration

8.5cm/3¼in

2cm/¾in

2.65cm/10½in

21cm/8¼in

Base

4.5cm/1¾in

Gable (cut 2)

18cm/7in

23.5cm/9¼in

21cm/8¼in

Step 1

16.8cm/6½in

22cm/8¾in

Step 2

15.6cm/6¼in

21cm/8¼in

Step 3

15.6cm/6¼in

21cm/8¼in

Ceiling

SEASIDE-STYLE BIRD TABLE, page 112

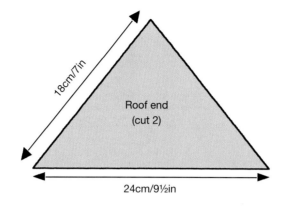

Roof end
(cut 2)

18cm/7in

24cm/9½in

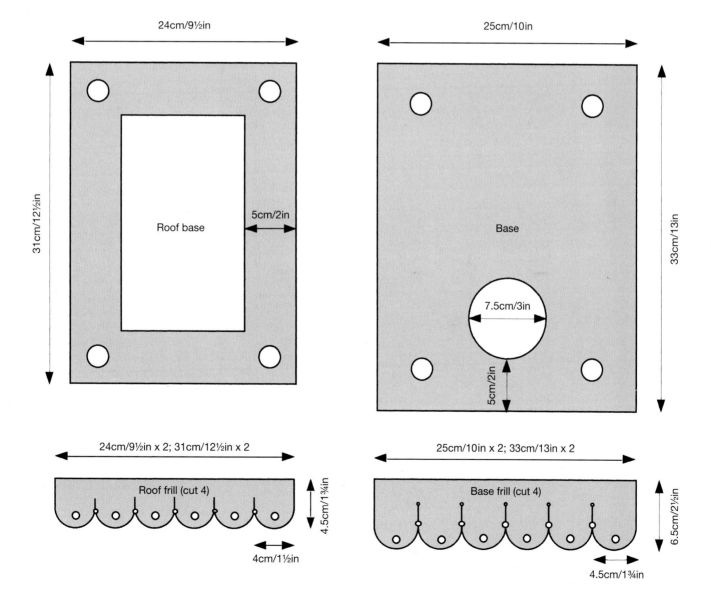

24cm/9½in

Roof base

5cm/2in

31cm/12½in

25cm/10in

Base

7.5cm/3in

33cm/13in

5cm/2in

24cm/9½in x 2; 31cm/12½in x 2

Roof frill (cut 4)

4.5cm/1¾in

4cm/1½in

25cm/10in x 2; 33cm/13in x 2

Base frill (cut 4)

6.5cm/2½in

4.5cm/1¾in

SNUG NESTING BOX, page 126

OPEN-FRONTED NEST BOX, page 140

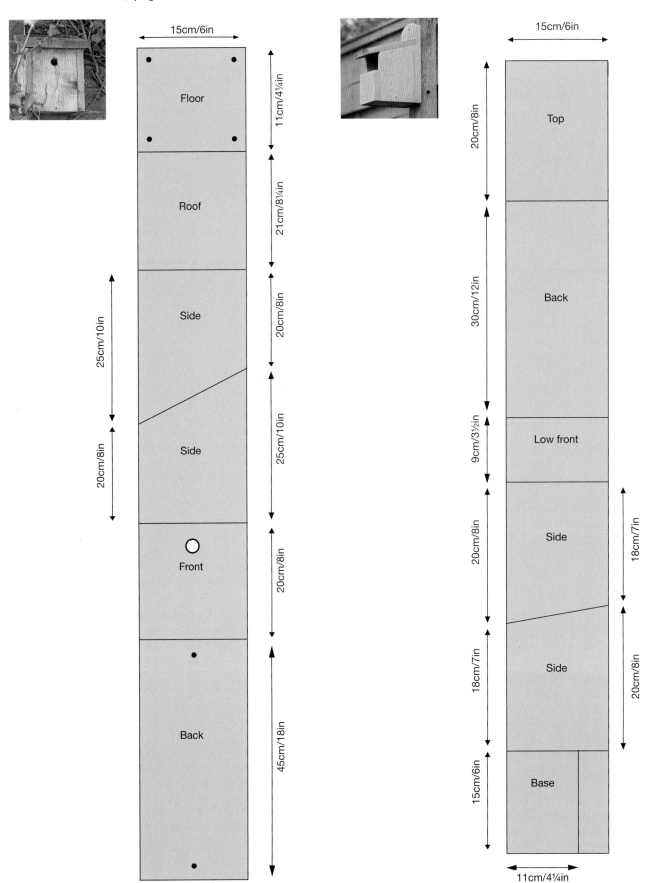

FOLK-ART BIRD BOX, page 128

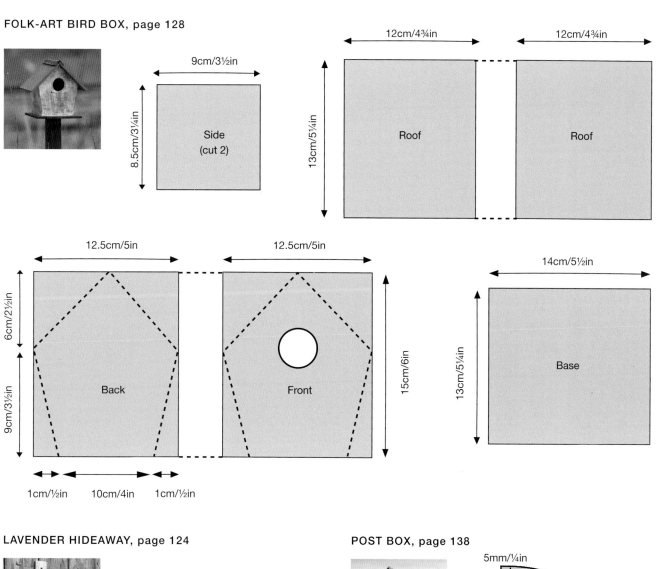

9cm/3½in

Side
(cut 2)

8.5cm/3¼in

12cm/4¾in

Roof

12cm/4¾in

Roof

13cm/5¼in

12.5cm/5in

Back

6cm/2½in

9cm/3½in

12.5cm/5in

Front

15cm/6in

1cm/½in   10cm/4in   1cm/½in

14cm/5½in

Base

13cm/5¼in

LAVENDER HIDEAWAY, page 124

POST BOX, page 138

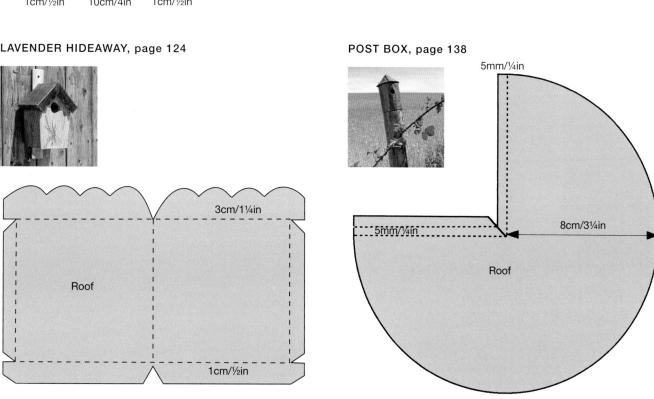

Roof

3cm/1¼in

1cm/½in

5mm/¼in

5mm/¼in

8cm/3¼in

Roof

PEBBLE AND THATCH HOUSE, page 130

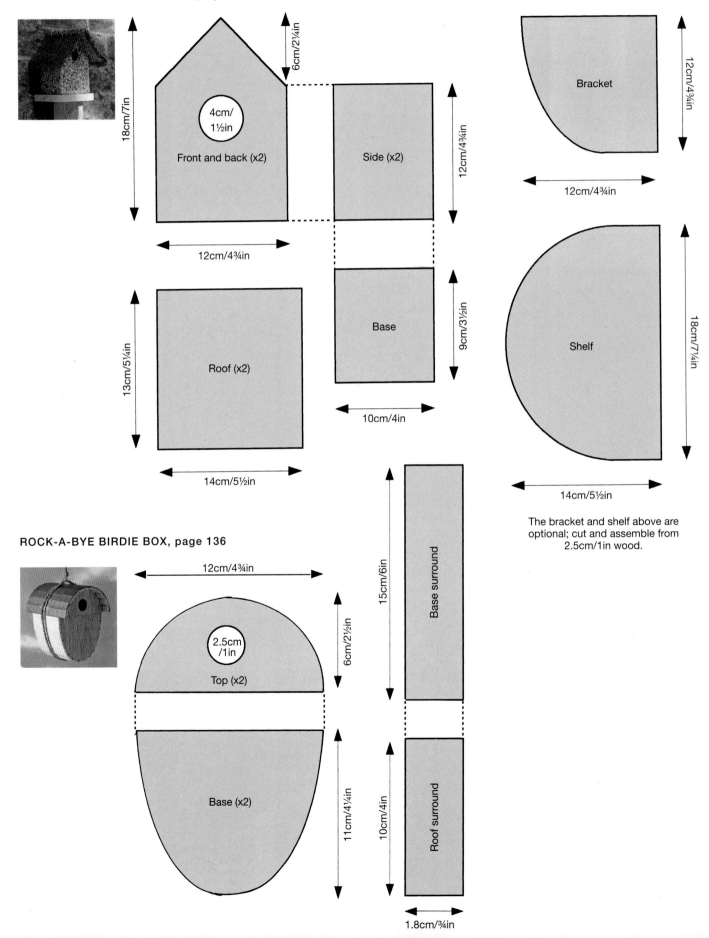

4cm/
1½in

Front and back (x2)

18cm/7in

6cm/2¼in

12cm/4¾in

Side (x2)

12cm/4¾in

Base

9cm/3½in

10cm/4in

Roof (x2)

13cm/5¼in

14cm/5½in

Bracket

12cm/4¾in

12cm/4¾in

Shelf

18cm/7¼in

14cm/5½in

The bracket and shelf above are optional; cut and assemble from 2.5cm/1in wood.

ROCK-A-BYE BIRDIE BOX, page 136

12cm/4¾in

2.5cm
/1in

Top (x2)

6cm/2½in

Base (x2)

11cm/4¼in

Base surround

15cm/6in

Roof surround

10cm/4in

1.8cm/¾in

DUPLEX LIVING, page 144

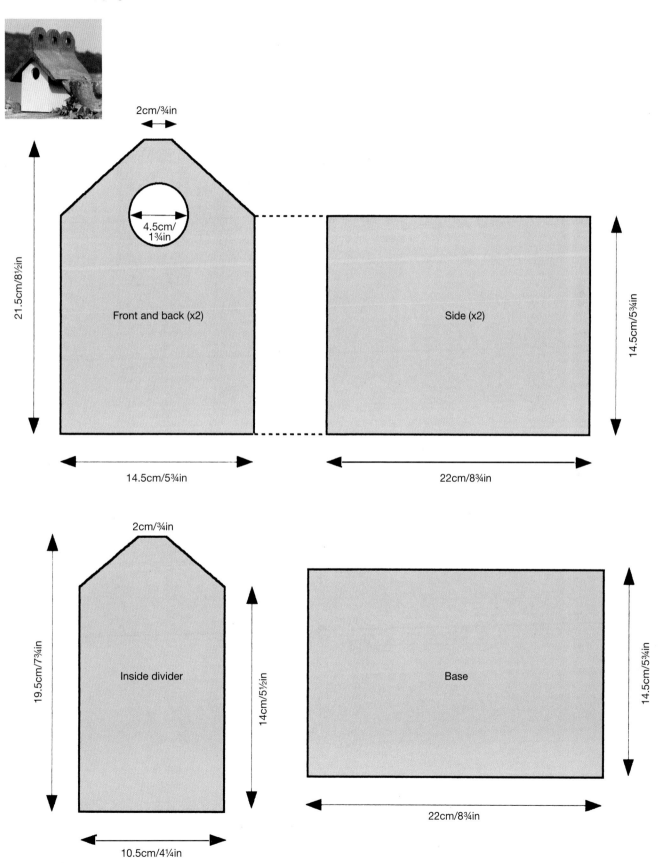

2cm/¾in

21.5cm/8½in

4.5cm/1¾in

Front and back (x2)

14.5cm/5¾in

Side (x2)

14.5cm/5¾in

22cm/8¾in

2cm/¾in

19.5cm/7¾in

Inside divider

14cm/5½in

Base

14.5cm/5¾in

10.5cm/4¼in

22cm/8¾in

SWIFT NURSERY, page 148

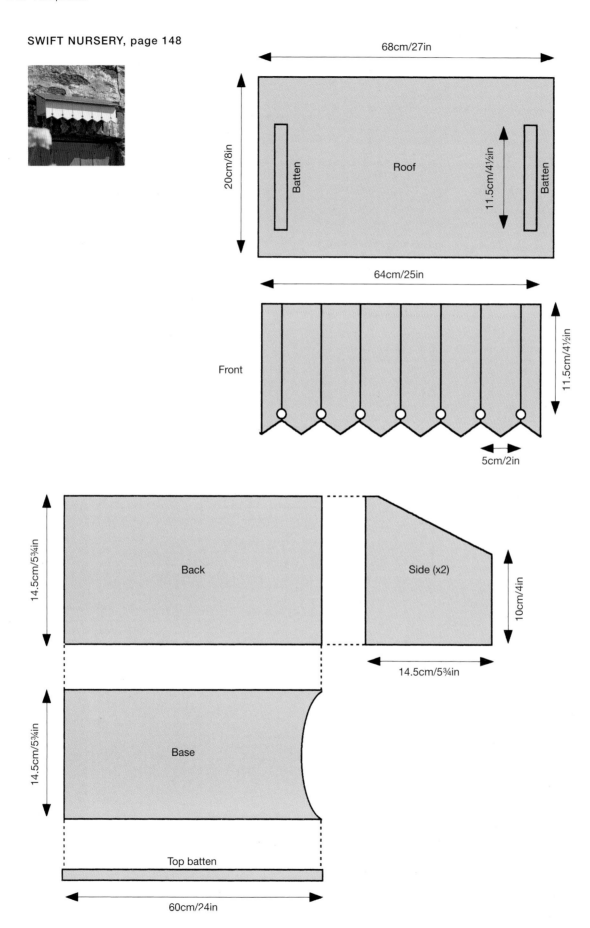

68cm/27in

20cm/8in

Batten

Roof

11.5cm/4½in

Batten

64cm/25in

Front

11.5cm/4½in

5cm/2in

14.5cm/5¾in

Back

Side (x2)

10cm/4in

14.5cm/5¾in

14.5cm/5¾in

Base

Top batten

60cm/24in

DOVECOTE, page 150

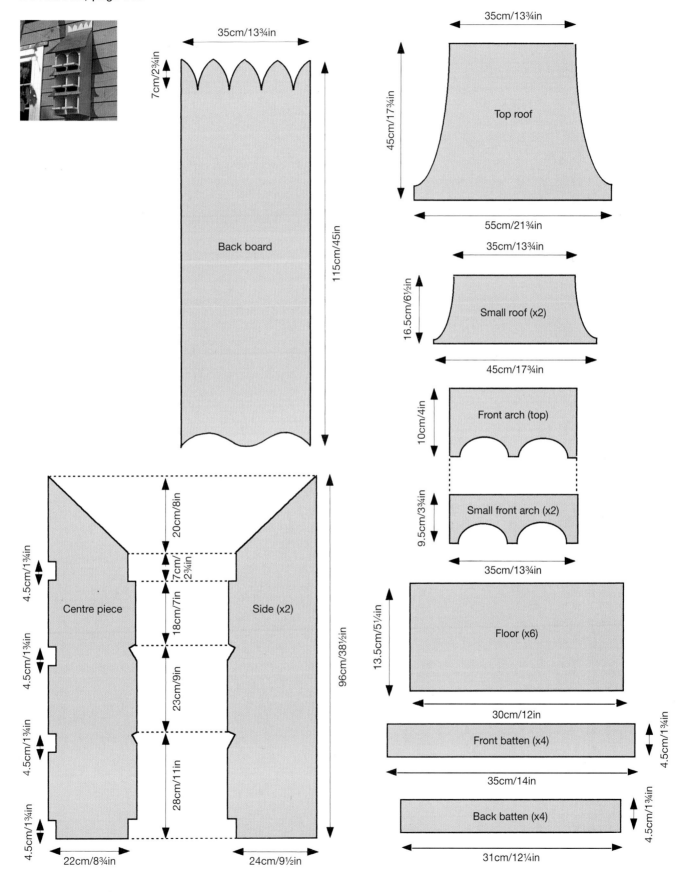

35cm/13¾in

7cm/2¾in

Back board

115cm/45in

35cm/13¾in

Top roof

45cm/17¾in

55cm/21¾in

35cm/13¾in

Small roof (x2)

16.5cm/6½in

45cm/17¾in

Front arch (top)

10cm/4in

Small front arch (x2)

9.5cm/3¾in

35cm/13¾in

Floor (x6)

13.5cm/5¼in

30cm/12in

Front batten (x4)

4.5cm/1¾in

35cm/14in

Back batten (x4)

4.5cm/1¾in

31cm/12¼in

Centre piece

Side (x2)

20cm/8in

7cm/2¾in

18cm/7in

23cm/9in

28cm/11in

96cm/38½in

4.5cm/1¾in

4.5cm/1¾in

4.5cm/1¾in

4.5cm/1¾in

22cm/8¾in

24cm/9½in

NEST BOX SIZES

The dimensions given here will enable you to modify basic nest box designs to suit a wide range of bird species. You may need to alter the dimensions slightly according to the thickness of your wood. Inner surfaces can be left rough, but you should drill a few small holes in the floor of the box for drainage.

ENCLOSED NEST BOXES

This style of nest box has a small, round entrance hole positioned high on the front face. Enclosed nest boxes are suitable for birds that usually nest in tree holes, such as wrens, tits, titmice, chickadees, sparrows, nuthatches, bluebirds, martins, finches, flycatchers and some swallows. Larger bird species, such as starlings, jackdaws, woodpeckers, flickers, owls, American kestrels and Carolina wood ducks, will nest in a larger box of this type, with a bigger entrance hole.

	Floor size	Depth of box	Height of entrance above floor	Diameter of entrance hole	Height above ground
EUROPE					
Wren	10 x 10cm/4 x 4in	15–20cm/6–8in	12cm/4½in	3cm/1¼in	Low in vegetation
Tits	15 x 12cm/6 x 4½in	20–25cm/8–10in	12cm/4½in	3cm/1¼in	2m/7ft
Sparrows	15 x 15cm/6 x 6in	20–25cm/8–10in	15cm/6in	3cm/1¼in	2–4m/7–14ft
Nuthatch	15 x 15cm/6 x 6in	20–25cm//8–10in	12cm/4½in	3cm/1¼in	3.6–6m/12–20ft
Starling	15 x 15cm/6 x 6in	40–45cm/16–18in	30cm/12in	5cm/2in	5m/16ft
Woodpeckers	15 x 15cm/6 x 6in	30–38cm/12–15in	40cm/16in	6cm/2½in	3–5m/10–16ft
Jackdaw	20 x 20cm/8 x 8in	30–38cm/12–15in	40cm/16in	15cm/6in	3–5m/10–16ft
Street pigeon	20 x 20cm/8 x 8in	30–38cm/12–15in	10cm/4in	10cm/4in	3–5m/10–16ft
NORTH AMERICA					
Chickadee	10 x 10cm/4 x 4in	8–10cm/20–25in	15–20cm/6–8in	3cm/1¼in	1.8–4.5m/6–15ft
Titmouse	10 x 10cm/4 x 4in	8–10cm/20–25in	15–20cm/6–8in	3cm/1¼in	1.8–4.5m/6–15ft
Nuthatch	10 x 10cm/4 x 4in	8–10cm/20–25in	15–20cm/6–8in	3cm/1¼in	3.6–6m/12–20ft
Wrens					
House wren	10 x 10cm/4 x 4in	15–20cm/6–8in	10–15cm/4–6in	2.5–3cm/1–1¼in	1.8–3m/6–10ft
Bewick's and					
Carolina wren	10 x 10cm/4 x 4in	15–20cm/6–8in	10–15cm/4–6in	3cm/1¼in	1.8–3m/6–10ft
Winter wren	10 x 10cm/4 x 4in	15–20cm/6–8in	10–15cm/4–6in	3cm/1¼in	1.8–3m/6–10ft
Bluebird	13 x 13cm/5 x 5in	20cm/8in	15cm/6in	4cm/1½in	1.5–3m/5–10ft
Violet-green swallow					
and Tree swallow	13 x 13cm/5 x 5in	15–20cm/6–8in	2.5–13cm/1–5in	4cm/1½in	3–4.5m/10–15ft
Purple martin	15 x 15cm/6 x 6in	15cm/6in	2.5cm/1in	6cm/2½in	4.5–6m/15–20ft
House finch	15 x 15cm/6 x 6in	15cm/6in	10cm/4in	5cm/2in	2.4–3.6m/8–12ft
Crested flycatcher	15 x 15cm/6 x 6in	8–10cm/20–25in	15–20cm/6–8in	5cm/2in	2.4–6m/8–20ft
Starling	15 x 15cm/6 x 6in	40–46cm/16–18in	36–40cm/14–16in	5cm/2in	3–7.6m/10–25ft
Woodpeckers					
Downy	10 x 10cm/4 x 4in	8–10cm/20–25in	15–20cm/6–8in	3cm/1¼in	1.8–6m/6–20ft
Golden-fronted	15 x 15cm/6 x 6in	30–38cm/12–15in	22–30cm/9–12in	5cm/2in	3.6–6m/12–20ft
Red-headed	15 x 15cm/6 x 6in	30–38cm/12–15in	22–30cm/9–12in	5cm/2in	3.6–6m/12–20ft
Hairy	15 x 15cm/6 x 6in	30–38cm/12–15in	22–30cm/9–12in	4cm/1½in	3.6–6m/12–20ft
Flicker	18 x 18cm/7 x 7in	40–46cm/16–18in	36–40cm/14–16in	6cm/2½in	1.8–6m/6–20ft
Owls					
Saw-whet	15 x 15cm/6 x 6in	25–30cm/10–12in	20–25cm/8–10in	6cm/2½in	3.6–6m/12–20ft
Screech	20 x 20cm/8 x 8in	30–38cm/12–15in	22–30cm/9–12in	7.5cm/3in	3–9m/10–30ft
Barn	25 x 46cm/10 x 18in	38–46cm/15–18in	10cm/4in	15cm/6in	3.6–5.5m/12–18ft
American kestrel	20 x 20cm/8 x 8in	30–38cm/12–15in	22–30cm/9–12in	7.5cm/3in	3–9m/10–30ft
Carolina wood duck	25 x 46cm/10 x 18in	25–60cm/10–24in	30–40cm/12–16in	36cm/14in	3–6m/10–20ft

OPEN-FRONTED NEST BOXES

Not all birds like nest boxes with small entrance holes. The open-fronted types have a larger, rectangular entrance area at the front. This style of box is suitable for wrens and robins. A kestrel will nest in a larger box of this type.

	Floor size	Depth of box	Height to top of front	Positioning/comments
EUROPE				
Wren	10 x 10cm/4 x 4in	15cm/6in	10cm/4in	Low in dense vegetation
Robin	10 x 10cm/4 x 4in	15cm/6in	5cm/2in	1.5–5.5m/5–18ft above ground
Kestrel	30 x 50cm/12 x 20in	30cm/12in	15cm/6in	5m/16ft above ground

BIRD SHELVES

Nesting shelves – also known as roosting boxes – have an entirely open front, and may used for resting and sleeping as well as nesting. They are suitable for wagtails, spotted flycatchers, blackbirds, song sparrows, American robins, barn swallows and phoebes. Other species, such as blue jays and cardinals, may also roost or nest in this type of box.

	Floor size	Depth of box	Positioning/comments
EUROPE			
Pied wagtail	10 x 10cm/4 x 4in	10cm/4in	1.5–5.5m/5–18ft above ground
Spotted flycatcher	15 x 15cm/6 x 6in	10cm/4in	1.5–5.5m/5–18ft above ground
Blackbird	20 x 20cm/8 x 8in	20cm/8in	In dense vegetation
NORTH AMERICA			
Song sparrow	15 x 15cm/6 x 6in	15cm/6in	30–90cm/1–3ft above ground
American robin	15 x 15cm/6 x 6in	20cm/8in	1.8–4.5m/6–15ft above ground
Barn swallow	15 x 15cm/6 x 6in	15cm/6in	2.4–3.6m/8–12ft above ground
Phoebe	15 x 15cm/6 x 6in	15cm/6in	2.4–3.6m/8–12ft above ground

UNUSUAL NEST BOXES

Some species, such as members of the swift family, owls and ducks, require special types of nest boxes. Most are constructed of wood, but cup nests for swallows and house martins can be made of papier-mâché or a wood-chip mix.

	Description	Positioning/comments
EUROPE		
Swallow	Cup-shaped nest	On shed or stable
House martin	Cup-shaped nest	Fix under eaves of house or shed
Swift	Oblong box, 60 x 15 x 15cm/24 x 6 x 6in, with an entrance underneath	Place horizontally under eaves of house
Barn owl	Oblong box, 25 x 46 x 40cm/10 x 18 x 16in	4.5m/15ft above ground
Tawny owl	Oblong box, 76 x 26 x 22cm/30 x10½ x 9in	In a tree under a branch
Little owl	20 x 120 x 26cm/8in x 4ft x 10in, with a 10cm/4in hole 30cm/12in from the floor	In a tree
Mallard	35 x 35 x 33cm/14 x 14 x 13in	On an island or raft
NORTH AMERICA		
Mallard	35 x 35 x 33cm/14 x 14 x 13in	On an island or raft

Right: A mallard house should be positioned on an island or raft to provide protection from predators. The ramp should have horizontal struts so that the ducks' feet do not slip when walking.

USEFUL ADDRESSES

UNITED KINGDOM
Organizations
British Birds Rarities Committee
www.bbrc.org.uk

British Garden Birds
www.garden-birds.co.uk

British Ornithologists' Club
www.boc-online.org

British Ornithologists' Union
www.bou.org.uk

British Trust for Ornithology (BTO)
www.bto.org.uk

BTO Garden Birdwatch
www.bto.org/gbw

Fat Birder
www.fatbirder.com

Hawk Conservancy
www.hawk-conservancy.org

Hawk and Owl Trust
www.hawkandowl.org

Rare Breeding Birds Panel
www.rbbp.org.uk

Royal Society for the Protection
of Birds (RSPB)
www.rspb.org.uk

Wildfowl & Wetlands Trust
www.wwt.org.uk

Advice on gardening for birds
Field Studies Council
www.field-studies-council.org

RSPB advice on gardening
www.rspb.org.uk/advice/gardening

The Wildlife Trusts
www.wildlifetrusts.org

Bird box and food suppliers
CJ WildBird Foods Ltd
www.birdfood.co.uk

Food for Wild Birds
www.food4wildbirds.co.uk

Garden Bird Supplies
www.gardenbird.com

Garden Wildlife Direct
www.gardenwildlifedirect.co.uk

RSPB Shop: bird feeders and food
shopping.rspb.org.uk

The Really Wild Bird Food Company
www.reallywildfoodfood.co.uk

Vine House Farm Bird Foods
vinehousefarm.co.uk

WWF Wildlife Shop
shop.wwf.org.uk/wildlife

NORTH AMERICA
Organizations
American Bird Conservancy
www.abcbirds.org

American Birding Association
www.aba.org

American Ornithologists' Union
www.aou.org

Audubon Society state contacts
www.audubon.org/chapter/
(Append the state abbreviation at the
end of this URL, for example for Alaska,
type in: www.audubon.org/chapter/ak)

Bird Studies Canada
www.bsc-eoc.org

Bird Watcher's Digest magazine
www.birdwatchersdigest.com

Birdnet.com
www.nmnh.si.edu/BIRDNET

Birdzilla.com
www.birdzilla.com

Nature Canada
www.naturecanada.ca

Canadian Peregrine Foundation
www.peregrine-foundation.ca

Canadian Wildlife Federation
www.cwf-fcf.org

Cornell Lab of Ornithology
birds.cornell.edu

National Audubon Society
www.audubon.org

National Parks, Forests, Wilderness
Areas
www.wildlifeleadershipacademy.org

National Wildlife Federation
www.nwf.org

North American Bird Sounds
www.birdsounds.net

North American Rare Bird
Alert
www.narba.org

Sierra Club Canada
www.sierraclub.org

US Fish & Wildlife Service
www.fws.gov

Advice on gardening for birds
Cornell Lab of Ornithology
www.birds.cornell.edu/AllAboutBirds/
attracting/landscaping

Council on the Environment of New York City
www.grownyc.org/files/citylot/Birds_in_
Urban_Gardens.pdf

National Wildlife Federation
www.nwf.org/backyard

NSiS: Florida Native Plants
www.nsis.org/garden/garden-native-birds.
html

Bird box and food suppliers
The Backyard Bird Company
www.backyardbird.com

Duncraft
www.duncraft.com/

National Bird-Feeding Society
www.birdfeeding.org

Wild Bird Habitat Store
www.wildbirdhabitatstore.com

CENTRAL & SOUTH AMERICA
Caribbean Species Listings
www.camacdonald.com/birding/
Comparisons-Caribbean.htm

Central American Species Listings
www.camacdonald.com/birding/
Comparisons-CentralAm.htm

Neotropical Bird Club
www.neotropicalbirdclub.org

South American Species Listings
www.camacdonald.com/birding/
Comparisons-SouthAmerica.htm

AUSTRALIA AND NEW ZEALAND
Birdlife Australia
birdlife.org.au

Birding New Zealand
www.birdingnz.co.nz

Bird Observers Club of
Australia
www.birdobservers.org.au

Birds New Zealand
www.osnz.org.nz

New Zealand Birds
www.nzbirds.com

Forest & Bird Protection Society
of New Zealand
www.forestandbird.org.nz

ASIA
Oriental Bird Club
www.orientalbirdclub.org

EUROPE/MIDDLE EAST
Ornithological Society of the Middle East
osme.org

AFRICA
African Bird Club
www.africanbirdclub.org

Birdlife South Africa
www.birdlife.org.za

West African Ornithological Society
www.malimbus.org

**INTERNATIONAL
ORGANIZATIONS**
BirdLife International
www.birdlife.org

European Ornithologists' Union
eounion.org

Neotropical Bird Club
www.neotropicalbirdclub.org

Pacific Seabird Group
pacificseabirdgroup.org

INDEX

PICTURE CREDITS

The publisher would like to thank the following for allowing their photographs to be reproduced in the book (l = left, r = right, t = top, c = centre, b = bottom):
Ardea: 13b. iStockphoto: 2, 3bl, 3br, 5tr, 8, 9b, 9r, 11tl, 11tr, 11cl, 11cr, 11bl, 11bc, 12br, 13t, 13r, 14l, 14tr, 17bl, 17br, 18bl, 19tl, 19bl, 19br, 20t, 20bl, 20br, 21t, 21b, 23tl, 24t, 25tr, 25br, 26bl, 26ct, 26tr, 27t, 27bl, 30t, 30b, 31tr, 31br, 32b, 32cl, 32bl, 35tl, 35tc, 35tr, 36br, 37bl, 37br, 38tl, 38tr, 38bl, 46bl, 46t, 47tr, 48tl, 48tr, 48b, 52tr, 53bl, 54bl, 55tl, 58l, 60br, 63tl, 63tr, 64t, 64bl, 68bl, 69t, 70t, 71bl, 71bcr, 72tr, 73t, 75tl, 77tr, 78tl, 80t, 84t, 85tl, 85b, 86tl, 86tr, 87bl, 87br, 88bl, 88br, 89bc, 89br, 90bc, 94tl, 94br, 104tl, 106tl, 108tl, 114tl, 124bl, 130tl, 132tl, 134tl, 136tl, 140tl, 144br, 146tl, 150tl, 152, 153bl, 153bc, 153br, 197bl, 197bc, 197br, 250, 251t, 251b, 252, 253, 254, 255, 256. NHPA/Photoshot: 27br, 120tl, 148tl. Nigel Partridge: 47tl. Photolibrary Group: 12l, 23br. Shutterstock: 1, 5tl, 6, 41t, 47br, 50tr, 58b, 58t, 59tl, 59tc, 59b, 65tr, 65br, 74bl, 78tr, 101. Woodfall/Photoshot: 25cl. Dan Brown: nesting shelf, 50tr.

ABOUT THE AUTHORS

David Alderton is an international best-selling authority on birds. An award-winning writer, his books on avian subjects and the wider natural world have sold more than 7 million copies worldwide and have been published in 31 languages. David has studied birds on all continents apart from Antarctica, and he has also been a long-standing volunteer at a wild bird hospital, helping to rehabilitate sick and injured wild birds, as well as having chaired the National Council for Aviculture. He has appeared regularly on television, and he has also taken part in many radio programmes about birds, including the BBC's Natural History programme.
Dr Jen Green, consultant, is a writer specializing in nature and the environment.